Freud's Traumatic Memory

Freud's Traumatic Memory

Reclaiming Seduction Theory and Revisiting Oedipus

Mary Marcel

Duquesne University Press
Pittsburgh, Pennsylvania

Library of Congress Cataloging-in-Publication Data

Marcel, Mary, 1961–
Freud's traumatic memory : reclaiming seduction theory and revisiting Oedipus / by Mary Marcel.
p. cm.
Includes bibliographical references and index.
ISBN 0-8207-0364-8 (hardcover : alk. paper)—ISBN 0-8207-0365-6 (pbk. : alk. paper)
1. Freud, Sigmund, 1856–1939. 2. Oedipus complex. 3. Seduction—Psychological aspects—History. I. Title.
BF109.F74M35 2005
150.19'52'092—dc22

2004023891

∞ Printed on acid-free paper.

This book is dedicated to
my husband, Alejandro Marcel
todos, siempre

Contents

ACKNOWLEDGMENTS

Without the help of many people, this book would have been a project interminable. The librarians at Brandeis University Library, Northeastern University Library and the Library of Congress were helpful in innumerable ways. I would especially like to express my gratitude to Catherine Cronin, Sheila Ekman and Marcia McKoy of the Solomon Baker Library at Bentley College for their unending patience and good cheer. I am grateful to Catherine Carlin for unstinting editorial help, and to Susan Wadsworth-Booth and anonymous reviewers of Duquesne University Press for their support of this project. Suzanne Hinton generously arranged travel funds from the Bentley College Gender Issues Council to support research at the Library of Congress. The Faculty Development Committee of Bentley College also provided support. I am grateful to Aaron Nurick for his encouraging comments on earlier drafts of this manuscript. I would also like to thank Emily Bergmann and Charlie Hadlock for accompanying me through some of the most difficult parts with clear-eyed certainty and faith.

The errors and shortcomings of this book belong to me alone. To my husband Alejandro Marcel, who extended unfailing protection against the cold winds of doubt, and who repeatedly called me to articulate a book worthy both of the material and myself, I give my greatest and deepest thanks.

My thanks to the following for permission to use materials included in this study:

Permission to quote from Robert Graves, *The Greek Myths*, © 1955, is granted by Carcanet Press Ltd., Manchester.

Permission to quote Bernard Sergent, *L'homosexualité dans la mythologie grecque* (© 1984, Editions Payot) is granted by Editions Payot, Paris; English translation, *Homosexuality and Greek Myth*, translated by Arthur Goldhammer, © 1984, Beacon Press, Boston.

Permission to quote from Judith Herman, *Trauma and Recovery*, © 1992, is granted by Perseus Books LLC.

Permission to quote from Josef Sajner, "Sigmund Freuds Beziehungen zu seinem Geburtsort Freiberg und zu Mähren," *Clio Medica*, 3 (1968): 167-80, © 1968, is granted by Editions Rodopi BV, Amsterdam.

Permission to quote from *The Complete Letters of Sigmund Freud to Wilhelm Fliess 1887-1904*, translated and edited by Jeffrey Moussaieff Masson, p. 398, Cambridge, Mass.: The Belknap Press of Harvard University Press, © 1985 and under the Bern Convention by Sigmund Freud Copyrights, Ltd., © 1985 by J. M. Masson for translation and editorial matter.

Material from *The Complete Psychological Works of Sigmund Freud* (Standard Edition), © 1955, 1958, 1962, 1963, Hogarth Press and the Institute of Psychoanalysis, London, reproduced by arrangement with Paterson Marsh, Ltd., London.

Permission to quote from *The Basic Writings of Sigmund Freud*, translated by A. A. Brill, is granted by the Estate of A. A. Brill.

Permission to quote Hans Licht, *Sexual Life in Ancient Greece*, translated by J. H. Freese (© 1994, Constable) is granted by Thomson Publishing. Originally published as *Sittengeschichte Griechenland: in zwei Bänden und einem Ergänzungsband* by P. Aretz, Dresden, Zürich and Berlin, © 1925-1929.

Permission to quote from Jean-Pierre Vernant, *Myth and Tragedy in Ancient Greece*, translated by Janet Lloyd (© 1988 Zone Books) is granted by Zone Books, New York.

INTRODUCTION

The Asymmetry of Taboo and the Unbearable Idea

The Oedipus complex concerns a neurosis, not a trauma. This book is about the trauma behind the Oedipus complex.

There are three strands of research in psychoanalysis in which this book participates. The first is the genre of works that seeks to gain insight into Freud's psychoanalytic theorizing by examining Freud's biography. The second is the recent spate of works that very closely reads Freud's shift in the years between 1897 and 1900, from the so-called seduction theory to the beginnings of the development of the Oedipus complex (which Freud continued to elaborate over the next 25 years), the analysis of dreams, and what has become associated with the core of Freud's psychoanalytic theories. The third has to do with Freud's uptake of the Oedipus stories, and the particularities of his reading of them.

The first strand includes quite interesting contributions to the search for insights about theory via the examination of Freud's own life. An early effort in this vein is the intriguing work by Ian Suttie, *The Origins of Love and Hate,* originally published in 1935.[1] Suttie, who died very shortly after the publication of his book, was arguably more sympathetic to what would become the object relations strand of psychoanalysis. He believed that human relationships and the quality of their experience by the individual were formative in both personality and neurotic formations. He makes an astute critique of several dogmatic issues in early psychoanalysis, including the problematic assertion by Freud that all expressions of "tenderness" (80) stem from a sexual root, and that children have innately aggressive tendencies toward their parents. Suttie clearly articulates some of Freud's limitations, especially in the areas of compassion and the formation of relationships. He also forwards his own theories about the sources of aggression and hatred in children. However, his mother-positive views in this work somewhat diminish his capacity to imagine the effects of relationships with adults that actually violate the child sexually or physically. Thus, while focusing on Freud's shortcomings in other areas, Suttie does not examine the difficulties experienced by children or adults who recollect being sexually violated. However, he makes strong arguments against Freud's overvaluation of the sexual and misapprehension of nonsexual love and nurturing, especially in the childhood context. Suttie primarily uses Freud's letters to bolster his analysis.

Erich Fromm, from a critical philosophical perspective, also engages in an examination of Freud's life and tendencies in the formation of Freudian theory. Fromm's concerns include the effect of Freud's subject position as a male bourgeois, a patriarch, his central European Jewish background, and his commitment to science and the supremacy of reason. In *Sigmund Freud's Mission,* Fromm primarily uses Jones's biography as his source material.[2] He cites one of Freud's letters to Fliess from the 1954 collection in English and one unpublished letter to Fliess, as well as a handful of other sources within and outside the Freudian canon to examine the development of theories in light of Freud's life details. He notes Freud's asymmetrical relationship with his mother versus his father, and his need for her approval in everything. Fromm also discusses in some detail Freud's authoritarian personality, both within his family and in analysis with patients, and his culturally supported notions of male dominance and male superiority. While Fromm gets closer to the facts of his subject's life than does Suttie, one could say that Fromm in 1959 is still hampered by the highly selected and edited version of Freud's correspondence, particularly to Wilhelm Fliess, which was available at that time.

Morton Schatzman's 1973 *Soul Murder: Persecution in the Family,* while not concerned with Freud's biography directly, does develop a method for reconsidering accounts of mental illness in light of related biographical materials. [3] Schatzman compares the writings of Daniel Paul Schreber, famously psychoanalyzed by Freud, with those of his father, Daniel Gottlieb Moritz Schreber, who was a doctor and a prolific writer on the education — moral, physical and otherwise — of children. Schreber *pere*'s methods involved extreme forms of both thought control and physical constraints (including implements of his own design), as well as exercises, the use of cold baths and other rough practices to rid children of their own thoughts and spontaneous reactions to the world. Schatzman concludes that what were taken as paranoid delusions in Schreber *fils* were in fact the residues of abuses — verbal formulas and physical practices — enacted upon him by his father. In this, Schatzman's method can be said to have enormously developed the path of inquiry that looks at environmental influences and experiences as psychically salient and with long-lived emotional sequelae. Schatzman also demonstrates the shortcomings in Freud's analysis of the writings of Schreber *fils*, in neglecting relevant evidence outside the memoirs that appears to have materially affected the development of his mental illness.

More recent efforts to analyze Freudian theory in light of Freudian biography include Marianne Krüll's 1986 *Freud and His Father* and Marie Balmary's 1982 *Psychoanalyzing Psychoanalysis: Freud and the Hidden Fault of the Father.*[4] Krüll uses the very interesting archival research of Sajner in Czechoslovakia to bolster her argument that the decisive fact of Freud's life with respect to his theorizing was the prosecution and imprisonment of Freud's uncle for counterfeiting when Freud himself was quite young. Freud's older half-brothers may also have been involved in the scheme. Krüll concludes that the shock of this affair to his father, and a subsequent dream in which Freud's father told him not to look too closely at things, or try to know too much, served as Freud's greatest intellectual inhibition. I will examine her work and Sajner's archival findings in greater depth in this book. Balmary's work, on the other hand, is rather more speculative, and regards the possibility that Freud's mother was pregnant when his father married her, among other things.

All of these works and others in this vein advance our understanding of the relationship between Freud's life and his theories. However, the unexpurgated version of Freud's letters to Wilhelm Fliess, a critical resource for information about Freud's everyday life and experiences during the period in question, was not available until 1985. Not long after that point, the ground on which Freud's theories would be debated changed dramatically.

Starting in 1980, the occasional paper or book criticizing some aspect of Freudian thought became such a common and at times virulent occurrence that "Freud bashing" soon seemed to take on a life of its own. As with any scientific or scholarly set of hypotheses, we should certainly expect that, over time, both new discoveries and the reexamination of core texts and testing of core concepts would yield fresh insights and serve to modify our estimate of the original theses. And so it has been with Freud. In particular, there have been many examinations of why Freud abandoned the "seduction theory" of the etiology of hysteria around 1897 and subsequently developed the body of work that has come to be known as "psychoanalytic theory."

Three distinct lines of attack and defense regarding Freud's work have hardened in the last two decades. One important attack has to do with scientific method and the extent to which Freudian concepts and evidence can be tested in scientifically satisfactory ways. Frank Sulloway and Adolf Grünbaum have been perhaps the most penetrating critics in this area. Alan Esterson focuses on the early period, to suggest that Freud tainted all of his cases by heavyhanded suggestion of "memories" his patients never remembered having.[5]

Freudians respond in a variety of ways. Psychoanalysis is not "scientific" in the way that the physical or biological sciences are, but its value is not thereby vitiated. Psychoanalytic concepts have been tested in a variety of ways; some have panned out and other have not. Bennett Simon and Rachel Blass argue that the Oedipus complex has not been borne out, for example, while Judith Herman argues that repression after trauma is a well-attested phenomenon.[6] And finally, some argue that Freud himself rejected his own early work on the seduction theory, and was right to do so. Criticisms of it are therefore moot.

Another line of critique has to do with Freud's work as a "hermeneutic," a way of understanding or interpreting valuable material about our humanity that would otherwise remain obscure to us. Feminists and others have suggested that Freud's hermeneutic simply encodes misogyny and sexism, and has become yet another means by which women are not liberated but "managed" and even exploited. Freudians respond widely, starting with the concept of resistance and ending with the assertion that psychoanalytic precepts are as timeless and universal as Freud stated them. The appeal of the Oedipus complex, whatever its faults, remains widespread, and the work of Lacan, sexist and misogynist in the extreme, is still the lingua franca of much psychoanalytic literary criticism.

A third critical approach has examined therapeutic efficacy. Many therapists and nontherapists concerned with the psychological health and well-being of patients have pointed to the analyst-analysand relationship as inherently exploitative and destructive for patients who have genuinely suffered trauma. In response, analysts such as David Sachs and Marshall Edelman appeal to what might be called the personal resonance test. If Freudian premises ring true to one's own experiences and sensibilities, then one will be able to accept the power of Freud's thoughts.[7]

These positions constitute a great part of what came to be known as the Freud wars. The last 20 years in particular have been especially productive for both attacks against and defenses of Freud's work and legacy. What emerges from much of the scholarship, however, is another, perhaps more thematic question. Many authors who have taken Freud to task have done so on the basis that he abandoned his early position, wherein the etiology of hysteria and neurosis is rooted in childhood sexual abuses, most generally but not exclusively perpetrated by adults. Jeffrey Masson, following on the heels of feminists who had begun this tradition of rejection, argues that Freud essentially acted in bad faith when he abandoned his belief in the veracity of his patients' stories. By standing down from the radical but correct position that his patients had been abused, Masson argues, Freud becomes a collaborator with the forces of oppression, and does not deserve his status either as culture hero or as humanistic liberator. His abandonment left generations of patients, especially women, in the cruel position of being told either that they were "making it all up" or that it was "only in their heads" anyway.[8] A great many more successful therapeutic approaches for survivors of childhood sexual abuse have been launched out of this lacuna in psychoanalysis.

Those who defend Freud's later work, on the other hand, turn to the Freudian corpus to suggest that the interpretive turn Freud takes, marked by the publication of *The Interpretation of Dreams* and the development of the Oedipus complex, resulted in enormous intellectual productivity and great conceptual richness. Even the abandonment of the therapeutic ideal of "curing" patients gave rise to the process of psychoanalysis itself. And surely, they say, the insights concerning memory, the unconscious, child sexuality, repression, transference and projection, to name a partial list, justify Freud's decision to turn away from a simple faith in his patients' verbatim stories. In a sense, this position agrees with part of the scientific critique. Freud gave up the seduction theory because it could not be proved and was likely wrong.

Judith Herman's formulation regarding Freud's inability to sustain the seduction theory is, however, perhaps the most historically informed in terms of the larger picture of clinicians who were Freud's contemporaries and who also failed to sustain the viability of approaches that granted credibility to victims' accounts of their abuses. French researchers, whose work had been buoyed by a nascent feminist movement, also abandoned their work by 1900. Herman writes: "As long as the study of hysteria was part of an ideological crusade, discoveries in the field were widely applauded and scientific investigators were esteemed for their humanity and courage. But once the political impetus had faded, these same investigators found themselves compromised by the nature of their discoveries and by their close involvement with their women patients" (17). Herman notes that Josef Breuer, Freud's mentor, was uncomfortable with his work with hysterical young women. Of Freud's own turn from the sexual etiology theory, she makes two important historical observations. First, regarding Freud's "recantation," which has come under particularly bitter attack in recent years:

> to engage in this kind of *ad hominem* attack seems like a curious relic of Freud's own era, in which advances in knowledge were understood as Promethean acts of solitary male genius. No matter how cogent his arguments or how valid his observations, Freud's discovery could not gain acceptance in the absence of a political and social context that would support the investigation of hysteria, wherever it might lead. Such a context had never existed in Vienna and was fast disappearing in France. Freud's rival Janet, who never abandoned his traumatic theory of hysteria and who never retreated from his hysterical patients, lived to see his works forgotten and his ideas neglected. (18)

Thus, narrow critics of Freud who have construed his retreat as opportunism or ambition or a character flaw have failed to notice the general climate of hostility in which he and his fellow researchers in France had worked.

But Herman offers an even more telling insight regarding the tremendous difficulty of the material Freud faced; namely, the real events that had so traumatized his patients:

> Perhaps the sweeping character of Freud's recantation is understandable, given the extremity of the challenge he faced. To hold fast to his theory would have been to recognize the depths of sexual oppression of women and children. The only potential source of intellectual validation and support for this position was the nascent feminist movement, which threatened Freud's cherished patriarchal values. To ally himself with such a movement was unthinkable for a man of Freud's political beliefs and professional ambitions. Protesting too much, he dissociated himself at once from the study of psychological trauma and from women. He went on to develop a theory of human development in which the inferiority and mendacity of women were fundamental points of doctrine. In an antifeminist political climate, this theory prospered and thrived. (19)

Here we see the connection drawn between Freud's subsequent theories regarding women's intellectual and moral "inferiority" to men, and his rejection of the feminist movement. He understood, in short, that he was not going to ride to triumph as the white knight by championing the human rights of sexually abused women.

Herman's argument is more comprehensive historically than the majority of critics who narrowly focus on Freud as the sole, rather than a representative, researcher in this area in his time. She also makes the important connection to the social taint of being associated with sexually "damaged" women, regardless of their social class. Her arguments are compelling and, as subsequent chapters will show, well corroborated. This book takes the analysis of Freud's antifemale animus one step further by examining Freud's own experience of "seduction," prior to the age of three, by his Czechoslovakian nurse in Freiberg.

By analyzing the material regarding Freud's experiences of infantile sexual abuse in his letters to his friend and confidante Wilhelm Fliess and from other sources, we will come to understand a new dimension in Freud's shift away from the seduction theory which has until now remained unanalyzed by researchers. With it, we will uncover, I believe, perhaps the deepest evidence regarding both Freud's humanity and the limitations worked upon it by untreated psychological trauma.

Freud replaced the "seduction theory" with the idea of the Oedipus complex, which became his primary theoretical innovation in that period, along with the idea of the unconscious and the significance of dreams. This transition was completed gradually over the next 14 years. But while Freud sought in the Greek myth of Oedipus and the oracle's curse to move toward a drive-based explanation of human behavior and away from the salience of experience or environment in psychic life, wittingly or unwittingly his theory remains tied to an initial act of sexual violence against a child. For as Freud may or may not have known, Oedipus was cursed because his father Laius had raped a royal boy named Chrysippus.[9]

For this reason, there has been a long tradition within classics scholarship which rejects Freudian interpretations, particularly as they apprehend Greek myth. The simple objection is that Freud's construction of Oedipus's motives and the structure of the complex itself have nothing to do with how the Greeks who authored the myth and the plays understood the same story.[10]

Strikingly, this camp has not participated in any noticeable way in the recent Freud controversies, and that is a pity. Both Freudians and their active antagonists have very little discussed how Freud read Oedipus, and there has been little consideration of what he understood and may not have understood about the play he took as the representative anecdote for all human development. There have always been popular objections that Freud's insistence on the "universality" of his Oedipal formula, hating the father and wanting sex with the mother, were unfounded and unconfirmed. But apart from classicists and a very few psychoanalysts such as Georges Devereux, scholars have little considered that Freud's interpretation of Oedipus and his omission of Chrysippus might be problematic, and that such problems might have larger implications for the psychoanalytic project as Freud envisioned it — including its "scientific" elements. [11]

So this book will also undertake an examination of Greek myths that explore both mother-son and father-daughter incest. In this way, the asymmetry of the incest taboo, which Freud was at pains to claim was universal and uniform, appears in its true light. That is to say, because mother-son incest threatens the sovereignty of paternal power, it is held up as a horror and an outrage. Father-daughter incest, however, is not only not uniformly punished. In one myth, the king secures his throne by raping his daughter and using the child born of the rape to eliminate his rivals. The same oracle who announced Laius's curse tells King Thyestes to go forward and father a child by his daughter!

In the final chapter, I assess the weight on the outlines of Freud's theory, of the asymmetrical taboo and the unbearable idea that Freud and his society could not accept or integrate, despite the reality of the traumas they caused and continue to cause. It seems clear that Freud himself was in dire need of a therapist. Winnicott has said that without someone else, there is no baby.[12] By this he means that the child's state of utter dependency requires the presence of an adult caregiver in order for normal development to occur. A baby cannot survive without nurturing care, without help. One can say the same thing about trauma victims. Without therapists there are no trauma patients — no one able to pursue healing, because healing requires help. Instead, they may identify with their perpetrators and repeat in some form the crimes committed against them. Or they may develop posttraumatic symptoms and suffer in that way. How different might have been the course of psychoanalytic history if Freud had been able, at least for a while, to be the patient.

ONE

Freud's Seduction

In the same important letter in which Sigmund Freud announces his "discovery" of the "universal" situation of Oedipus, he also tells Wilhelm Fliess that "fleetingly the thought passed through my head that the same thing might be at the bottom of Hamlet as well."[1] He first states that he believes "that a real event stimulated the poet to his representation, in that his unconscious understood the unconscious of his hero . . . How better than through the torment he suffers from the obscure memory that he himself had contemplated the same deed against his father out of passion for his mother . . . His conscience is his unconscious sense of guilt" (272–73). Here his remarks have to do with the content, not the technique of psychoanalysis. Freud's speculation about the motivation for Hamlet's hesitation seeks to make Hamlet's reasons "Oedipal."[2] And yet what he says about Shakespeare writing Hamlet might apply equally so to himself. What of the possibility that a "real event" stimulated Freud to create his fictional masterpiece, the Oedipus complex?

When Jeffrey Masson published his edition of the Freud-Fliess letters and "discovered" the great betrayal, that Freud had at first believed his patients' stories about seduction but then changed his mind in the face of professional hostility to his thesis — the focus was on the (mostly) women patients Freud affected. What Masson did not explore were the difficulties Freud himself reported having as he tried to sort out the painful detritus of his childhood memories of molestation. Since then, however, no one seems to have taken up Freud's accounts to Fliess about his own early childhood sexual experiences. For example, Ernest Jones, Marianne Krüll, Peter Gay, Frank Sulloway, Gerald Izenberg, Peter Newton, Alan Esterson, Richard Webster and Sander Gilman each consider the transition from Freud's ascription to the "seduction theory" to his abandonment of it.[3] Most include material from his letters to Fliess regarding Freud's earliest formulations of the Oedipus complex. But none of these authors analyzes Freud's discussions about his nurse's sexual "lessons," with the exception of Gilman and Krüll. Gilman's narrative, however, concerns the dangers faced by Jewish children in nineteenth century Austria from Christians who abducted and converted them. And Krüll refers to the abuse as "sexual games," clearly not considering them problematic.

Revelation in Self-Analysis

In the midst of his self-analysis, Freud had dreams each night that he felt were helping him clarify his theories about neurosis. He wrote to Fliess on October 3, 1897:

> To put it in writing is more difficult than anything else for me; it also would take me too far afield. I can only indicate that the old man plays no active part in my case, but that no doubt I drew an inference by analogy from myself onto him; that in my case the "prime originator" was an ugly, elderly, but clever woman, who told me a great deal about God Almighty and hell and who instilled in me a high opinion of my own capacities; that later (between two and two and a half years) my libido toward ***matrem*** was awakened, namely, on the occasion of a journey with her from Leipzig to Vienna, during which we must have spent the night together and there must have been an opportunity of seeing her ***nudam*** (you inferred the consequences of this for your son long ago, as a remark revealed to me) . . .
>
> I have not yet grasped anything at all of the scenes themselves which lie at the bottom of the story. If they come [to light] and I succeed in resolving my own hysteria, then I shall be grateful to the memory of the old woman who provided me at such an early age with the means for living and going on living. (268–69)

Since Freud is talking about the origins of neurosis at this point, which he had until very recently been associating with the sexual abuse of children, when he speaks of the nurse as his "prime originator," we can reasonably presume that he is referring to the origin of his own neurosis in a "seduction." Significantly, he says "libido" toward his mother is awakened *later*, between the age of two and two and a half years, by seeing his mother nude, *after* his experiences with the clever old woman. Peter Gay pushes his age to four for this episode (11). But, following the dictates of his own seduction theory, where traumatic sexual episodes in childhood form the etiology of hysteria, he connects his dreams about this old woman and the resolution of his own hysteria.

At this point in his career, Freud was in the midst of revising his theories. In September 1897 he had written to Fliess rejecting the notion that child sexual abuse was as widespread as it appeared to be, and seeming to recant his earlier commitment to his "seduction theory" as the sole etiology of hysteria. But he had maintained that neurosis was linked to child sexual abuse, and continued to mention cases sporadically to Fliess for another year. So while it is not wholly clear in this passage whether he is referring to his nurse as the "originator" of his sexual abuse, or if he is asserting some other basis for neurosis, probability suggests the former.

Other letters add layers of detail to the relationship between the infant and toddler Freud and his nurse. He reports that she regularly took him to church (she was Catholic) and preached to him about God and hell. On October 4, 1897, he writes:

> The children arrived. The fine weather is gone. Today's dream has, under the strangest disguises, produced the following: she was my teacher in sexual matters and complained because I was clumsy and unable to do anything.
>
> (Neurotic incompetence always comes about in this way. The fear of not being able to do anything at all in school thus obtains its sexual substratum.) At the same time I saw the skull of a small animal and in the dream I thought "pig," but in the analysis I associated it with your wish two years ago that I might find, as Goethe once did, a skull on the Lido to enlighten me. But I did not find it. So [I was] a "little blockhead" [literally, a sheep's head]. The whole dream was full of the most

> terrifying allusions to my present impotence as a therapist. Perhaps this is where the inclination to believe in the incurability of hysteria begins. Moreover, she washed me in reddish water in which she had previously washed herself. (The interpretation is not difficult; I find nothing like this in the chain of my memories; so I regard it as a genuine ancient discovery.) And she made me steal zehners (ten-kreuzer coins) to give them to her. There is a long chain from these first silver zehners to the heap of paper ten-florin notes which I saw in the dream as Martha's weekly housekeeping money. The dream could be summed up as "bad treatment." Just as the old woman got money from me for her bad treatment, so today I get money for the bad treatment of my patients. (269)

In this remarkable passage, we see Freud further reconstructing from dreams the memory of his nurse, identified by Josef Sajner in 1968 as Monika Zajic.[4]

In a photograph published in Peter Gay's *Freud: A Life for Our Times,* the house Schlossergasse 117 in Freiberg has "J. Zajic" in large letters on the outside.[5] Gay states that Freud was born above a blacksmith (9); perhaps Monika Zajic was the blacksmith's wife or other close relation. Sajner in a later article casts doubt upon the certainty that Monika Zajic was Sigmund's nurse, because the Roznau Spa Register for June 5, 1857 lists Amalia Freud and a nursemaid by the name of Resi (Theresa) Wittek.[6] However, Zajic's close proximity to the Freuds is attested by the fact that she was registered as the "Dienstmagd" for Maria Freud, who lived across the hall from Amalia, Josef and Sigmund Freud. Theresa Wittek was never listed with the city registers in Freiberg as being employed by Jakob and Amalia Freud. I will return to this matter later.

There are many striking observations in this letter. To begin with, Freud draws the conclusion from his dream analysis that his nurse "was my teacher in sexual matters and complained because I was clumsy and unable to do anything." These statements echo a passage in the *Aetiology* lecture of 1896, where Freud paints a picture for his psychiatric colleagues of what transpires between adults and children in "sexual scenes":

> All the singular conditions under which the ill-matched pair conduct their love-relations — on the one hand the adult, who cannot escape his share in the mutual dependence necessarily implied by a sexual relationship, and who is yet armed with complete authority and the right to punish, and can exchange the one role for the other to the uninhibited satisfaction of his moods, and on the other hand the child, who in his helplessness is at the mercy of this arbitrary will, who is prematurely aroused to every kind of sensibility and exposed to every sort of disappointment, and whose performance of the sexual activities assigned to him is often interrupted by his imperfect control of his natural needs — all these grotesque and yet tragic incongruities reveal themselves as stamped upon the later development of the individual and of his neurosis, in countless permanent effects which deserve to be traced in the greatest detail.[7]

In the letter to Fliess, Freud presents in clear terms his recollection that his nurse engaged in some kind of sexual activity with him, in the years before he was three. What she was trying to "teach" Freud sexually, he does not stipulate. But he does recall her complaints that he was "clumsy and unable to do anything."

Yet in contrast to the etiology lecture just cited, where Freud describes with painful poignancy the inevitably disappointing, coercive and humiliating sexual dynamic between an adult and child, he shows little or no compassion for his own infantile sexual failings at the hands of a trusted adult caregiver. In fact, he relates the dream of his infantile incapacity to his present "impotence as a therapist." In the etiology lecture, his sympathies are surely with the child victim. Here in recollecting his own life, however, he harshly internalizes the feelings of failure and inability to complete the required task, as if the toddling child should ever have any sexual demands made of him or her by others, let alone expect to fulfill them. Freud remarks about the "most terrifying allusions" to his therapeutic failures, and then avers, "perhaps this is where the inclination to believe in the incurability of hysteria begins." He feels so overwhelmed, but by shortcomings that were by rights not his to own, that he feels he will be unable to succeed at the project he set out to do, namely, to develop a cure for hysteria. The clarity with which he had set out a sad and damning picture of the damaging effects of the premature sexualization of a child by an adult in the *Aetiology* lecture is here smudged and made over by his internalization of the demands of his abuser as legitimate, and the delegitimation of self he feels in his failure to fulfill them.

This reversal of sympathy is made clear in a truly stunning psychoanalytic linkage. The woman made the toddling Freud steal coins to pay her for her "bad treatment" of him — meaning she had him pay her to molest him. In the same way, he says, his patients also pay him for "bad treatment." To be required to pay someone to abuse oneself — to give the torturer recompense for her or his pains — is an assault in addition to the primary acts of abuse on the person. The unwilling innocent is abused and then is required to pay his abuser for her pains — but this is not how Freud characterizes the situation. "Just as the old woman got money from me for her bad treatment" hardly does justice to the fate of an infant, a little person in diapers, barely able to walk, to speak, to feed himself or go to sleep without help, whom an adult woman takes as her sexual "student." By likening his own difficulties in treating his patients to the abusiveness of his nurse, we see a transformation at midpoint: from the doctor whose sympathies lie with his patients sexually abused in childhood presented in the etiology lecture of 1896; to the confused victim of 1897 whose failings as a therapist he identifies as rooted in his childhood sexual abuse; to the author in 1900 of *The Interpretation of Dreams,* whose creation of the Oedipus complex shifts the guilt of childhood "sexuality" squarely onto the instinctual life of the child. Freud takes to heart his infant sexual failings. He cannot summon, nor does Fliess seem to offer, any sympathy for himself, any rational or even moral means to absolve a baby for the guilt of not sexually satisfying his adult abuser. It is as if in this passage he is saying: She wanted me to do certain things and I couldn't, so that makes me a bad baby and now a bad doctor.

That Freud expresses no surprise or outrage that this beloved and trusted adult could make such outrageous demands of her tiny charge may suggest that he has grown accustomed, even hardened to such cases. Based on the etiology lecture, we can say with some certainty that he has heard almost a score of patients recount such things to him in sessions. In this letter, he is no longer the salvithic knight of 1896 riding into the midst of his psychiatric colleagues with a cure in hand (they rejected the sexual abuse theory stonily). He is the vulnerable, abused boy so beholden to his perpetrator that he stole money to pay her for her "bad treatment" of him. But rather than read his reduced state in terms of appropriate vulnerability and trust violated by abuse, he remembers his deep and "terrifying" feelings of *sexual impotence* — being unable to do what he ought never have been asked to do, but childlike, took as his brief anyhow. Despite his complete inability to perform sexually at the age of *two*, the depiction of those encounters as failures haunts him, and he takes the failures as his own.

On the one hand, we can read this passage in the letters with some astonishment, if we think of Freud as a psychoanalyst. He has uncovered in himself the kind of memory he has found in his own patients. We could say that he struggles to depict his self-analytical findings with the same composure and detachment he would use with an other. However, the extremity of his feelings here, which he has told Fliess are so hard to put into words, leads me to conclude that this is a case of a genuine affect-laden memory that Freud has uncovered in his self-analysis. He tries, seemingly, to make the unbearable thing more bearable by calling her his teacher, rather than his molester; he minimizes her agency and power over him by eliding her role into something more acceptable for a woman in a child's life. And in his dream, he turns *her* reproaches into genuine *self*-reproaches for his failed therapies. From a distance, each of these moves reveals an intellectual approach at work that is incredibly sad in its inadequacy to master the terrible emotional objective correlative.

In the 1896 etiology lecture, in the run-up to the description of the abuse scenes, Freud makes no statement about the description's source. He does not stipulate that "such things as the following have been reported to me by patients," for example, which might have strengthened the authority of his case. Nor does he say that these are matters that he has (like a proper archaeologist) reconstructed from patient material.

And yet one is struck both by what he says and does not say. One wonders about the sex of the people involved and what acts he was alluding to. Contemporary accounts by both survivors and male perpetrators are frequently much more unequivocal about what transpires, often describing more force or violence than here alluded to.[8] A child being penetrated or forced to give fellatio (the "anal and buccal cavities" having been cited by Freud just before this passage in the lecture) is not "performing" in that sense, so much as being acted upon. The intrusion of the child's "natural needs" could refer to defecation, urination, bleeding or vomiting in the course of such abusive episodes. For a boy, perhaps he means the child might urinate when his penis was stimulated.

Freud's halfhearted retrospective bravado about this desire to master the molestation comes through in his words to Fliess: "she was my teacher in sexual matters and complained because I was clumsy and unable to do anything" (*Letters,* 269). Freud rewrites his sexual molestation at ages prior to two and a half at the hands of an elderly woman as if it were a teenage boy's first visit to a prostitute. Reread the passage, bearing in mind that the sexual teacher's pupil is perhaps a year old, perhaps unable to speak very many words yet, and probably not even toilet trained — and the pathos and denial become overwhelming. What exactly is a one- or two-year-old boy supposed to be able to do to sexually satisfy an adult woman? The only healthy answer is, nothing. And yet Freud, thrust back into the humiliation of being unable to perform what he could not perform, and should never have been expected to perform, tries to rewrite the scene as a precocious sexual initiation at which he failed.

Though this material has been widely available since the publication of Masson's edition of the *Letters* in 1983, I have found it observed but ignored. This seems odd, despite its clear relevance to Freud's project. But then, the heroic incest of the adult King Oedipus on the Queen Mother confers far more glory than the sad story of a toddler boy molested by an old lady in a provincial town in Czechoslovakia.

In these few pages we have Freud's own expressions about his childhood molestation by his nurse. For the sake of argument, since Freud cannot be further questioned on the matter, I will proceed as if this admission is what it appears to be on its face: that the nurse was the molester. Indeed, the thorough and authoritative Peter Gay has no trouble characterizing the episode as Freud does, though after noting it he moves on. And yet it is a heartbreaking story to a contemporary reader. This is Freud at his most vulnerable; Freud closest to breaking through his own ego defenses; to remembering, and in the moment of remembering, being overwhelmed by the affect and reality of the events he himself had repressed. We are less able to assess the quality of Fliess's response, since Freud burned all his letters. Thus a crucial part of a prototherapeutic process that had been played out with a friend has been lost to us.

Freud makes another connection between the mother and the nurse in his next letter to Fliess on October 15, 1897. He relates that he was able to confirm with his mother some facts about the nurse.

> I asked my mother whether she still remembered the nurse. "Of course," she said, "an elderly person, very clever, she was always carrying you off to some church; when you returned home you preached and told us all about God Almighty. During my confinement with Anna (two and a half years younger), it was discovered that she was a thief, and all the shiny new kreuzers and zehners and all the toys that had been given to you were found in her possession. Your brother Philipp himself fetched the policeman; she then was given ten months in prison." Now look at how this confirms the conclusions of my dream interpretation. It was easy for me to explain the only possible mistake. I wrote to you that she induced me to steal zehners and give them to her. In truth, the dream meant that she stole them herself. For the dream was a memory of my taking money from the mother of a doctor — that is, wrongfully. The correct interpretation is: I = she, and the mother of the doctor equals my mother. So far was I from knowing she was a thief that I made a wrong interpretation. (*Letters,* 271)

This passage provides both confirmation and correction to Freud's interpretation of the material. So he believed he had stolen money from the mother of a doctor, when in fact the nurse had stolen money from his mother. He had preserved her version of the events. What becomes clear in this letter is that, in attempting to reconstruct events from earliest childhood, Freud has difficulty keeping straight in his mind who is responsible for what. In this same letter of October 15, 1897, he states that he found, in his case, that he loved his mother and was jealous of his father, and that now he understands the power of Oedipus, above all "the objections that reason raises against the presupposition of fate" (*Letters,* 272). After having stated that his father did not figure in his own case of neurosis, he adumbrates his theory that Oedipus is the same as mother-love and father-hatred.

Freud discovers, with information added by his mother, that it was not he, the child, who had stolen money and toys, but his nurse. He had remembered that she had "induced" him to steal the money, when in fact it had been she who had stolen it. Here we may witness the essential reversal of guilt between the adult sexual perpetrator and her child victim, which becomes the cornerstone of the Oedipus complex. Freud remembers that *he* had stolen the money, and that *the nurse had induced him to do it.* His mother, however, corrects him by saying that the *nurse* in fact stole money from the family. So in the uncorrected residue of his childhood memory, he had taken the blame for stealing the money, when in fact the woman had stolen it herself. This, I think, is an apt metaphor for the sexual abuse. In his mind, the young Freud thinks he is in charge of the sexual activity (the stealing of the money) when in fact it is the woman who is "induc[ing]" him to "steal." That he thinks about this matter with respect to his mother may suggest a child's belief that he somehow "belongs" to his mother, and that this woman who is not his mother, by taking something from him, is by extension taking something from his mother.

The issue of post hoc reasoning becomes operative in Freud's self-analysis. He reveals that his nurse sexually molested him, and recalls that some time after that he saw his mother nude. Immediately he creates the idea of the Oedipus complex. And yet, we could say in his own case, post hoc, ergo propter hoc. It was not that he first had sexual thoughts about his mother and was jealous of his father, and that this becomes proof positive of the "universality" of the Oedipus complex. Rather, his sexual feelings were prematurely aroused by the "sexual lessons" carried out on him by his nurse. As he makes clear in the letters, sexual feelings for the mother came later.

But the shame of being a boy molested by a woman, the low social station of the nurse, and her subsequent incarceration for stealing from the Freuds, make it rather less compelling a story than to say that the little boy Freud "seduced" his *nurse*. Freud himself recoils from saying that he was in love with the woman who actually molested him. Rather, at a subsequent point, when he sees his *mother* nude, one would hypothesize that his sexual feelings, which had been initially aroused by the nurse, are re-aroused at the sight of his mother. He then re-cathects the mixed feelings he had for his nurse to his mother.

But since, presumably, his mother does not proceed to molest him, Freud can take on all the guilt to himself. He has sexual thoughts about *her*, therefore *he* is the initiator of the Oedipus mechanism. In this case, the mother is indeed innocent, while the molested boy is left to sort out his precociously and traumatically aroused feelings. The fact that he feels guilty about the episode with his mother suggests, in that case, that the feelings were only on his side, and his mother did nothing untoward with him. In the *Aetiology* lecture of 1896, Freud posits the mechanism whereby children who are first molested may go on to molest other children. One can say by extension that it is possible and indeed likely that a child who has been molested might also have sexual thoughts or impulses that she or he feels toward subsequent persons, but which the child does not act upon. The trigger for little Sigmund would be seeing the grown woman nude. In his mind, this is associated with sexual acts or stimulation, such as he experienced with his nurse. He feels aroused based on his previous experiences with his nurse. But instead of acting upon him, his mother simply changes her clothes. His mother does not act out her expected role as molester. So the toddler is left with his own feelings, about which he now feels guilt and embarrassment. Contemporary clinical work indeed confirms this hypothesis.

In the same letter of October 15, 1897, Freud recounts a story about missing his mother and crying terribly because she was not there.

His brother Philipp, 20 years older than Freud, unlocks and opens a wardrobe for him, but his mother is not inside, and he cries even more. Then his mother appears through the door, and Freud states:

> I had asked him to [unlock] the wardrobe. When I missed my mother, I was afraid she had vanished from me, just as the old woman had a short time before. So I must have heard that the old woman had been locked up and therefore must have believed that my mother had been locked up too — or rather, had been "boxed up" — for my brother Philipp, who is now sixty-three years old, to this very day is still fond of using such puns. The fact that I turned to him in particular proves that I was well aware of his share in the disappearance of the nurse. (*Letters,* 271–72)

This passage suggests the toddler Freud's close association between his nurse and his mother, and his anxiety that his mother, like his nurse, might be removed from him. It happened that the nurse had been caught stealing money from the family, and Philipp had called the police and had her taken away. It also demonstrates that in fact it was Freud's older brother, and not his father, who dispatched the nurse from their household. This underscores the weakness of Jacob Freud, in this case through his apparent absence, in being able to regulate his home.

It also may tell us something about Freud's idealized castrating father. Freud thus far has reversed the vector of agency with respect to sex. If we apply this notion of reversing the vector of action to the Oedipus complex, another view of it emerges. Let us hypothesize that part of Freud's fantasy reversal includes ascribing incestuous desire to the boy, even though we will assume for purposes here that such desire comes from the adult. Let us then for a moment treat it as something the child takes on, rather than originates. The castrating father then can be said to intervene between the attacking *mother* and the fearful boy. He thereby stops, not the boy from carrying out his fantasies of sex with his mother, *but the mother from carrying out her desire for sex with the boy.* The castrating father is, then, a wished-for rescuer. At the manifest level, the abused child wants someone to help him not carry out the associations from his nurse that he is having in the presence of his nude mother, which are not reciprocated or acted upon by his mother, and which therefore cause the child to feel there is something wrong with his responses. The image of the castrating father is created in the child's mind to prevent him, from the outside, from acting upon feelings coming from the inside, as the residue of his previous abuse. At the latent level, the child may wish that the father had been there to prevent the old woman from acting out her wish to "marry" him in the first place. The wish for a rescuer in a traumatic scene, in short, might take a myriad of forms.

Oedipus

If the nurse molested him, Freud's later "awakening" of his toddler "libido" toward his mother might have been a safer or more preferable way for the adult Freud to understand, and mask, what had happened to him. The Greek Oedipus has no libido toward his mother when he solves the riddle of the Sphinx and is allowed to marry Jocasta as an adult man. The idea of the Oedipal sexual desire for the mother is a Freudian invention. But, as with every invention, we must ask: what does the Oedipus complex do better, and for whom, than the evidence of the bare elements in the ancient plot?

Doing something he did not want to do (kill his father, marry his mother), without knowledge of it, and then discovering that he had in fact done it, is the basis of Oedipus's tragedy. If there had been any hint that he had come to Thebes in order to marry his mother, Oedipus would no doubt have been killed, not simply exiled. Equally, though, it is entirely outside the Greek Oedipus to suggest that he *unconsciously* wanted to "marry" his mother.

Leopold Constans's *La Légende d'Œdipe* is in Freud's library at Maresfield Garden, with passages on the incest between Oedipus and Jocasta marked (35–42).[9] The pages concerning Laius and the rape of Chrysippus (26–29) contain no marginalia or other marks.[10] In 1898, however, when Freud writes to Fliess that he needs to "read up on the Oedipus legend" (*Letters,* 304), he makes no mention of knowing where to look. This suggests that he got and read Constans at a later time; or that he had read and disregarded the passage if he had the book at that time. At this point, it seems that he is still relying solely on Sophocles.

I believe that Freud's reinvention of Oedipus, or perhaps more simply his cooptation of it, helps him explain to himself what happened to him *in terms he is prepared to accept and integrate.* The shift, the libidinization of a child-Oedipus, allows Freud, with respect to his own toddler "libido," to put a more emotionally tolerable interpretation on a *prior* event, namely, the experience of having been molested by his nurse. His version, including the invention of the altered Oedipus, becomes compensatory for the shame and anger he feels about having been overpowered and abused by a woman caregiver, and not having been protected or saved by his father in the process.

The childhood logic of victimization is to take responsibility for whatever has been done to the child in order to master the overwhelming and unbearable feelings attached to the traumatic experience.[11] The children of divorced parents sometimes attempt to master their unbearable grief and fear by believing they themselves are the cause of their parents' breakup. The son Jude in Hardy's *Jude the Obscure,* when told his family would have to leave their lodgings because the landlord felt there were "too many of them [children]," waits for his parents to step out and then smothers his two siblings and hangs himself. *Children cannot handle the overwhelming anxiety of feeling that their parents are out of control.* To do so would mean having to reconcile two unbearable truths: that they are utterly dependent upon their parents, and that their parents are incapable of successfully caring for them. Taking the blame on themselves reorganizes their psychic worlds. It brings events under control, if only speciously so, by putting painful and potentially obliterating episodes under *their own* control.

Freud's somewhat shocking inability post-1900 to empathize with his patients' suffering comes, in fact, from the resolution of his own "seduction"-generated neurosis: to master it by denying its power over him. He does this by taking responsibility for his arousal at the sight of his nude mother, which occurs after his molestation by the nurse. That is why he makes Oedipus responsible for his fate in a way that the

Greeks did not. Freud's prescribed therapy is for the patient to get over her or his suffering by bucking up; by accepting that she or he wanted the sex; by blaming the patient for being attached to her or his illness; and by substituting his version of why the patient is suffering for the patient's own understanding of what happened.

The supremely painful idea that Freud cannot accept or integrate, ultimately, was that someone, and most especially a woman, took absolute control of his body at an age when he could do nothing to prevent her, at an age when no one else who should have stopped her stepped in to save him. That for Freud was the idea, the reality, that most had to be resisted — because he could not integrate it into the rest of his personal psychic infrastructure of beliefs, values and experiences. And so, ironically, by arguing that the libido of the child was responsible for the subsequent arousal at the sight of the mother, the child is in control again. By arguing that real episodes are fantasies, Freud builds his own kind of seduction kettle logic. You were not molested by someone who overpowered you. If you were, you wanted it anyway. But it was not really a molestation because you just fantasized it; it never really happened.

In his moment of reckoning, Freud takes on undeserved guilt at having been aroused at the sight of his mother's body. But he also thereby erases or sweeps away the memory of the nurse who first used him for her own gratification — an experience that he may have known from his own patients had the power to make him hysterical. He follows the archaeological procedure of the *Aetiology* lecture in reverse. Seeing his mother nude at the age of two and a half or four and being aroused by her is the inadequate objective correlative for the magnitude of his later guilt feelings. In his patients, had they remembered the mother scene first, he would have pushed them to go deeper. What child of two fears castration because his mother is in his presence naked? Such a response is out of proportion, overreaction at the sight of a handkerchief. His process of self-analysis, however, has given him access, perhaps because of his lowered resistance to these possibilities, to the "primordial" scenes. And they are with his nurse. But those are unbearable, humiliating, intolerable scenes to remember.

Conjuring up a castrating father restores limits to a scene of the child's troubling arousal. Such limits, such a castrator, were not available during the scenes of real molestation that preceded the upsetting episode of seeing *matrem nudam* on the train.[12]

The Freudian persistence in calling child sexual abuse *seduction* simply perpetuates the idea that children want sexual contact with adults. Any adult who participates in it is exonerated, as real acts are shifted into having taken place in the child's fantasy. It is striking that Freud never seems to have treated a woman or girl made pregnant by such an attack. Such incontrovertible evidence of sexual contact between an adult and child could have been taken by Freud as evidence that no repression had taken place, and thus he would presume such a rape victim, by incest or otherwise, would not be "neurotic" or "hysterical." Molestation of very young and prepubescent boys by adult women, by contrast, or prepubescent girls by men, would not result in pregnancy — never in any circumstance leave such a trace. And so such contacts become easy to rationalize away, as a baby cannot be. It is also arguable why children are more vulnerable to sexual attack by selfish and unscrupulous adults. The crime can often be covered up by a simple denial. Additionally, the sterility of children makes them attractive targets. Solon, the great Athenian lawgiver, commended man-boy pederasty , in epochs before effective birth control, as an honorable means for male citizens to prevent a population explosion.

The Nurse and the Flight from Freiberg

We know little about Freud's nurse, other than his references to her. Joseph Sajner has identified the nurse as Monika Zajic, while Sander Gilman and Marianne Krüll name her as Theresa Wittek.[13] Krüll considers a listing of visitors from a spa in Roznau in June 1857 significant. Amalia Freud, the wool merchant's wife, is entry number 180, along with her son Sigmund and the "Dienstmädchen" [maid] Resi Wittek (Krüll, 245). However, Sajner also observes the following:

> Jews were allowed to have servants, but they had to register them with the public authorities. Since in the "Register of those holding servants, Freiberg 1857," no other servants of the Freud family are noted, I

> assume that Monika Zajic, most likely a member of the family of Jakob Freud's landlord in the Schlossergasse, in this way earned some additional income. She was officially regularly registered with Maria Freud and could simultaneously have cared for the little Sigmund, taken him for walks, spoken to him in Czech, and often taken him to church.
>
> It is most unlikely that Jakob Freud in those days could have employed an unregistered person. In a draft of a notice . . . of December 19, 1857, "relating to the already three-times fruitless summons in Freiberg of foreign Jews delaying conscription," it states that "Kabut Magdalene" lives with Mrs. Maria Freud as maidservant. All persons mentioned should within 24 hours pay a fine of 8 florins, or be expelled. That the name Kabut never again appears in the archives means that Magdalene Kabut left Freiberg immediately. I mention this fact as confirmation of my thesis that the authorities were very well informed about the employment of people, especially by Jews. (Sajner, 174–75; my translation)

Thus, while Wittek may have been listed in the summer of 1857 on a guest register as the maidservant of Amalia Freud, at home in Freiberg there is no attestation of her presence. Rather, the only "Dienstmagd" [maid] listed for any Freud in this period is Monika Zajic. Thus, barring further archival evidence to the contrary, I find Sajner's earlier reading consistent with the likelihood that Wittek, though perhaps employed for a brief time, was not the person Freud remembers as having molested him and stolen money and toys. Indeed, if there were an issue about foreigners, it seems all the more probable that a Catholic fourth-generation resident of the town would be a more likely and long-term solution for the Freuds' need for servants, than someone liable to be expelled or fined. In any case, there are no Freiberg records to suggest Wittek and not Zajic was the salient person in Freud's recall. Importantly, she was Catholic.

Siegfried Bernfield and Suzanne Cassirer Bernfield describe the house Freud's family inhabited in Freiberg, 117 Schlossergasse, as near to the marketplace, "fields and pastures."[14] The house, they write, "built around 1800, was extremely simple — a detached, rather small, two-story house, without ornamentation, constructed of plastered bricks, with a slate roof" (109). It was a freestanding building. Sajner reports, from Freiberg town records, that

> from 1852 the produce trader Jakob Freud, 38 years old, lives with his wife Rebecca (32 years old) and his sons Emanuel (21 years old) and his spouse (18 years old) and Philipp (16 years old); he is licensed in Klogsdorf; he possesses Housing Certificate Number 195 of the municipality of Klogsdorf as of October 1852; and that he lived there alone from 1840; from 1852 his second wife and sons all stay with him. (170–71; my translation)

Sajner notes that it is not exactly clear when Jakob Freud, Sigmund's father, left the place in which he had been living, owned by a Frau Raska at number 417 (his son Phillipp occupying number 416, owned by August Weber). It is also still an unresolved question as to what became of Jakob Freud's second wife Rebecca, here attested, who is clearly too young to have been the mother of these two sons.

But it does seem clear that Jakob Freud, aged 40, moved into house number 117 on the Schlossergasse after his marriage to the 19-year-old Viennese Amalia Nathansohn. Here, in March or May 1856, Sigmund Freud was born (171–72). The house had been owned by the Zajic family for four generations. The Zajic family were locksmiths (not blacksmiths, as Jones and others report). Sajner states, based on information from a surviving descendant, that the Zajic family had always been locksmiths, and had their workplace on the ground [first] floor of the house (Erdegeschoss). "The Freuds lived in a room in the first [second] floor of the house, while the second room of the same floor was occupied by the owner with his family" (172; my translation). This was a common arrangement, Sajner tells us, for families with businesses involving handiwork. Vitezslava Balcarkova, the daughter of Johann Zajic (1850–1924), tells Sajner that her father remembered Freud well, and was always a warmly welcomed guest of Freud's when he visited Vienna (173). Sajner reports that Monika Zajic was employed as the "Dienstmagd" (hired maid) of Maria Freud, the wife of Freud's older half-brother Emanuel. Sajner finds the likelihood overwhelming that Monika Zajic was a member of Jakob Freud's landlord's family (174). Emanuel and Maria lived in house number 42, with a Frau Blazek (174) very near Jakob and Amalia's place.

Ernest Jones and the Bernfelds have associated the Freuds' departure from Freiberg with the loss of the father's fortunes. The Bernfelds write:

> Cloth manufacture, which was [Freiberg's] main source of income, had been on the down grade since 1835 — and Jacob Freud was a wool merchant. Everywhere in Central Europe the introduction of machines threatened handwork increasingly. In the Forties the new Northern railway, from Vienna to Germany and to Galicia, had bypassed Freiberg. This dislocated trade there and put increasing numbers of artisans out of business. Jacob Freud's business was directly affected. Furthermore, a serious inflation from 1852 on increased the poverty of the town, which, by the year 1859, was pretty well ruined. The Austro-Italian War in 1859 added its bit to make the future still more dark. For the Freud's [sic], these facts made it seem advisable, if not imperative, to move away from Freiberg . . .
>
> The revolution [of 1848–1851] had definitely established Czech nationalism as a power in Austrian politics and consequently had fanned the Czech hate against the Germans, the ruling class in Bohemia and Moravia. Now the Jews, whose language and education were German, became the objects of Czech anti-Semitism. (113–14)

Jones's line of analysis in the first volume of his biography of Freud follows this passage exactly, without attribution (11–12). Didier Anzieu, on the other hand, attributes the departure of the Freuds from Freiberg to "an initial economic crisis caused by mechanisation" (10).

Alternatively, Marianne Krüll has suggested that Jakob Freud's sons Emanuel and Philipp emigrated to Manchester, England at around this time in order to avoid conscription in the Austrian army, which was at that point engaged in fighting the Sardinians (144–45). Philipp, in fact, had been identified by the authorities as eligible for conscription as early as May 1857 (144). Krüll's thesis in full, however, is that Jakob was eager to separate his son Philipp from his wife, with whom she presumes he was engaged in some kind of love affair, at least of an emotional nature. She speculates that Jakob sold his business and gave the proceeds to his older two sons to set themselves up in England. As they later were implicated in a counterfeiting scheme, she draws the conclusion that they left with the intention of engaging in it, and that Jakob Freud hoped "that his generosity would pay dividends"

(145). She believes he was trusting that his Viennese relatives would support him until he got his business going again. There are good reasons to accept her theory; the chain of events and the links she makes are not improbable.

Less probable is her idea that the nurse, having served her ten-month prison term, would come back to visit Amalia and her two children before they left in October. Krüll here is trying to account for a dream analyzed in *The Interpretation of Dreams,* which Freud had in adulthood (146). I find it hard to imagine that a woman so disgraced would come back to say goodbye to her charges after serving a prison term due to their apprehension of her thievery. Instead, it seems more clearly a wish fulfillment on the part of Freud, who almost certainly never got to say goodbye to his nurse, since it is most likely that she was in prison when his family removed to Leipzig.

Sajner and Krüll both dispute the Bernfelds' speculation, also used by Jones, that, even though there were no wealthy Jewish textile merchants in Freiberg, it is possible that in the revolt of 1848–1849 the local Czechs may have scapegoated the Jewish wool handlers (176). Instead, using Sajner's well-documented archival work of 1968, a different explanation suggests itself.

Sajner observes that "The three most important experiences in Sigmund's childhood, namely, the birth of his sister Anna, on December 31, 1858, the dismissal of his nurse and the resettlement out of Freiberg, followed shortly one after the other within two months" (176; my translation). Regarding the birth, Freud quotes his mother in his letter to Fliess of October 15, 1897; her words have been translated as "confinement" in reference to the time during which the nurse was found to have stolen money. She states to Sigmund (per his reportage to Fliess), "Als ich in Wochenbett mit Anna war" (quoted in Sajner, 174). The nurse Zajic was taken away by the police, whom half-brother Philipp had summoned, and sentenced to ten months in prison. Sajner reports that on February 26, 1859, the mayor of Klogsdorf certified that Jakob, Amalie and their two children were entitled to housing in his jurisdiction and, so long as they did not secure citizenship elsewhere, were entitled to return. The mayor further certified that Jakob and Amalie were in good standing in every relationship — presumably he was certifying that they were leaving no bad debts behind, and that on the contrary, there were no blemishes on their reputation whatsoever (176). From there, the family traveled to Leipzig, and then permanently resettled to Vienna a year later. Sajner and Renee Gickelhorn's subsequent work uncovered another affadavit of good standing from the Freiberg authorities of March 23, 1859. Jones is the source given by Krüll that Jakob, Emanuel and Philipp "traveled from Freiberg to Saxony in about June 1859, and that Amalia, Sigmund, and Anna arrived in Leipzig in October of the same year" (Krüll, 261). Jones does not give the source of his dates, which Krüll notes are missing altogether from the German edition of the biography (261). Amalia's date of arrival in Leipzig can be better fixed. She was issued a passport in Brno to continue a stay in Leipzig on August 11, 1859 (140).

These latter dates call into question Sajner's earlier conclusion, that the three most important events of the Freiberg years for Freud occurred within a two-month span. We do not have an exact fix on the date of the nursemaid's apprehension for theft. What we can deduce from the extant evidence would be a date in January, most likely, or perhaps February, when Amalia would still have been confined and Philipp would still have been in Freiberg. My contention would be, however, that there was no catastrophe per se at the time of the departure from Freiberg. Though Freud, as the pseudo-analysand in the screen memories paper, suggests such a chronology, as of March 23, 1859, Jakob and Amalia were issued a certificate of good standing. Presumably, if there had been debts or other difficulties, the municipal authorities might either have noted them, or refused such a "good conduct" certification altogether.

In his paper on screen memories, Freud's "patient," whom editors have identified as a thinly veiled version of Freud himself, reports to Freud the psychoanalyst that "When I was about three, the branch of industry in which my father was concerned met with a catastrophe. He lost all his means and we were forced to leave the place and move to a large town. Long and difficult years followed, of which, as it seems to me, nothing was worth remembering. I never felt really comfortable in the town."[15] If we use this passage and attempt to discern from it something about the circumstances and times surrounding the Freuds' departure from Freiberg, a few things stand out. For while Freud's patient avers that it was a catastrophe in business that drove the Freuds from the idyllic little town in which he had spent his first three years, it is to a large town that they move. The analysand does not detail two moves, from Freiberg to Leipzig and then on to Vienna, as was actually the case for Sigmund Freud. But he does elide together all the years *after* the idyllic town of birth as full of difficulty — all the years after his father's economic loss.

Since the authorities certify the good reputation and good standing of the Freuds as of February and March 1859, another possibility suggests itself. In addition to the reasons supplied by Krüll regarding the avoidance of conscription for the older brothers, and perhaps the initiation of the counterfeiting scheme necessitating emigration, the business with the nurse is worth considering. One wonders what would have been the impact upon the family of Jakob and Amalia Freud, living in close quarters with their Catholic landlords, when a member of the landlords' family, who happened to be a nursemaid taking care of Sigmund and his niece and nephew, was caught stealing from the Jakob Freuds, taken off by the police, and sentenced to ten months in jail. The money she took from the Freuds was found to be "in her possession," according to Freud, so while she was living with Emanuel and his wife it seems clear that Philipp Freud, a bachelor who also lived nearby, had sufficient traffic with all three families to discover her crime. They lived only steps away from each other, according to Sajner.

Is it possible that the difficulty this discovery inflicted upon the living arrangements of the Freuds and Zajics contributed to the decision to leave Freiberg so shortly after the birth of Anna on New Year's Eve, 1858? If the mayor wrote a letter certifying the good standing of Jakob and Amalia on February 26, 1859, it seems plausible to conclude that the Freuds might have departed shortly thereafter. If confinement and *Wochenbett* can be taken to mean the time just after Anna's birth for when Monika Zajic's larceny was discovered, then the departure of the Freuds can be somewhat firmly established as perhaps March or early spring 1859. This corresponds to the screen memory analysand's assertion that he moved away from the beloved town around age three. Freud's own birthday would have fallen at the beginning of May 1859.

The catastrophe with Jakob Freud's brother Josef and the counterfeiting case, on the other hand, occurred in 1865 and 1866 (Gay, 8). And while it is likely that Jakob Freud was indeed affected in his business dealings by the general hard times depicted by the Bernfields, the suddenness of the departure in 1859 also suggests perhaps some connection with the discovery of the thieving nurse, and likely the touchiness her jailing might have engendered in her family, the Freuds' landlords. The counterfeiting business was indeed a catastrophe, which later caused Jakob Freud's hair to famously turn white in the space of a few days. There is no other clear indication of something happening in a short space of time in 1859 which would have precipitously reversed the family fortunes. It is, of course, possible for a small business to lose its capital over time and simply reach a point, undramatically, when going on becomes impossible. Perhaps that point was reached by pure coincidence in the same period that Anna was born and the nurse was discovered in her larceny. Perhaps, though, if Czech anti-Semitism was increasing after 1849, as the Bernfields suggest, such an incident might have strained the tolerance of the landlord-neighbors beyond the breaking point. It is perhaps also likely that if Jakob Freud had liquidated assets and turned the proceeds over to his sons as seed money for the counterfeiting scheme that would eventually become such a scandal and indeed a catastrophe, the eliding memory of the screen memory analysand might easily have collapsed the timeframe of the events in question. The nurse was stealing money given to the baby Sigmund; that suggests that there was cash lying around the family room to be had. At any rate, it is striking to me that even as thorough and usually sensible a reader as Krüll, who notes well the sexualization of the baby Freud by the nurse, would not imagine some negative fallout from this kind of event.

It is also strange to think that after more than 100 years, we still do not know Monika Zajic's exact relation to the Freuds' neighbors across the hall and landlords. Was she a widow? One of the landlord's relatives? An unmarried woman working as a lowly nursemaid for what little money she could get, perhaps even reduced to stealing? This seems possible, given that the Jakob Freuds were not officially employing her. Was she the landlord's wife? Or sister? And while Mrs. Freud reports years later that she received ten months in jail as her sentence, there has been no discussion of prison records, the trial, where she served her time, or any other matter relating to her arrest. While Philipp Freud's joke to his baby brother was that his mother was "eingekastelt," meaning both boxed up, jailed and confined, as in childbirth, there is another layer of resonance. Monika Zajic of the locksmith family was herself locked up.

In one sense, the Freuds' departure may seem overdetermined. So many factors may have conspired to make Freiberg untenable for the Jewish family of wool merchants to stay and prosper. At another level, it is important to underscore, as Sajner does, that Freud lost both his nurse and his beloved Freiberg in the same space of time. So the discovery of the nurse's wrongdoing and her dismissal, which in some sense represents effective justice, is associated with a cutting off from the beloved countryside that Freud would remember with the greatest fondness throughout his life. As with Oedipus, the discovery of wrongdoing between the older woman and the younger man [*sic*] results in unhappy exile.

Conclusion

I have tried to imagine why many male authors, and a few female, have not given these passages much weight or credence. Perhaps for them, as for Freud, the terrible pain of knowing that one was sexually violated in earliest infancy by a beloved and trusted nurse is simply unbearable. Perhaps the men who have written about Freud post publication of the Masson edition of the letters have, like Freud himself and the hostile *Verein,* found it hard if not impossible to compassionately identify with the feelings of a male victim of sexual abuse. Perhaps this difficulty is compounded by the fact that the abuser in this case was a woman — a person propagandized to be without sexual or other agency —, and the victim such a little boy. For whether we like it or not, boys also are propagandized, to be the sexual doers, not the done-to. Men at some level may cling to the fantasy, unavailable to women, that they are a sexually protected, sexually sovereign class. Outside prison, they consciously expect to encounter no unwanted sexual attack. Hence, any sexual attack that does take place is met with vigorous prosecution, or silence.

The poignancy and sadness with which Freud discloses this experience seem to have been lost on Fliess. Freud certainly makes no reference to his response to it in subsequent letters. If Fliess's response were flat or dismissive, especially in light of the failure of 1896, then that, too, would likely have been devastating for Freud. No plaudits for championing abuse victims; and then, no quarter from his best friend and only confidante.

One might say, though, that we see the enormous residue of what Freud *can* admit to himself about this time in the other significant memory associated with Monika Zajic, the theft of money and toys that had been given to him. This is where virtually all previous critical attention has been directed, and readers of Freud have had much to say about these events. But it seems as if much more was taken from him than material things. At the very point where Freud complains about his patients being evilly attached to their illnesses, he has found the key to his own, and yet he is unable to hold onto it.

Instead, the libidinal feelings aroused by the nurse's premature sexualization of Freud the child get transferred to Freud's mother. He sees his mother nude during a train trip and is aroused by her, but this occurs after the episodes of molestation by the nurse. And in the same way that he initially believed that he himself had stolen the money, his mother clarifies that it was in fact the nurse who did the stealing. Whereas he had perhaps wanted to believe that it was his idea to engage in sexual play with the nurse, what is entirely more likely is that it was her idea. But she convinced him, along with instilling in him a high opinion of his capacities, that it was his idea. Strikingly, this is precisely the reversed pattern of blame and agency that Freud will eventually use as a model for understanding child molestation and incest in a psychoanalytic context.

Are there other significant emotional events and losses which the very young Freud endured? To be sure. Louis Breger details the loss of Freud's grandfather just before he is born; the loss of his infant brother Julius when he is about two years old; and his mother's brother's death shortly before Julius's birth.[16] Her likely depression surrounding these deaths may indeed have made her "unavailable" to Freud emotionally, while making him feel "vulnerable and fearful that he too might die, become sick or disappear" (12). And yet, as Breger also concludes, this loss of care and attention seems to have wounded the young Freud even more deeply because of the loss of his nurse, Monika Zajic (14). The wrenching exile from his beloved and pastoral Freiberg and his extended family, precipitated according to Breger by Freud *pere*'s business incompetence (16) certainly consolidated Freud's later sense of catastrophe and poverty in this early period of his life.

Madelon Sprengnether intelligently describes Freud's later difficulties in attempting to reconcile the image of the pre-Oedipal, all-powerful and self-sufficient mother with the morally underdeveloped and sexually passive woman of later essays such as "Femininity."[17] She rightly reckons, I think, many of the problems and inadequacies in the "mothering," to use a Chodorowian term, that Freud received in earliest infancy and its effects on his later theorizing. She does not, however, see the nurse's abusive actions as intrinsically traumatic. She also reads the red water as a castration image, not considering the possibility of its representing Freud's own deflowering or loss of virginity.

What is salient for the present analysis is not the elimination of these experiences from consideration. Rather, I would emphasize their impact on Freud's emotional environment and its inadequacy for him as he struggled to deal with his feelings. Because his mother was both depressed and preoccupied by subsequent births, she was not available to him to comfort him in the loss of his nurse's attention. Breger, for example, sensitively connects Freud's own experience with the loss of maternal attention to the hatred Freud attributes to female children toward their mothers in "Femininity" (13–14). Sprengnether connects several elements in later case studies to Freud's own experiences in this period.

In such a state of emotional neglect and even disarray, it is perhaps not surprising that a child was abused, and that no one, not even his mother, was able to save him from it or to comfort him after it happened. In the public works, Freud emphasizes the physical separation from his nurse as the source of trauma. In his private accounts to Fliess, he describes her as his "sexual teacher" who berates him for his clumsiness, his inability to "do" anything. The first is an official grief to be mourned aloud in public. The second is a wound as well, but one that in his time shunned public attention, grief or consolation. He may have been the nurse's "little man." But when he experienced the same abuse-conditioned arousal before his mother, his mother seems not even to have noticed. Thus he felt shame at his inappropriate reaction and her nonresponse; anger, that he never was able to be his mother's little husband, even if he had wanted to. His nurse taught him that her attention and nurturing came with a sexual cost. It appears that his mother's attention would not come at all. The age-appropriate need, and here, loss, is nonsexualized nurture and loving attention, which all infants require and many receive. The great loss for Freud may have been that, after losing his mother to siblings and his nurse to crime, their attention was never replaced for him until well after the end of this most vulnerable period of his life.

Freud may have wished that there was as much protection for boys against sexual attack under Austrian law as there had been under the Athenian law, which treated the molestation of citizen boys as a punishable outrage. The reddish water in which the nurse bathes him, discolored for reasons uncertain to us, may have signified to him the loss of his virginity in his adult dream, in the way that the virginity of females, when lost, is associated with the bleeding of the hymen. The later paper of 1899 on screen memories revisits the theme of violent deflowering, though in that case the done-to is his coeval niece Pauline. In the fall of 1897, Freud was on the verge of experiencing a great remembered sadness. And then, abruptly, he turned away.

Two

Freud and French Forensic Medicine

In order to understand the development of Freud's "seduction theory," that repressed childhood sexual traumas sat at the base of hysterical symptom formation, it is useful to consider the postdoctoral work Freud completed with the leading lights of French forensic medicine during the late 1880s. While Freud's interest in the work of Charcot has been relatively well discussed, research on Freud's engagement with the work of his forensic colleagues has been much less incorporated into scholarly considerations of the development of the sexual trauma theory. Before we consider what became the central question about Freud in the 1980s and 1990s — why a theory that has become a standard tool for understanding trauma and treating traumatic psychological sequelae was cast aside by the man who first articulated it — it will be useful to consider the grounds upon which he first established it. Part of the answer lies in a close attention to the historical context in which Freud operated. Other critics have attributed Freud's turn to character flaws or rank ambition. Whatever weight these factors may have, additional light on the problem is also shed by a consideration of historical circumstances. Once he returned to Vienna, Freud would attack a problem much larger than himself. Unlike his French colleagues, however, he found himself working in virtual isolation.

In the autumn of 1885, Sigmund Freud traveled to Paris for additional studies at the end of his medical training. He remained there from October 3, 1885, to February 28, 1886.[1] While attending the famous lectures of the chair of the "legal" (forensic) medicine department, Paul Brouardel, it is likely that Freud saw Brouardel perform autopsies on, among others, raped and murdered children in the Paris morgue. Brouardel was the recognized authority on such cases in France, and had documented hundreds of them by the time Freud came to study with him. Much later Freud would allude to the role played by Brouardel, along with Charcot, in linking sexuality and mental illness (Masson, 33). This suggests that Brouardel offered insights about the mental states of both children who survived sexual assault and their perpetrators. At some point Freud, despite his meager means, purchased the forensic medical literature from the Paris school authored by Brouardel and others, which forcefully and comprehensively documented physical and sexual attacks upon children in France by parents, teachers and others who provided care for them (37–40). Thus, Freud had reasons from outside his own practice as well as within it to be interested in the sadly well-attested phenomenon of the physical and sexual abuse of minor children by adults.

More familiarly, Freud also watched Charcot proceed with extrinsic, externally observable manifestations of hysteria in live women patients and a wide variety of attendant symptoms. Charcot observed. Charcot hypnotized. But for him, the hysterical patient remained an object of study, not a speaking subject. He was interested in the manifestation of physical symptoms, but did not see patients as a source of information capable of contributing to an understanding of their etiology. Charcot remained content to attribute hysterical symptoms to heredity. This obviated the need to discuss or investigate any of the patient's experiences. As Jose Brunner points out, Charcot also worked primarily on the poorest members of society; his authority compared to their low station reinforced his conclusions but did little to engage them as sources capable of giving insight or relevant information.[2]

What we are accustomed to knowing about Freud's work at this point has to do with the discovery of the "talking cure." Freud's eventual breakthrough, some years after returning from France, was that he asked for and listened to his patients' stories. At some point, Freud must have made a decision that something parallel to a medical history-taking might reveal salient information regarding the etiology of inorganic hysterical symptoms. He got his patients to reveal the painful facts to him — including facts they had repressed. As he listened to the growing numbers of his patients, following an inductive pattern of thought, he was able to connect their *experience* of early sexual traumas with their current symptoms.

Since this is the point at which readers of Freud tend to separate into supporters and critics, let us consider for a moment what happened when Freud raised his observations to the level of a theory and presented them to his psychiatric colleagues in April 1896.

Like Hamlet, one can say that he had been let in on a great secret involving great crimes. And like Hamlet, he was stymied and unable to act. As a man of science, or, failing that, as one who would have had to defend himself against charges of libel and slander by those he accused, he was unable to either prove or disprove all of his patients' stories through third-party evidence. The legal and medical-scientific standards of proof are remarkably similar at this point, because, as in forensic medicine, they are inseparable.

Freud had a certain amount of data from patients he had seen in the 1880s and early 1890s, which became notable to him in the similarity of their symptoms and root causes. By the time he presented the "seduction" theory to the *Verein für Psychiatrie und Neurologie* in 1896, he was able to cite 18 cases.[3] Clearly numbers of cases are critical in the development of a theory through scientific induction, and this became a difficult issue for Freud. As early as 1893 in a letter to Fliess he had sketched out a kind of study design, of 100 cases of anxiety neurosis, and "a corresponding number of male and female cases of neurasthenia and the much rarer periodic mild depressions. A necessary counterpart would be a second series of one hundred cases of nonneurotics" for comparison.[4] There is no evidence, however, that he was able to follow through on this experimental design.[5] Given the sample size he envisioned, the small size of his own caseload, and the lack of trained colleagues who could collaborate in such data collection, this is not surprising. Freud also had third-party evidence, from the forensic medical sources of the French and the pediatricians' accounts he refers to in the 1896 lecture, that adult sexual abuse of children occurred.[6] It is uncertain and probably unlikely that this material attempted to construct hysterical symptoms as the adult psychological sequelae of persons abused as children.

Since Freud was working from his patients' memories and not the observations of coroners or pediatricians with fresh physical evidence before them, he necessarily struggled with how to cross-check and prove beyond a shadow of a doubt that what his patients were telling him was the whole and unimpaired truth. Brouardel, quoted by Masson, had written that men convicted of rape are often "excellent family men" (Masson, 34). Brouardel's predecessor, Paul Bernard, had published an article in 1886 stating that the reported rape of children 15 years or younger in France between 1827 and 1870 was four times the rate for adults (26). But the work of other helpful, would-be allies in France such as Alexandre Lacassagne, who argued in 1886 that "sexual assaults, even when repeated over a long period of time, and frequently engaged in, are capable of leaving absolutely no trace" was apparently not available to Freud.[7] By 1896 Freud believed he could establish a causal link between the experience of childhood sexual contacts and hysterical symptoms of an inorganic nature in later life. But in 1896 he was caught in a classic logical dilemma. He was stuck in the space between what he felt he knew, and what he could prove to the satisfaction of his own medical and scientific colleagues.

His problem was multiple and complex. First, he was attempting to connect past experiences patients reluctantly remembered with present *harm.* As I will discuss later, no previous person had attempted in a systematic way to argue against the sexual use of children *because it resulted in harm to the child.* And yet this is perhaps the most revolutionary aspect of Freud's perception of his patients: that what someone had done to them in childhood had personally and lastingly harmed them. We should not underestimate how striking such a suggestion would have been in a society accustomed, for example, to the severe and routine corporal punishment of children "for their own good." Second, while he seeks a singular cause for all hysteria, Freud must face the possibility that, on further examination, his cases might not all reduce to a unified etiology. Induction always depends at some level upon probability, and therefore always leaves open the potential for multiple causality. In that sense, Freud also had to be concerned that a larger sample of patients would not reproduce both the single and the same causality that he had asserted. Finally, from a legal and scientific standpoint, in his city and time, the testimony of hysterical women, and children especially, had standing tantamount to that of a ghost story. His witnesses were not considered credible in the eyes of law or science to give testimony about *direct observations,* let alone memories in which they were alleging that crimes had been committed, often by adult men, against their persons. From an evidentiary standpoint, for his audience, Freud was building a case on the shakiest grounds imaginable.[8]

To act, or in Freud's case, to present his findings, on the basis of the unprovable, the unfalsifiable, was to invite attack, even ruin. And yet, like Hamlet, he did so. Using a curious mixture of his own cases, calculated attacks on his colleagues, a fallacious appeal to ignorance, ignoring the weight of the French forensic medical literature, and avowing his unfamiliarity with the Viennese accounts he mentioned in passing, Freud presented his thesis: that *all* hysterias have at their source a sexual trauma. He had found, he told Fliess triumphantly, that sine qua non of nineteenth century European explorers, the head of the Nile (*Letters,* 184).

The reaction of Freud's colleagues was total rejection. Professionally he became completely isolated in Vienna. The paper was not printed, as was customary, in the proceedings of the *Verein*. There was a deafening silence growing around him.[9] Krafft-Ebing, the great authority on sexual matters, told Freud afterward, " 'It sounds like a scientific fairy tale' " (*Letters,* 184). He might as well have said "ghost story." Referrals from other physicians seem to have dried up, and with it, his chances to collect further cases and more data.

Freud's situation at this early juncture parallels Hamlet's in another important way. The people whom his victims accuse are mostly men — men of substance, men who pay the bills of his own patients. They are men who might be his colleagues. They are not serving boys; they are the king. It would presumably be easier to analyze and properly dispense with these perpetrators, were it not for their class positions. The French school of "the hysterical liar" often paints this image: that because the man accused of rape of the child is an upright and prosperous man, an accusation by a child cannot be sustained, ipso facto, precisely because the accused is an upright and prosperous man (Masson, 40–50). The work of Alfred Fournier is relevant in this connection, particularly a case from his work "Simulation d'attentats veneriens sur les jeunes enfants."

> A child of eight came into Fournier's office "literally bathed in yellow pus oozing from her vagina." Something in her account of how she was molested by a man awakened Fournier's suspicions and he decided to win her confidence by means of money, candy, sweet words, and finally "a doll whose eyes moved" which "decided my triumph." She told Fournier, with great difficulty, that "it was not a man who touched her, but that her mother, three times, brushed her sexual parts with a waxing brush, forbidding her to tell anyone about it, and threatening to do it more if she told."[10]

There is legitimate concern with Fournier's precipitous conclusion that the girl lied about the man, and the danger to which Fournier has exposed the girl with her mother, now that her secret has been told. The accused man, whom Fournier describes as "[a]n excellent and perfectly honorable man, father of a family, justly honored and absolutely incapable (I will gladly act as a guarantor) of any ignominious action" and who "allowed himself to be caught up in a trap of this kind" is construed as being a credible testifier because of his class position. Fournier states that "All circumstances, both moral and material, argued in his favor" (Masson, 43). The mother and her daughter, by contrast, were "poor and from the lower classes, hence, in Fournier's eyes, greedy. Moreover, they were of "*déplorables antécédents.*" Nevertheless, the man involved "agreed to pay the money demanded rather than be tried in court," though Fournier is confident he could have exonerated him (43).

In this instance there is no reference to testing the child and the man for venereal disease, as Fournier has determined the child's symptoms to be the result of a different cause. Fournier can easily cite four or five cases of simulated attacks and maintains that therefore such cases are not rare, as might commonly be believed ("Simulations," 502). His credibility might have been bolstered if he had set these simulated cases against the number of true venereal infections he has seen. There is also no follow-on concern by Fournier that the child has accused her mother of acts of sexual abuse, which have resulted in physical symptoms, what appears to be a severe infection. Once the "gentleman" has been exculpated to Fournier's satisfaction, the case is closed and he sends the mother home with a stern warning that if she does not withdraw the charge, he will tell the judge about the brush used to induce the child's infection ("Simulation," 503). He appears not to be concerned with the criminality of the child's mother. This might not be problematic were Fournier a lawyer, particularly for the defense. However, Alfred Fournier is a doctor, and one who was considered a world authority on syphilis.

We would expect a less biased expert to submit the evidence of infection to microscopic examination, and to turn over his evidence regarding the mother's attack on her daughter to the police. There is concern for the welfare of the child, and outrage at so blatant a class prejudice overshadowing the parts of the child's testimony which do not affect the gentleman involved. All that is as it should be. But there are also questions of method and bias that go to the larger issues of procedure in handling such cases legally and treating them medically.

From a legal standpoint, Fournier is generous in his detail as to how he coerced testimony from a reluctant, young and apparently infected witness. There is no apparent concern on Fournier's part for the niceties of being able to provide complete testimony without fear of reprisal. But there is also no construction or analysis of the child's subject position as extremely *dependent* — on her mother, and indeed all adults, who have literally the power of life and death over her.

Fournier states that the main causes of such criminal cases are attempts to extort money or extract vengeance ("Simulation," 509–12). Fournier does not concern himself with the damage to the child's welfare, but only to the man's reputation that even an acquittal cannot erase. In such cases, it would seem that the evidence of science might prove extremely useful. What is the nature of the child's infection? Is it shared by anyone else in contact with her? While Fournier here seems to have discovered a simulated case of venereal infection, it begs the question of whether some cases might not be genuine. Only testing in every case would show this.

But further, there is clearly a prejudgment made by Fournier that the lower classes tell lies but the upper classes do not. At first, the child's testimony against the wealthy man is rejected. But later, when the child contradicts her impoverished mother's story and is the direct accuser (the mother has alleged that the man molested the girl, and the girl avers her mother induced the infection with a brush), the class overlay is to ignore the implications of the child's testimony altogether. In a contemporary setting, we would expect Fournier, after completing an examination of the girl, to at least turn the case over to a prosecutor for further investigation, since clearly something seems to have been done to her that should not have been done. Fournier's agenda, by contrast, seems narrower and easily revealed: to protect the "innocence" of the upper-class man. A more thorough forensic analysis seems likely to have yielded a charge of child abuse against the mother, assuming testing did not establish a venereal infectious link between the man and the girl. It certainly suggests the limits of the statutes and imagination of enforcing agencies that no investigation appears to have been carried out responding to the child's allegations regarding her mother.

Importantly, Linda Gordon and Louise Jackson both corroborate directly the class bias in favor of middle-class offenders and against lower-class victims in the United States and Britain during this time period. Jackson, for example, writes that in Britain, while trials for indicted offenses generally fell between 1830 and 1914, "the number of sexual offenses sent for trial — a large proportion of which involved the sexual assault of children — increased drastically . . . But, throughout the period, only a small proportion of reported cases of sexual abuse—probably less than a third — resulted in conviction" (3). She concludes:

> The likelihood of conviction was linked to social class, reputation and status of, on the one hand, the defendant and, on the other, the victim. The reputation of the girl child was gauged in terms of sexual knowledge and experience; that of a male defendant in relation to his occupational status and position as a family man. Perhaps because child sexual abuse was defined as such a horrible and brutal crime, juries found it harder to believe that a "normal," "respectable" male, with a permanent job and family responsibilities, should wish to molest a child. The middle-class male, and, indeed, the middle-class home, was less likely to be the subject of surveillance or scrutiny. (8)

An indirect confirmation of this attitude is available from German sources as well. Of the 100 criminal incest cases reviewed by Eber (1937), who also compares his numbers with the earlier and magisterial Hentig, the greatest frequency is among trained manual laborers, untrained manual laborers, factory workers and farmers. Eber found only one case among the "higher strata," an engineer, and concluded that the authorities had so few such cases because they actually seldom occurred (18).

A key argument against the legitimacy of Freud's abandonment of the seduction theory is that Freud was well acquainted with the French "legal medical establishment," as it were, more properly rendered as the *forensic* medical establishment, by his studies in Paris. He would have known about the autopsies on children brutalized to death by parents and caregivers, including those children who had been raped prior to death. He owned several of the key works from the French experts in this area, Brouardel, Tardieu, and Bernard (Masson, 37–40). And so the argument from probability suggests that Freud was indeed familiar with this material, and, in one construction of the facts, chose to deliberately ignore it, making him and his followers morally reprehensible and therapeutically bankrupt.

There is, however, an important qualifier regarding the influence of the French material. Commenting on a study by a Dr. Nidart of a girl who, between the ages of 8 and 17 had been physically and sexually tortured by her parents, Dr. Tardieu, author of a comprehensive work on sexual assault from a forensic medical approach, wrote in 1879: "This study, undertaken eighteen years ago, is the first to have been attempted on this subject, about which writers in the field of legal medicine have subsequently remained completely silent" (Masson, 22). The reception of the work of the sympathetic French doctor stands in further historical perspective:

> The singular importance of this work has been ignored for more than 120 years. No trace of any influence it may have had has survived in any direct form (it was never quoted in subsequent literature on infanticide, for example, which became a popular theme in European medico-legal literature of the late nineteenth century). The work which brought Tardieu temporary fame, his *Étude médico-légale sur les atentats aux moeurs* (A Medico-Legal Study of Assaults on Decency), first published in 1857, has never been quoted in the psychoanalytic or psychiatric literature. It is the first such book written in Europe. (22)

The seventh and last edition of the book appeared in 1878. One author suggests that, apart from a 1968 medical doctoral thesis in France and a 1972 paper by a Stanford pediatrician and radiologist, there are no references in any subsequent literature of these important works (22).

The magnitude of suffering described in the French scholarship, along with the British, American and German material, certainly provides a strong basis in hindsight for response and action. From the standpoint of the community of male opinion, however, both medical and psychiatric, in which Freud would come to operate, a singular excoriation of Freud does not bear scrutiny. If the work of French doctors involving autopsies on children brutalized to death by their parents and caregivers was not widely accepted and built upon, we should perhaps be less ready to single out Freud for particular disapprobation and censure for his work on the more difficult cases involving memory and inorganic symptomologies in sexual abuse survivors. Tardieu served as "professor of legal medicine at the University of Paris, dean of the Faculty of Medicine, and president of the Academy of Medicine in Paris, 'the most eminent representative of French legal medicine'" (Masson, 15). I would add that he was probably also Catholic in a Catholic country. From a rhetorical standpoint, one should assess how even a man so fully vested in the medical and academic establishment in France could not gain the day with his colleagues and subsequent generations of physicians. Tardieu possessed all of the force of title, position, education, academic stature, and a breathtaking body of incontrovertible evidence for the crimes, both physical and sexual, committed on the bodies of children. Between 1858 and 1869, 79 percent of all reported rape or attempted rape cases in France were on children under 16 years of age, mostly girls, with the majority of cases between ages 4 and 12. Tardieu, quoted by Masson, observed that of the 616 cases of alleged assault which he personally examined, "339 were of rape or attempted rape of children under the age of eleven" (23). And yet despite this astounding and careful body of work, filled with legally compelling evidence against the perpetrators, Tardieu's research in the fields of medicine and psychiatry largely remained a dead letter until a century later.

Rhetorically, using an Aristotelian framework of ethos, pathos and logos as the chief means of proof in establishing a persuasive argument, I would suggest the following: Tardieu and his sympathetic colleagues possessed both ethos — that is, the force of their expertise and moral character, and the logos, or sound argument, necessary to carry the day, from the perspective of twentieth century critics. What critics fail to weigh adequately, however, is the nature of the reception of the material — the pathos, or how such material would affect the emotions of its intended audience.

It seems clear, given the specificity with which Tardieu was able to document his perpetrators, that fathers as well as mothers, teachers, clergy and others in authority in children's lives were perfectly capable of committing horrifying acts of cruelty and torture, even unto death, upon the bodies of their innocent and dependent charges. Thus, in the most extreme cases, meaning those resulting in the death of the child, male perpetrators as well as female could be named. The courts' hand was closest to being forced here, when even a powerful man or father would fall under the net of law and punishment. I do not know how many of Tardieu's perpetrators were prosecuted, however, nor the outcome of their cases.

The basis for prosecution and punishment was present, from the standpoint of one and a half centuries hence. But however compelling Tardieu, Brouardel and Bernard's work was for the prosecution, and the children and women it would have protected, children and women were not the agents of authority. If we look at the intended audience of the French forensic school, we see that it is comprised of men — doctors, lawyers, judges, all, indeed, "men of substance." As Fournier so deftly reminds us, arguments of probability in such a social system will always favor the credibility of wealthy, educated family men over poorer and socially disenfranchised children and women.[11] Rhetorically, the major premise is clear. In cases where the accused is a man "of substance," the accuser perforce must be an extortionist or mentally unsound.[12] Men of substance do not sexually or physically abuse women and children. M. —— is a man of substance; therefore, he did not commit this abuse. What was at stake was the credibility of the ruling class, that is, powerful men. They had no incentive, in this time before the political enfranchisement of women and the extension of protective rights toward children, to allow, except in the most incontrovertible cases, any encroachment on their hereditary privilege of male caste membership. The ideal, seemingly, was to minimize the damage to the caste as a whole by making the bar for prosecution and punishment so high, only the deaths of victims would warrant criminal investigation.

In cases that failed to provide evidence of a positive and legally sufficient nature, it was possible in such a climate, and even routine, to cast doubtful shadows on or dismiss entirely the charges made by children and women. Fournier, and later Motet, made a small specialty of arguing that children lie about sexual and physical abuse. The nineteenth century assumption was that children did this to extort money and favors, and "hysterical" women did so because of mental "degeneration" (Masson, 40–50). From twentieth century data, we know that, in fact, most child abuse does indeed stop short of murder, though its effects are usually still devastating for those who suffer it. In such cases, the best one can hope for is treatment and the ability to remove the survivor from the reach of the perpetrator. Prosecution and punishment of the perpetrator are luxuries, a standard of justice never to be experienced by most victims.

Importantly, the legal standard comes to serve as the de facto medical and psychiatric standard for agreeing about whether or not someone abused another. The attitude of the French forensic medical school of "lying children" said, in essence, that without legal proof positive, one must assume the child is lying. The effect of this understanding was to render legally unprosecutable any molestation or attack that either left no lasting physical evidence or was unwitnessed. *Any* doubt became the standard for exculpation of the accused. Such a category of alleged but not legally provable cases comprises, as experts know, the vast majority of all sexual abuses committed on children. Freud himself alludes to this when he describes, in 1896, the strangers who knew "how to avoid inflicting gross, mechanical injury" (208). Rather than the French legal standard of "guilty but not proved," which at least provided a basis for sympathetic treatment for the victim, an Anglo-Saxon standard of "not proved beyond the shadow of a doubt" became the basis for denying even sympathetic therapy for the victim. It created a psychiatric and psychoanalytic environment in which the accused would always be exculpated, and the survivor would have to choose between reconciling herself or himself to the attack, or being labeled insane or degenerate.[13]

In this we hear the echoes of René Girard's analysis of the scapegoat situation.[14] Girard defines a (human) scapegoat as someone capable of being loaded with the guilt felt by the polluting elements in the community, and then being banished or killed, thereby bearing the communal guilt or pollution away with him or her in death. In pre-judicial or nonjudicial societies or situations, a substitute wrongdoer, a scapegoat, must be found. If the actual wrongdoer were held responsible, due to his social stature his death or punishment would have to be avenged by his family. Any hurt to the person or reputation of a powerful person must be answered. This necessity, however, would unleash a potentially unending spiral of reciprocal violence, as each side would repeatedly attack a worthy person from among their enemy's group.

The utilitarian purpose of the scapegoat, then, is precisely this: he or she is the one character in the piece whose death will not be protested, and therefore not avenged, the primary characteristic which makes him or her suitable as a scapegoat. Girard even notes those classes of people who provide good scapegoats. Chief among them are unmarried women, slaves (we might add nurses and maids) and children (140–42, 12). The law, however, recognized this class as such in many ways prior to the twentieth century. Adult sex with children, especially very young children, was at times given lesser penalties than for sexual contact or rape of older children or adults. As recently as 1947, the Swiss legal scholar Hans-Ulrich Gebhart characterized as ludicrous the increased penalties on adult sex with young children, which had been instituted in Austria in 1927 (64). Although Gebhart noted in his review of post-Enlightenment European incest laws that children under the age of 16 were usually unpunished if it was shown that they had been seduced, it was also frequently the case that those over 16 were punished with imprisonment or other means.[15] We may therefore infer that young children who could be construed as *not* having been seduced could also be subject at least in some cases to punishment along with the adult perpetrator(s). Gebhart does not review the actual outcomes of prosecutions in the European jurisdictions he examines; however, there is evidence that the girls themselves could be and were punished, even if they were below the age of consent. Gordon, for example, writes directly of the Victorian notion of the girl herself as "polluted" (216) and notes that girl victims of sexual abuse "were usually punished more than culprits" (217).

The significance for the nineteenth century French material is straightforward. When it is possible, due to political, social or economic disenfranchisement, to carry out crimes on a group that lacks the means to defend itself or exact justice or retribution, even a judicial society functions, in essence, as a scapegoat society. That French society felt itself to be polluted seems to be demonstrated by Tardieu, Brouardel, Bernard and others. Incest per se has throughout western history repeatedly been referred to as unspeakable, the very greatest horror and pollution imaginable, often carrying the death penalty in early times.[16] As Kenneth Burke and René Girard remind us, however, pollution or guilt must be purified in order for society to carry on.[17] Cases came to the attention of Tardieu and the courts that could not be denied or dismissed, given the courts' own standards of proof and legal statutes governing rape and murder. It cannot be said that no cases were ever prosecuted. But an exchange also took place. The powerful perpetrators, who sometimes did get caught, devised arguments and standards that carried away from themselves guilt for crimes short of gonorrheal rape or impregnating rape or murder. As Lacassagne had observed with alarm, in cases where sexual crimes were committed on the persons of children and women which left no physical proof, the standard would simply be that the accuser was lying. With proof, the victim still had no guarantee of justice. By the same token, the existence of laws against incest, for example, created a climate in which adult men in particular could be legally accused and charged. Making such charges, directly or indirectly, was not a thing to be done or taken lightly.

In the prosecution of crimes lacking definitive physical evidence from the bodies of the persons involved, the alternative rhetorical strategy of the *contrarium* seems not to have held the day. The figure contrarium operates in this way: If the less likely thing can be shown to have happened, then we should accept that the more likely thing is certainly happening, even if it is more difficult to demonstrate. Here, the less likely thing is that parents would so abuse and torture their own children that those children would die from their wounds. Tardieu and his colleagues showed definitively that, time and again, such things did happen. If parents were willing to commit sexual and violent crimes against their children that might result in their own prosecution and punishment because they left physical and even fatal marks, how much more likely would they be to commit crimes for which they would never have to fear punishment? How many sexual abuses may be perpetrated without the creation of a physical trace adequate for forensic standards? This represents criminal opportunity. History is replete with admonitions to parents not to avail themselves of such opportunities.[18] Where the perpetrator is gaining sexual and other pleasurable gratification in the process, how much more motivation might there be? This represents criminal motive, and would be the argument by contrarium. For the nineteenth century audience, however, such arguments proved unpersuasive.

Although it is customary in our times to express public outrage at the sexual abuse of children, even recent history indicates that law and custom have been far from solicitous on behalf of children in Europe and the United States. Behlmer, Jackson and Hooper provide detailed accounts, both of the abused and neglected condition of many Victorian children in Britain, and of the enormous efforts required by reformers to pass laws intended to protect them. Lloyd DeMause's comprehensive work in this area is a landmark in a field whose literature has grown to staggering proportions. This represents a shift in attitudes, both among the public and among academicians, that children have human rights as well as adults, and that the violation of such rights represents a concern, if not an outrage. But while France and England may have experienced decades of social reforming around child sex abuse just before and after the turn of the nineteenth century, there is much less evidence that German and Austrian societies experienced such a transformation. Freud's difficulties and his inability to attract any other champion to his cause are consistent with this historical picture.

Tardieu's argument is made nowadays by proponents of the false memory syndrome. Perfectly fine families have been ruined, they say, because of the (necessarily) false accusations of suggestible children. The virtue of families, by virtue of being families, is put above the possibility or likelihood of a crime having been committed, and the suggestibility of some children is used to vitiate the veracity of all.[19] Two important elements can be lifted out of this discourse: One is the continuing class bias in analyses of men who are successfully prosecuted for sexual crimes. A reasonable body of evidence suggests that sexual crimes against children have a pattern of prosecution not unlike that of other crimes. Lower-class men have traditionally been more heavily scrutinized and punished for such crimes, along with men construed as gay, or nonfathers, such as priests, than have middle- and upper-class married or heterosexual men.[20]

There is also a simple but important methodological rule to employ when attempting to ascertain the veracity of testimony. Apply the same standards to adults as to children — in other words, do not begin from an assumption that one group is any more or less prone to lie than the other. While false memory syndrome theorists have built a case that children are suggestible and may testify to remembering something they never in fact experienced, there is the obvious attendant corollary concerning the credibility of adults. Because some adults sometimes lie or misremember, shall we conclude that all adults always do? Hans Joachim Schneider suggests that children are indeed capable of producing credible testimony, citing the 92–98 percent accuracy of statements by children up to 14 years of age (the youngest children proved most reliable).[21] Judith Herman and Mary Harvey have shown experimentally that victims also forget traumatic crimes committed on their persons, and that perpetrators forget crimes for which they were legally convicted.[22]

There is quite a rich body of contemporary literature on the clinical ramifications of trauma on memory, which will be discussed later in this book. At this point, however, there is the still terribly difficult situation of false accusations. Children, in their utter dependence on their parents and caregivers for survival, might conceivably take on an adult's desire or suggestion that they accuse, say, an estranged spouse or family member or caregiver. In custody situations, or cases where a parent or adult might be projecting his or her own experiences onto the child, pressure on children from unethical or unaware adults to produce accounts of abuse in order to incriminate other family members or caregivers must at times be overwhelming. We accept that adults may be extorted or coerced. It would seem sensible to continue to pursue research on the question of undue influence on children in a legal setting as well.

In the last 15 years in particular, the weight of these difficult questions often led to extreme positions. The camps implicated in the

"Freud wars" often divided into all or nothing positions. Childhood accounts were either all true and necessarily always to be accepted in law courts, or all false, and all to be thrown out, with complaining victims treated as fantasists or malingerers. Freud's French contemporaries grappled with the same questions about the reliability of children's testimony (Masson, 40–54), as had English, American and other western jurists. The difficult fact remains: crimes are often committed that cannot be proved in court. The legal system that operates in this fashion is intended to protect the innocent. In child sex abuse cases, we have yet to devise adequate and fair means to ensure that the innocent accused and the guilty accused are reliably distinguishable from each other. Until we do, one test of the bias of authorities should be the robustness with which they are willing to support access to treatment for an alleged victim, short of "proof positive," as the courts now construe it. The scandal of child sex abuse by Catholic priests in the early years of the new millenium has showed greater credibility being extended to the claims of victims, against the Church's attempt through the decades to settle those claims quietly through monetary awards and "rehabilitation" for offenders. Here at least was the beginning of a recognition that perpetrators, too, had psychiatric problems.

For the French, however, as for Freud, the same presumptions ultimately applied. For them, the testimony of adult, white, prosperous, heterosexual men would almost always prevail. The king remained the king despite the charges. We should remember: it was not other fathers who executed Laius, the father of Oedipus. Laius became king after the rape of Chrysippus. Laius was punished by his son.

Conclusion

In France, Freud was acquainted with a well-developed forensic medical establishment. The work of Brouardel, Tardieu, Bernard, Lacassagne and others may have gone some way toward planting in Freud's mind the awareness that adults were perpetrating terrible crimes, including sexual crimes, upon the bodies of children. The process by which Freud was ultimately able to link such sexual crimes with the symptoms of "hysteria," so-called, constituted the formation of the "talking cure," and the first iterations of psychoanalysis as a method and technique for treating such patients. The "unspeakable" things Freud witnessed in Paris, and could only allude to in his letters to Martha Bernays, may well have set his mind racing and stimulated his competitive energies, as Judith Herman has suggested.[23]

And yet despite his desire to differentiate himself from his French colleagues, Freud ultimately returned to the simple economy of blaming the less well-defended party, namely the child. This tracked with the work of Fournier and the "hysterical liar" school. Instead of lying, however, which attributed a vicious motive to the child, Freud would develop, post-1897, the fantasy theory inherent in the Oedipus complex.

On the other hand, Freud's defenders aver that Freud never denied that adults do sexually molest children. In cases not involving repressed memories or hysterical symptoms, they note that Freud never defended the perpetrators. Jose Brunner, for example, writes:

> a closer look at Freud's references to child abuse in his later writings reveals that this divide was less deep than it might appear from the dramatic emplotment in Freud's autobiographical essays and Masson's problematic attempt at debunking Freud. In 1907 Freud still advised Karl Abraham that some patients' accounts of sexual traumas were real. In January 1913 he wrote to the Swiss pastor Oskar Pfister that he himself had "analysed and cured several cases of real incest (of the most severe kind)." In 1931 he described the seduction of children as "common enough" and as an experience leaving behind "extensive and lasting consequences." Finally, in *An Outline of Psycho-Analysis*, written shortly before his death, he repeated this statement, albeit in a somewhat different wording.[24]

The first two references are in letters, which occur in private communication published decades after his death. These can hardly be taken as public avowals. His expressions to Abraham may be considered to be genuine, given the latter's own contributions in this area. One may wonder, however, where in his case histories and clinical notes are the several cases of "real incest" that Freud cured. If he had achieved such therapeutic successes and believed that such crimes and their treatments were important, would he not have written about them for public consumption?

We also might wonder what Freud means here by "real." It is not clear if he is referring to cases where the victim never forgot or repressed the experience, and thus the problem of the intermingling of memory and "phantasy" about which Freud was always concerned was not material, or cases where he was able to confirm by some third-party means that incest had taken place. Does "real" here simply mean cases where Freud was sure beyond the shadow of a doubt? Does "real" amount to clearly and definitely confirmed? Are these cases different from the more difficult cases of recalled repressed memories, which might be more vague and less easy to ascertain but are nevertheless "real" to their victims?

If by "real" Freud means the former, it would undercut his previous thesis that psychic damage only occurs when repression has taken place. As Brunner characterizes Freud's position, "those who had the moral and mental strength to consciously acknowledge and remember that they had been victimized in early childhood were able to stay healthy."[25] But if Freud "cured" such cases of "the most severe kind" of incest, then presumably even always-remembered incest can cause damage.

On the other hand, Freud is also at pains in the *Introductory Lectures* of 1916–1917 to point out that, while patients' accounts of sexual abuse ought not to be taken simply at face value as true, they should also not be dismissed out of hand as fabrications: "You must not suppose, however, that sexual abuse of a child by its nearest male relatives belongs entirely to the realm of phantasy. Most analysts will have treated cases in which such events were real and could be unimpeachably established."[26] This may have been his principal step forward, for it seems clear that in cases short of death or extreme injury, many Victorian medical and legal authorities were unwilling to accept the child's credibility over the adult's.

But a laxity in characterizing the acceptability of sexual contact between adults and minors persists even in recent times, in writings by contemporary psychoanalysts. The eminent Charles Rycroft, for example, delivers a crisp critique of Ferenczi's terminological slippages in a 1932 paper asserting evidence of the widespread nature of child sexual abuse by adults, including among the educated and monied classes:

> According to Ferenczi, "Even children of respected, high-minded puritanical families fall victim to real rape much more frequently than one had dared to suspect. Either the parents themselves seek substitution for their lack of (sexual) satisfaction in this pathological manner, or else trusted persons such as relatives (uncles, aunts, grandparents), tutors, servants, abuse the ignorance and innocence of children." This corresponds exactly to what Freud had said in his 1896 paper, but Ferenczi goes on to add something that Freud did not say: "The obvious objection that we are dealing with sexual fantasies of the child himself, that is, with hysterical lies, unfortunately is weakened by the multitude of confessions of this kind, on the part of patients in analysis, to assaults on children." But, curiously, Ferenczi does not go on to cite any of the "multitude of confessions" made to him by patients in analysis but to the much weaker "Thus I was not surprised when a short time ago an educator known for his high-minded philanthropy came to see me in a veritable state of despair to tell me that thus far he had been unfortunate enough to discover fine families of good society in which the governesses lived in a regular conjugal state with nine-to-eleven year old boys."[27]

Rycroft takes issue with Ferenczi on a number of grounds, but in terms of the status of the last claim, he refutes its significance by the following statement: "Now, it may or may not be a good thing for nine-to-eleven-year-old boys to sleep with their governesses, but 'living in a regular conjugal state' with a governess is certainly neither rape nor assault, though it does suggest that some seduction may have been going on."[28] The first extraordinary thing about this statement is that, in the eyes of the law, such a situation would be considered statutory rape. A child who is considered in the eyes of the law not to be able to withhold consent from a sexual act cannot be categorically excluded from rape, regardless of the level of force used to secure sexual contact. Rycroft's gallant assertion of the nonseriousness of such contact has nothing to do with any knowledge of how this contact is experienced by the children involved, including the possibility of their own inappropriate sexual behavior as a result toward other children — another piece of the scenario Freud discussed in 1896. Are we to presume that such arrangements are not noxious because the adult is a female of lower class than her prepubescent male charges? Would Rycroft be equally nonchalant if Ferenczi had related knowing of five girls of that age in conjugal arrangements with their male tutors? Would he be as dismissive had the adults been male tutors engaged in sexual acts with their male students?

The issue of coercion is also important. Many adults report great distress and psychological damage from childhood sexual contacts with adults that were not at the time experienced as painful, coercive or punishing. "Seduction" is the great undefined term here. It suggests some resistance on the part of the child victim that must be overcome. Perhaps Rycroft feels, contra the clinical evidence, that only forcible rape has traumatic sequelae. In any event, it seems shockingly irresponsible for Rycroft to suggest, as late as 1991, that sexual contact of the kind Ferenczi described should be considered benign and unproblematic for either the adult or the child. While Ferenczi fails to give details, apart from the fact that adults admit perpetrating such acts, including rape, in analysis, surely the burden of proof is on Rycroft to show that such sexual contact has no short- or long-term negative consequences for anyone involved. The implicit bravado is there — for boys that age, Rycroft seems to suggest, such an arrangement is in fact a godsend devoutly to be wished. We should not be so sure, I think. The obvious difference between woman-boy and man-girl contact is that boys' social reputations are supposed to be enhanced by sexual contact with women — even before they are old enough to ejaculate, implies Rycroft. Girls, on the other hand, who were engaged in such relations would hardly escape scot-free. The deeper questions have to do with the other kinds of emotional damage we would anticipate relating from both kinds of relations. Interestingly, in the eyes of contemporary U.S. law, even the apparent consent of the younger party is not enough to absolve the adult of legal culpability. It would appear that even the law, in this instance, has progressed beyond psychoanalysis.

But Rycroft's characterization *is* consonant with the Victorian attitude, where we have also seen no categorical criminal response to any sexual contact between an adult and a minor. The poor Parisian mother of the child with the infection who accused the gentleman seems not to have come under judicial scrutiny for assaulting her daughter. What is significant about this period, from the standpoint of factors which would or would not support Freud's seduction theory, is that the letter of the law was generally weak, and even where it was not, it resulted in very few convictions for adult sexual contact with children.

Some defenders of Freud have suggested that his theory of childhood sexuality and the Oedipus complex were hardly more palatable to his colleagues than the seduction theory. But in this they miss an important point. From a rhetorical standpoint, the contrarium is operative here. Against the backdrop of the social beliefs held by Freud's contemporaries, it would be easier to argue to grown men that little girls desire sex with them, than to argue that grown men who engage in sexual acts with little girls are doing something wrong, even harmful to the child. The British, after all, had lowered the age of consent during periods of syphilis so that men could have sex with ever younger virgins.[29] Children of the lower classes may have been especially vulnerable to such depredations. But we should not be blinded by conventional or received notions of Victorian sexual propriety either. Incest, after all, was not made a crime in Great Britain (though it had been an ecclesiastical offense) until 1908.

To suggest that sex with children has lasting traumatic consequences for the children involved would have been tantamount, in some ways, to suggesting that corporal punishment also had negative psychological sequelae — an idea that did not gain currency in the United States or Europe until well into the twentieth century. On a more depressing but probably real note, any adults engaged in such behaviors would hardly welcome the idea that that they should stop their own illicit activities — including those who by virtue of their titles were being told to prevent such things and intervene appropriately. Even priests, as we now know, were not above engaging in such crimes, nor was the Catholic Church above protecting them after they had done so. At a base level, we should expect that those committing acts that *become* criminalized will first blame others for their wrongdoing, before eventually and grudgingly consenting to give up a free pleasure, a free power, that they desire and secretly enjoy.

Unpalatable as the theory of childhood sexuality may have been, it did allow adult men (and women) to speak for children, and assert through denial or minimization the harmlessness of sexual practices that brought pleasure to adults. The child's reaction and ability to give or withhold consent, along with any damaging effects upon the child, were washed away. In claiming that children desire seduction, the child's agency is in every case turned over to the service of adult wishes. By arguing that the child has sexual desires, adults can more easily rationalize "satisfying" those desires. They can vitiate the chasm of difference in their power by speciously re-creating the child as a sexual equal or even provocateur.

On the other hand, accusing adults of harming children through sexual contact exposes adults to the prospect of legal punishment and social ostracism. It becomes an occasion for legal examination of a charge, and the possibility of accounting for damage its victim may have sustained. Though adults may fear false accusations, the absence of legal inquiry means society will never arrive at an agreement over whether an accused person committed a crime. Such a system, however, presupposes that a society agrees there should be no sexual contact between adults and children. Victorian Europe, in both law and fact, was rather far from that standard.

The seduction theory meant accusing adult men of criminally abusing children. It also meant acknowledging the sexual agency of women abusers, a point that Freud, at least, seemed unprepared to defend, and, based on his own history, against which he needed devoutly to defend. However distasteful child sexuality within the Oedipus complex may have sounded to Victorians, history shows that Freud was taken up by other doctors and the public when he sexualized children — not when he criminalized their adult sexual perpetrators.

THREE

Analyzing Freud's Arguments in "The Aetiology of Hysteria"

Having examined the general climate of opinion regarding the sexual abuse of children in Europe and the United States at the turn of the nineteenth century, the contentions that Freud recanted his views due to opportunism or moral collapse take on a different cast. Freud at that point was probably less aware of the overall sense of his times than he was sensitive to the conditions immediately before him and the reception he had received among his immediate colleagues in Vienna. It may be easier to understand Freud's unsympathetic reaction to his own memories of sexual abuse if we look at how his "seduction theory" was received by medical colleagues the previous year. Though Freud believed that in linking hysterical symptoms to repressed episodes of childhood sexual abuse he had found "the head of the Nile," his colleagues at the Vienna *Verien für Psychiatrie* were uniformly hostile in their reaction. Thus, a year before he came to grips with his own abuse, Freud had suffered enormous public humiliation as the champion of childhood abuse victims, and as a result had found himself on the verge of professional ruin and the collapse of his practice. It is hardly a circumstance one could describe as supportive of the victim's position or therapeutic needs. And while it is not in itself the reason for Freud's collapse of sympathy, it does provide a telling prelude to the doctor's reconstruction of his own abuse, and his response to it, in the creation of the Oedipus complex.

Masson observes that no one in the French school seems to have linked such acts as survivable rape or attempted rape with psychological sequelae for the victim (Masson, 36, 52). These, of course, constitute the set from which Freud's subset of cases — patients with "hysterical" symptoms deriving from the repressed memory of sexual abuse — derive. Freud concerned himself not with cases where there was forensic evidence of sexual abuse in the present or most recent past; nor was he interested in cases where the person had always actively remembered the abusive episodes. He considered such people as free of hysterical symptoms — though he apparently was not curious about what other psychological difficulties they might be experiencing as a result. Freud's special purview was cases involving repressed memory — abuses pushed beneath conscious recall, yet, as he came to believe, capable of subsequently causing symptoms that had no apparent organic cause.

In terms of legal standards of proof, such cases on their face presented enormous challenges. Freud was making a new case for a link that no one before him had tried systematically to establish. What was at the root of so-called "hysterical" symptoms? Freud's answer, his discovery of "the head of the Nile," was sexual abuse in childhood. But such an answer represented a drastic change in clinical understanding. And Freud clearly understood, as the 1896 lecture shows, that he had an enormous persuasive task before him as he addressed his psychiatric colleagues.

This chapter explores Freud's arguments before the Vienna *Verein* on April 21, 1896, in a lecture subsequently known as "The Aetiology of Hysteria." This lecture develops further some ideas in his earlier lecture before the Vienna Medical Club on January 11, 1893, "On the Psychical Mechanism of Hysterical Phenomena,"[1] in which he asserts that "*hysterical patients suffer from incompletely abreacted psychical traumas*" (38; italics in original). In the 1893 lecture, he attempts to establish that

> "*There is a complete analogy between traumatic paralysis and common, non-traumatic hysteria.*" The only difference is that in the former there is seldom a *single* major event to be signalized, but rather a *series* of affective impressions — a whole story of suffering. But there is nothing

> forced in equating such a story, which appears as the determining factor in hysterical patients, with the accident which occurs in traumatic hysteria. For no one doubts any longer to-day that even in the case of the major mechanical trauma in traumatic hysteria what produces the result is not the mechanical factor but the affect of fright, the *psychical* trauma. The first thing that follows from all this, then, is that the pattern of traumatic hysteria, as was laid down by Charcot for hysterical paralyses, applies quite generally to all hysterical phenomena, or at least to the great majority of them. In every case what we have to deal with is the operation of psychical traumas, which unambiguously determine the nature of the symptoms which arise. (30–31; italics in original)

The lecture develops the idea that hysteria may develop both due to a physically traumatic injury as well as to a severe fright or other "psychical" trauma. If this earlier lecture, which does suggest innovative approaches to hysteria of a (presumably) nonphysical trauma, was accepted more readily by colleagues, that may have been due to its technical nature and to Freud's close association with Josef Breuer at this time. Their joint treatise *On The Psychical Mechanism of Hysterical Phenomena: A Preliminary Communication* appeared in 1893 as well.[2]

Here we will explore how Freud makes his case in the more controversial 1896 lecture. It is clear from the outset that he understands himself to have a difficult persuasive task. He seems to sense he is facing an audience that is at best skeptical, at worst hostile. The method Freud asserts for establishing a technically, professionally and clinically defensible case for the "seduction theory" at this early stage of his career is rhetorically revelatory.

Freud's Objectives

Freud begins the "Aetiology" lecture by setting out some of the technical precepts he and presumably other psychiatrists in his audience used in examining patients and seeking diagnoses. The opening passage reveals the way in which Freud seeks mastery over the notoriously Protean phenomenon of hysteria. His dissatisfaction with the procedure of questioning the patient directly is also clear. The idea that the patient almost necessarily gives faulty or incomplete information is critical as an impetus for improved technique as well as therapeutic efficacy. The presumption is that the true basis of the neurosis is "hidden" from the patient, who therefore cannot directly comment upon it.

> Gentlemen — When we set out to form an opinion about the causation of a pathological state such as hysteria, we begin by adopting the method of anamnestic investigation: we question the patient or those about him in order to find out to what harmful influences they themselves attribute his having fallen ill and developed these neurotic symptoms. What we discover in this way is, of course, falsified by all the factors which commonly hide the knowledge of his own state from a patient — by his lack of scientific understanding of aetiological influences, by the fallacy of *post hoc, ergo propter hoc,* by his reluctance to think about or mention certain noxae and traumas. Thus in making an anamnestic investigation of this sort, we keep to the principle of not adopting the patients' belief without a thorough critical examination, of not allowing them to lay down our scientific opinion for us on the aetiology of the neurosis. ("Aetiology," 191)

In other words, the doctor must be in charge of the diagnosis. The patient's account is not a self-evident, fully self-revealing or complete text, nor is the patient a reliable narrator.

Freud's use of the term of argumentative fallacy, post hoc ergo propter hoc, is notable, for it reveals a rather sophisticated rhetorical sense: that the patient's information can be flawed because she or he mistakes a correlation for a cause, "after the fact, therefore because of the fact." Freud senses the inadequacy, because of the disproportionality, between symptoms and past experiences that some patients connect. Freud describes how he pushes his patients to go back further in memory, to find the more distant past event that carried sufficient emotional charge to cause trenchant current symptoms. He pushes them, in short, to find a sufficient objective correlative.

Patients are also blind to the possibility of inherited neurosis, he asserts. Freud credits Charcot for this contribution ("Aetiology," 191). Charcot, as Freud notes in his obituary of the French doctor, came to believe that heredity was the sole factor in the development of neuroses, and events in the patient's life merely "*agents provocateurs*" that brought forth symptoms.[3] The rest of the lecture is not consistent with Charcot's position at all, in that Freud will argue for an experienced event or set of events as the basis for neurosis (as he does in the 1893 lecture). But as a researcher he must account for or at least acknowledge a leading theory that conflicts with his position, and he does so.

Thus, in the opening paragraph, Freud has introduced a method by which the doctor attempts to establish the etiology of the neurosis, made up of several factors: the patient's account, which is presumed to be incomplete; the testimony provided by family, friends and others in a position to provide information about "harmful influences" the patient may have fallen under; and the additional factor of heredity. But for Freud, all these factors rest on the unsound foundation of the patient's testimony. In essence, patients are often unwilling, unable, or both, to reveal information that might truly shed light on the causes of the illness. He continues by suggesting that "You will readily admit that it would be a good thing to have a second method of arriving at the aetiology of hysteria, one in which we should feel less dependent on the assertions of the patients themselves" ("Aetiology," 191). He sees the problem of the Ghost.

What Freud seeks, and what he intends to offer his colleagues, is a method that does not depend on the cooperation of the patient, or even necessarily on the awareness of the patient. Likening the patient's mind to an archaeologically interesting ruin, in a place now inhabited by "semi-barbaric" people ("Aetiology," 192), he suggests the superiority of the archaeologist, who uses picks and other tools to reveal the true nature of the original structure rather than having to depend on the current inhabitants to act as informants about the structure now in ruins. His desire is for a method like that of the dermatologist, who diagnoses a blister based on his own scientific knowledge, not what the patient tells him. He also invokes the work of the forensic pathologist, who works on the bodies of the dead and arrives at the cause of death or injury without testimony, let alone cooperation, from the patient. Freud's argument proceeds here by analogy. In every example, the mind of the patient is, in the condition of the desideratum, as inert and voiceless as a stone, a sore or a dead body. These images, I think, represent fantasies of control that Freud desires to have over the wayward symptoms of his hysterical patients. But they also advert to the influence of the French forensic doctors, whom he saw working on corpses.

Freud seeks a more reliable, unbiased and extrinsically confirmable source of information about the cause of the hysteria. He suggests the preferred method, derived from Breuer's famous discovery regarding trauma and its sequelae:

> If we try . . . to induce the symptoms of hysteria to make themselves heard as witnesses to the history of the origin of the illness, we must take our start from Josef Breuer's momentous discovery: *the symptoms of hysteria . . . are determined by certain experiences of the patient's which have operated in a traumatic fashion and which are being reproduced in his psychical life in the form of mnemic symbols.* (192–93; italics in original)

Importantly, hysterical symptoms, according to Breuer, derive from experiences.

Freud commends Breuer's formulation of etiology, but characterizes the resulting therapeutic method in rather mechanical terms:

> What we have to do is apply Breuer's method — or one which is essentially the same — so as to lead the patient's attention back from his symptoms to the scene in which and through which that symptom arose; and having thus located the scene, we remove the symptom by bringing about, during the reproduction of the traumatic scene, a subsequent correction of the psychical course of events which took place at the time. (193)

What this correction is, Freud does not specify. The procedure is vaguely surgical, and surely logical rather than emotional. The symptom is "removed" by the doctor making a "correction" in what he and Breuer in "The Psychical Mechanism" refer to as symptoms resulting from an "idea":

> *each individual hysterical symptom immediately and permanently disappeared when we had succeeded in bringing clearly to light the memory of the event by which it was provoked and in arousing its accompanying effect, and when the patient had described that event in the greatest possible detail and had put the affect into words.* (6)

> *It brings to an end the operative force of the idea which was not abreacted in the first instance, by allowing its strangulated affect to find a way out through speech; and it subjects it to associative correction by introducing it into normal consciousness (under light hypnosis) or by removing it through the physician's suggestion, as is done in somnambulism accompanied by amnesia.* (17)[4]

The "affect," which we take as the patient's heretofore unexpressed emotional reaction to the *old* precipitating event, is the only affect mentioned. Freud does not report in 1893 any new affect in the therapeutic situation resulting from the revelation of the old "idea." Notably, the symptom is resolved through *speech.*

The 1896 description suggests that the doctor leads the patient back to the scene of the crime, as it were, in a fairly synchronic way. There is a sense of the situation being in the control of the doctor. The patient is present, but is also being acted upon by the doctor. There is little to suggest that the patient is an active participant in the procedure, or that the patient's feelings or present affect during and about the whole procedure might either get in the way or help the process along. The patient, in a sense, is ideally irrelevant to the treatment or the therapeutic procedure.

Freud proceeds by showing, however, that memories and traumatic scenes are not as directly related as one might wish. He relates that symptoms and scenes concatenate in genealogical trees of association ("Aetiology," 194–98). Such symptoms, he states, do not arise from experience alone, but must have the participation of memory to become activated. After several pages describing an example of how this phenomenon manifests itself, he jumps to an amazing and controversial assertion: that the wide variety of traumatic scenes from whence symptoms emerge invariably relates back even further to a single set of causes: "Whatever case and whatever symptom we take as our point of departure, *in the end we infallibly come to the field of sexual experience.* So here for the first time we seem to have discovered an aetiological precondition for hysterical symptoms" (199). This is Freud's proud discovery, his "head of the Nile."

The shift, to clarify, between the Breuer/Freud position of 1893 and his new outlook in 1896 is the elimination of *all* other possible causes of hysteria besides the sexual. Freud is making an epidemiological statement of sweeping proportions, given the commonness of hysteria in his day. On the basis of 18 cases, he will assert "universal validity" (199). He will stake his reputation on a claim that is not qualified or limited by the expression of any reservation or alternative factors. In a rhetorical sense, he has not primed the audience very well for receiving his claim.

He knows that his contention will be controversial because his next sentence goes on the defensive, and then the attack:

> From previous experience I can foresee that it is precisely against this assertion or against its universal validity that your contradiction, Gentlemen, will be directed. Perhaps it would be better to say, your *inclination* to contradict; for none of you, no doubt, have as yet any investigations at your disposal which, based upon the same procedure, might have yielded a different result. (199; italics in original)

At this point in the lecture, Freud has offered his conclusion in advance of giving any evidence, any case studies, or even any mention of how many cases he has used to formulate his notion about the "universal" validity of his finding. And yet in the same moment, he essentially insults his listeners with a rhetorical fallacy, namely, an appeal to ignorance: Since none of you is in a position to contradict me because you lack such clinical information as I have collected, I am therefore automatically right in my conclusions. Since they cannot at that moment disprove him, he is correct. This flies in the face of all notions of scientific inquiry, where results must be produced and reproduced before they can be considered valid. Freud here rejects a Baconian notion of reproducibility, and the humility of a Boyle who would not claim his results until he had been able to demonstrate them repeatedly for observers. At this juncture Freud seems decidedly unscientific, in both his method and his method of argument.

It is only after hurling this barb that Freud begins to offer his reasons for having come to such a conclusion. But even here, his language is defensive and rhetorically tense, as he attempts to eliminate charges of bias or preconception, and to depict himself as a reluctant testifier to what he has found:

> As regards the controversial matter itself, I will only remark that the singling out of the sexual factor in the aetiology of hysteria springs at least from no preconceived opinion on my part. The two investigators as whose pupil I began my studies of hysteria, Charcot and Breuer, were far from having any such presupposition; in fact they had a personal disinclination to it which I originally shared. Only the most laborious and detailed investigations have converted me, and that slowly enough, to the view I hold to-day. (199)

This is his reluctant testimony. Though he is inclined to find it incredible himself, he nevertheless has been convinced by his own evidence, as if persuading himself, and not his colleagues, were the primary objective of the talk. And his evidence, he asserts, has been derived in both a "laborious" and "detailed" manner. He implies that he has developed his data precisely. But was he accurate?

Only after these qualifiers does Freud offer his evidence: 18 cases in which he claims every symptom was able to be connected to a sexual basis, and every symptom subsequently resolved by therapy based on this finding (199). It seems somewhat odd not to even mention the work of Tardieu and Bernard in this light as providing a basis in prior research for his hypothesis.[5] Perhaps, as Masson suggests, Freud is loathe to admit the influence on his own notions of his French experiences and researches (Masson, 136–38). Perhaps he believes his psychiatric audience will not be impressed by such work. It seems strange indeed that he would not make the simple argument that, given forensic evidence, his audience had to already understand that adults did terrible sexual things to children, which sometimes resulted in their deaths. Freud is certainly rhetorically capable of mounting the argument that, in such a light, psychiatrists should expect a person surviving less grave sexual attacks to have some psychic residues, which could, like physical attacks (accidents, for example, mentioned in the 1893 lecture), result in psychic trauma as well. In any event, it seems singular that Freud decides to make such a daring claim in such a truly weakened form.

Freud next addresses himself precisely to the kind of objection contemporary medical and scientific researchers consider in studies with human subjects. Eighteen is a very small number of cases, and certainly too small as a basis for a claim of universality. One anticipates Grünbaum's tally argument.[6] Freud refutes the putative objection in several ways. First, these 18 represent his entire caseload of hysteria patients to date. The problem for his audience would be that they had not come to the same conclusion in their own complete caseloads, and might perhaps have "hysteria" cases that could legitimately be linked to nonsexual causes. Later experience, with patients witnessing shootings, war, natural disasters, accidents and other traumatizing events, lent credence to the idea that trauma, not sexual abuse per se, was the common factor in certain patterns of psychological and physical symptoms formerly thought of as "hysteria."[7]

Second, Freud argues, his cases were not preselected by him, but rather represent a somewhat random group of patients whom he happened to treat because their presenting diagnosis was hysteria ("Aetiology," 200). Again, though, the question must be asked, why did Freud not attempt to crosscheck his caseload and diagnoses with those of some or at least one of his colleagues, to test whether the asserted randomness was true or simply an artifact of his own practice?

Without having tested these factors, which might have impinged on his claim's universality or conversely helped to bolster it, he does admit that his enthusiasm for his thesis "run[s] ahead of the evidential force of the observations I have so far made" (200). But he is prepared to do this. He allows that at a "subjective" level, he is simply prepared to assert that in the "physiological and psychological mechanism of hysteria," "the participation of the sexual motive forces" constitutes "an indispensable premiss" (200). In one sense, he is being honest; in another sense, he is being completely foolhardy if he wants to win over his detractors. The relevant question from the standpoint of the Freud wars may not be why Freud recants, but rather why he feels impelled to make his case public when his data are at a rather premature state. At the minimum, those data can be not unreasonably viewed as insufficient to support the sweeping conclusions he draws from them at that early time.

Freud makes some rather interesting admissions and assertions in this paper regarding other researchers who might corroborate his findings. In response to the argument that sexual acts committed on the bodies of children are too rare to suffice as the explanation for such a wide variety of cases as represented by hysterics, Freud points to the work of some colleagues.

> It seems certain to me that our children are far more often exposed to sexual assaults than the few precautions taken by parents in this connection would lead us to expect. When I first made enquiries about what was known on the subject, I learnt from colleagues that there are several publications by paediatricians which stigmatize the frequency of sexual practices by nurses and nursery maids, carried out even on infants in arms; and in the last few weeks I have come across a discussion of 'Coitus in Childhood' by Dr. Stekel (1895) in Vienna. I have not had time to collect other published evidence; but even if it were only scanty, it is to be expected that increased attention to the subject will very soon confirm the great frequency of sexual experiences and sexual activity in childhood. ("Aetiology," 207)

Historically, we know that there is very good supporting evidence for the statements Freud makes here. But that same historical scholarship makes clear that, socially and legally, the acknowledgment of such matters was, with few exceptions, considered highly unpalatable. One wonders here why, given the steep resistance he knew he would face, Freud did not more fully avail himself of the corroboration that he asserts is available, or at least wait until he could review the published evidence and judge its potential value to his case before offering his lecture. In our own time, the matter of reliably establishing the incidence of sexual abuse of children is still difficult, though we perhaps on the whole are more ready to accept that it occurs and may even occur frequently. And this objection is not trivial to Freud's position. Hysteria is widespread and multiplex — this premise was accepted as perhaps the very basis of his psychiatric colleagues' professional practice. By contrast, sexual abuse of children, especially incest, was for Victorian

Vienna barely a crime to be spoken about, and thus required far more effort on Freud's part to establish positively in the minds of his audience. Again, it has been customary to castigate Freud for "abandoning" the seduction theory. Here I hope it becomes more evident that if Freud comes out of this lecture professionally isolated, he certainly has provided a weakened account of his own work and ideas. He seems repeatedly to forswear himself any corroboration from the work of others, which might have increased the chance of the audience's acceptance. This is admittedly a difficult case to make at this point in time.

The lecture's next section details Freud's case observations. He divides them into three groups. The first is primarily comprised of girls, abused on one or a few occasions by mostly strangers who knew "how to avoid inflicting gross, mechanical injury" (208). In the second, an adult known to the child, "a nursery maid or governess or tutor, or, unhappily all too often, a close relative" (208) initiates a "love-relationship" that may go on for years. The third group consists of brother-sister relationships. Freud notes that for several of his patients, more than one of these situations is operative. A brother initiating sexual contact with a sister sometimes had been previously abused themselves by an adult woman (208).

In the next paragraph, Freud makes two of his strongest statements for the effects of actual sexual contact, and against the weight of the heredity hypothesis:

> In view of this, I am inclined to suppose that children cannot find their way to acts of sexual aggression unless they have been seduced previously. The foundation for neurosis would accordingly always be laid in childhood by adults, and the children themselves would transfer to one another the disposition to fall ill of hysteria later. I will ask you to consider . . . the special frequency with which sexual relations in childhood occur precisely between brothers and sisters and cousins, as a result of their opportunities for being together so often; supposing, then, ten or fifteen years later several members of the younger generation of the family are found to be ill, might not this appearance of a family neurosis naturally lead to the false supposition that a hereditary disposition is present where there is only a pseudo-heredity and where in fact what has taken place is a handing-on, an infection in childhood? (208–9)

I quote this passage at length because it gives some of the greatest support to those who believe Freud abandoned his most useful theses in favor of more dubious ones. In this section of the lecture he is arguing for two crucial factors. First, he emphasizes that adults sexually attack children, not the other way around, in cases understood to him through recovered memory only. This is the point from which he will later publicly turn away, to the dismay of some critics, including many feminists.

In the second important contention, he argues that "illness" arises from *experiences*, not constitution or instinct or some other immutable factor or intrinsic nature. What you do to a person has emotional consequences for her. Illnesses do not arise simply out of a diseased or weakened constitution without any other aggravating or stimulating cause. This passage holds adults accountable for the "infection" of their children and charges. But it also makes a subtle and important evidentiary assertion qua the Charcotian position that hysterical neurosis is simply inherited. In families where several generations have actually engaged in sexual contact with each other, there might be the appearance of biological heredity, when there is only a "pseudo-heredity" (209). In fact, the analogy is closer to an infection or illness. It is an environmental matter, in other words — passed at close quarters from one person to another. This assertion of the significance of negative experiences, of environmental factors, over against endogenous biological or instinctual ones, as having the potential to become psychological noxae has almost universal acceptance outside psychoanalytic circles. That Freud later steps back from it and toward a theory of intrapersonal factors (primarily drives) is another way of seeing the watershed between 1896 and 1900.

In response to the question of high prevalence, Freud makes an acute and still-used epidemiological argument. Based on his argument, child sexual abuse would have to be widespread, and more widespread than hysteria or neurosis. But this cannot be used as an argument against etiology. Because of a socially outrageous notion that child sexual abuse would be so ubiquitous, Freud must offer a method of discount. Etiology will have been established if two conditions can be satisfied. First, it is not necessary for everyone who is exposed to a particular noxa to become sick. He uses the analogy of smallpox, where the incidence of illness is less than the incidence of exposure. Second, regarding smallpox, "infection from a smallpox patient is almost the only known etiology of the disease" ("Aetiology," 209). This is the more difficult claim regarding hysteria; in fact, this is the link Freud is attempting to establish. In his 18 cases, 12 women and 6 men, Freud states that every case and every symptom devolved to a sexual cause. So, as far as Freud is concerned, as with smallpox, there is only one (now) known etiology for neurosis, and it is sexual. "It does not matter if many people experience infantile sexual scenes without becoming hysterics, provided only that all the people who become hysterics have experienced scenes of that kind" (209). Thus, Freud established both his major and minor premises and was set to deduce his conclusion.

Here, however, Freud created for himself what would become an evidentiary bind. In his commitment to the biologically based model of the single "infecting" cause, Freud wrongly narrowed the etiology of hysteria to a sexual root. Writing prior to World War I, he did not yet have access to the large body of clinical data from combat stress that would form the basis for the theory of posttraumatic stress disorder. This evidence, in turn, gave rise to comparisons, such as Judith Herman's, regarding the larger category of psychological trauma and its sequelae. In Freud's own practice, for example, he was uninterested in corporal childhood punishment experiences and their emotional consequences for patients like the Rat Man, physically abused in the name of discipline. It is striking, in a sense, to see Freud's own habits of mind at work, as he returned to the sexual time and again as that which has been repressed in memory. Other kinds of traumatic experiences, including torture, physical attacks and the experience of a natural disaster, have been proven both to result in repression and to bear powerful and distressing psychological sequelae, some of which resemble the now-obsolete diagnosis of hysteria. Yet Freud, on the basis of only 18 cases, was prepared to stake his claim on a single cause for all of them, namely sexual abuse in childhood.

The interesting point that partisans on both sides miss is that there are at least two aspects of the phenomenon: what happened and what the person makes of it. The post–1900 Freud can certainly be accused of neglecting to inquire about what happened, instead focusing exclusively on what the person made of the experience. Critics like Masson, on the other hand, stress the violating experience to the seeming neglect of how the sufferer makes sense of it, and what the lasting effects of varying coping abilities and strategies will be. We return momentarily to Freud's clinical experience, that not everyone who was exposed to "infantile sexual scenes" developed hysterical symptoms.

Both sides at times also miss the more subtle point made by Alice Miller and by object relations theorists such as D. W. Winnicott. People have or lack resources to deal with such traumas based on the state of their relationships with others. What Freud stumbled through, as he combed the logic of what belonged to what, was the nature of the person's experience and its aftermath, relative to the patient's other relationships and psychological resources. That is to say, did the patient experience the sexual contact in a traumatizing way, and did the patient have anyone to turn to for comfort or safe reassurance after the experience? These distinctions could account for why some people developed symptoms and others did not. Freud had a sense that some people were more likely to experience such things as damaging, and he attributed this to a combination of endogenous and exogamous factors ("Aetiology," 210). This leads to Freud's response to the next set of objections. Many people "have a very clear recollection of infantile sexual experiences and . . . nevertheless do not suffer from hysteria" (211). Freud's response is unequivocal. This objection has "no weight" because "the scenes must be present as unconscious memories; only so long as, and in so far as, they are unconscious are they able to create and maintain hysterical symptoms" (211).

In the third and final division of the lecture, Freud moves to perhaps the most distressing material, which he acknowledges will be most difficult for his audience to accept. Up to this point, he says, he has been describing the "*mechanism* of the formation of hysterical symptoms" (214). Now, however, he will undertake to describe the "*causation*" of such symptoms (214; italics in the original). In attempting to explain the kinds of physical symptoms patients experience, he states: "Among the latter are above all to be found the numerous and diverse sensations and paraesthesias of the genital organs and other parts of the body, these sensations and paraesthesias being phenomena which simply correspond to the sensory content of the infantile scenes, reproduced in a hallucinatory fashion, often painfully intensified" (214). So here he seeks to directly connect the patient's bodily experience of the originating physical aspects of the sexual attack with present symptoms. He spells these out for his colleagues, whom he no doubt assumes will have had such patterns of symptoms among their own hysterical patients, even if they had drawn differing conclusions regarding their origins:

> Another set of exceedingly common hysterical phenomena — painful need to urinate, the sensation accompanying defaecation, intestinal disturbances, choking and vomiting, indigestion and disgust at food — were shown in my analyses (and with surprising regularity) to be derivatives of the same childhood experiences and were explained without difficulty by certain invariable peculiarities of those experiences. For the idea of these infantile sexual scenes is very repellent to the feelings of a sexually normal individual; they include all the abuses known to debauched and impotent persons, among whom the buccal [oral] cavity and the rectum are misused for sexual purposes. (214)

Freud gives an inventory by which, in the moment, his audience might be shocked, as they consider such symptoms from their own cases as now possibly connected with sexual abuse. He gives a nod to his presumably sexually "normal" colleagues by acknowledging, in effect, that what he is talking about may strike them as "repellent," and then goes on to further stipulate the abuses. He attempts to steer the intense emotions his audience might be feeling by asserting that, "For physicians, astonishment at this soon gives way to a complete understanding" (214). He is surely hoping this will be the case for the physicians in the room, following his lead in the denouement of his great investigation. Then he returns to his material:

> People who have no hesitation in satisfying their sexual desires upon children cannot be expected to jib a finer shades in the methods of obtaining that satisfaction; and the sexual impotence which is inherent in children inevitably forces them into the same substitutive actions as those to which adults descend if they become impotent. All the singular

> conditions under which the ill-matched pair conduct their love-relations — on the one hand the adult, who cannot escape his share in the mutual dependence necessarily implied by a sexual relationship, and who is yet armed with complete authority and the right to punish, and can exchange the one role for the other to the uninhibited satisfaction of his moods, and on the other hand the child, who in his helplessness is at the mercy of this arbitrary will, who is prematurely aroused to every kind of sensibility and exposed to every sort of disappointment, and whose performance of the sexual activities assigned to him is often interrupted by his imperfect control of his natural needs — all these grotesque and yet tragic incongruities reveal themselves as stamped upon the later development of the individual and of his neurosis, in countless permanent effects which deserve to be traced in the greatest detail. (214–15)

This is perhaps the most compelling aspect of the entire lecture, in terms of pure emotional force. Freud's re-creation or representation of material presumably taken from the analyses of his patients reveals a level of compassion and empathy for the children involved that is deeply affecting. He refers to such relationships as "love relations," and then proceeds to develop a picture devoid of mutuality or the least consideration of the feelings and needs of the child partner. The child is subject not only to her or his own limitations, but the ever-present threat of punishment by the adult. We may infer that such "love relations" also partake of violence, or at the very least, coercion. And though the picture is that of scenes as they unfolded in time and not later memory, we also begin to develop some ideas about why the child might, under threat of punishment, repress such scenes as part of a larger psychic survival mechanism.

Freud then moves into the final crescendo of the lecture. He mentions children sexualizing children and once again emphasizes that this happens subsequent to sexual abuse by adults ("Aetiology," 215). He elucidates the matter of the sufficient objective correlative. First, he explains the principle that "*hysterical symptoms are overdetermined*" (216; italics in the original). By this he means they may have both a more conscious and recent experiential antecedent, and a more severe one from earliest childhood. He then drives home the point:

> The reaction of hysterics is only apparently exaggerated; it is bound to appear exaggerated to us because we know only a small part of the motives from which it arises.
>
> In reality, this reaction is proportionate to the exciting stimulus; thus it is normal and psychologically understandable. We see this at once when the analysis has added to the manifest motives, of which the patient is conscious, those other motives, which have been operative without his knowing about them, so that he could not tell us of them. (217)

In response to the customary characterization of hysterical patients as overly sensitive to slights, Freud likens the situation to a tinderbox. Because of the repressed material, it is not the apparently insignificant present action that calls for an extreme reaction from the hysteric. Rather, the repressed material represents the buildup of fuel, which permits the person to ignite over a single stray spark and to appear to overreact to innocuous thoughts, words or acts, by the self or others (217–18).

Only at the end of the lecture, where Freud considers the effects of future new data on the simplicity of his etiology and diagnoses of obsession and neurosis, does he acknowledge uncertainty. "The number of cases I have analysed is not large enough nor have the determining factors in them been sufficiently various" (220).

Freud's peroration returns to the problems he knows his arguments have met with in his audience. He begins his concluding paragraph: "I have now come to the end of what I have to say to-day. Prepared as I am to meet with contradiction and disbelief, I should like to say one thing more in support of my position" (220). He reassures his audience that his arguments are based not on "idle speculation," but "on a laborious individual examination of patients which has in most cases taken up a hundred or more hours of work" (220). Here it is not clear whether he means in total, or for each of his 18 cases. Indeed, 1,800 hours, using the yardstick of a 40-hour work week, comes close to being a solid year's worth of work. It is one way of compensating for the small number of cases, to point to the depth in which such cases have been analyzed.

Freud asks the audience, if they doubt his conclusions, to at least not dismiss his methods, which he again describes as a "modification of Breuer's procedure." He asks them not to "deny" his work using the standards of how patients are "customar[il]y" questioned, likening such a judgment to the rejection of findings discovered via microscope that would be invisible to the naked eye (220). His closing sentences reveal, however, his optimism for his new approaches:

> The new method of research gives wide access to a new element in the pyschical field of events, namely, to processes of thought which have remained unconscious — which, to use Breuer's expression, are "inadmissable to consciousness." Thus it inspires us with the hope of a new and better understanding of all functional psychic disturbances. I cannot believe that psychiatry will long hold back from making use of this new pathway to knowledge. (220–21)

Apparently, psychiatry decided it could indeed hold back, and spent the next 17 months doing so.

FOUR

Reconsidering Freud's Recanting

Scientific and Therapeutic Failures

When, in September 1897, Freud wrote to Fliess to tell him that he was abandoning his theory that gave credence to patients' stories, he gave him several reasons for doing so. His patients all left before he could complete analysis with them. He could not imagine all fathers were guilty of sexual crimes, as his theory supposed they must be. With no reality factor in the unconscious, he was unable to distinguish truth from fantasy in his patients' accounts. And, in cases of "deep-reaching psychosis," the unconscious was unable to break through and therefore nothing would ever be revealed (*Letters,* 264–65).

It should be clear, based on subsequent clinical experience, that there would be factors that had nothing to do with the correctness of Freud's etiological assertion for this set of cases, which might account for his premature sense of defeat.[1] There are indeed several factors that may have driven these early patients out of analysis before reaching a satisfactory completion, including problems with Freud's therapeutic technique, a limited capacity for patients to effect the safety necessary for therapeutic progress, and conflicts of interest for the patients' paying fathers. Additionally, Freud's ability to collect the magnitude of data necessary to establish his case of firm scientific grounds was constrained by limits on the size of his caseload and extreme time and financial pressures that he was not in a position to overcome in defense of the sexual etiology hypothesis.

Freud, interestingly, considers none of these possibilities at this juncture. Freudians who followed him have often accepted this abandonment as justified and not worthy of reconsideration in light of subsequent evidence. Critics have used his frankness with Fliess as the basis for rejecting both Freud and the etiological bath water. Some of the elements of therapeutic technique and the limitations on Freud's ability to engage in a broad-based scientific endeavor were more accurate reasons for Freud's sense of failure. Freud felt pressure not to correct these shortcomings with further improvements on his existing work, but to simply move on.

The Emotional Weight of Trauma Remembered

From the distance of 100 years, there is a striking, seemingly fundamental disconnect in Freud, that he cannot figure out that something so shocking or unbearable as to be "inadmissable to consciousness" would not also have potentially excruciating, even unbearable emotional concomitants when made available to consciousness. By 1896, Freud was no longer talking about affect or technique in therapy so much as about etiology and method. The work of psychoanalysis was just that: analysis, breaking into smaller pieces the rough stone of the unconscious. Perhaps his medical and scientific training had become a block to empathy. Here was Freud the dissectionist, the objective investigator accustomed to reading the signs of illness without the active input of the patient. In treating the patients' unconscious as a site to be excavated, Freud overlooks, it would seem, the distress that such opening to the light of day would cause them. Perhaps, too, he felt it was part of the task, for physicians often had to ask patients to endure pain "for their own good."

It is paradoxical that, while such traumas had resulted in sometimes debilitating symptoms while still repressed by the patient, Freud was apparently unable to grasp that such childhood scenes could inflict *new* emotional devastation to patients once the news was brought to light. For Freud, however, living in a different time, such abuses were by far not necessarily the worst things that might befall people — which I say without irony or ill-spiritedness. Children were still being caned in Germany, and dead babies were commonly thrown on open rubbish piles in London streets at the end of the nineteenth century.[2] Incest was not outlawed in England until 1908. Against the backdrop of everyday horrors that Western middle-class people in the twenty-first century would never expect to experience in their own daily lives, except perhaps through the distantiation of media, Freud's sense of proportion is likely not our own. The fact that in Imperial Austria, he does see that "infantile sexual scenes" have long-lasting and distressing effects on people, including women, and that he thinks such matters are worth paying attention to, is remarkable.

However, from the standpoint of what we now understand about trauma recovery, we see how inadequately he was able to estimate the devastating emotional impact of revelations on his patients. Even more, however, one may imagine, as the first cases to be talked out, how ill-equipped they must have been to cope with the anguish of analysis. One thinks especially of cases where the memories had been completely repressed and then uncovered *de novo* in analysis. First, given the sensibilities of women patients who had been socialized not to speak about sex, let alone childhood molestation or rape, uncovering this news must have been extremely upsetting. At another level, there is good reason to think that anything traumatic enough to be repressed in the first place would still be potent and upsetting to the person later recalling it. Second, it must have been impossible for patients who still lived in their perpetrators' homes to have any sense of personal safety, let alone to grieve this horrible news and experience all the attendant feelings that had previously been repressed, if the context of family settings still included the perpetrator. Even assuming a best case, where they would be living out of contact with their wrongdoers, they would still be left with the struggle to integrate this terrible remembered information into their lives in a way that would leave them psychologically intact and stable. For unmarried patients, there might have been questions about whether anyone would ever be willing to marry them, given this awful history, and a social mindset that always targeted the reputation of the woman rather than her abuser.

Freud, in other words, may have lost patients not because he was wrong about what was causing their symptoms, but because he was unprepared in his therapeutic technique to deal with the magnitude of emotional sequelae his cognitive revelations brought out. One could make the analogy to a surgeon who has discovered tumors as the source of certain symptoms in his patients. The patients die, however, because he fails to anesthetize them before operating, fails to sew them up once the tumor is out, and fails to keep their wounds from getting infected (or in Freud's case, reinfected) after the surgery. In short, they cannot withstand the pain of his treatment. What later clinicians would find necessary is precisely the kind of nurturing and holding relationship with a therapist that Freud seems here either incapable of providing or unaware of its being needed for therapeutic success.[3] Freud the Oedipus has unraveled the puzzle, but patients' lives and their psychological well-being were more than puzzles to be worked out. They needed caring for probably even more *after* they learned what had made them sick. This was the piece of therapeutic work that at this early point Freud apparently did not foresee or address.

The impact of admitting that he had been unable to "cure" anyone was devastating to Freud's 1896 thesis. Curing hysteria by revealing its etiology had formed one of the bedrocks of his argument before the *Verein*. Using a standard medical model, he had reasoned that if a particular remedy cures a particular malady, then one can speak about causation. Presumably a different malady would not respond to that remedy. The second analogy was to tuberculosis, where science had been able to find the singular germ that causes the illness. Again, Freud struggled to make a transition between his purely medical and physical training and vocabulary, to a model of illness whose emotional as well as cognitive elements could be successfully addressed by therapy. With the apparent failure of psychoanalytic treatment, Freud began to doubt whether he had gotten to the source of the malady.

Misapprehending the Perpetrating Classes

In his recantatory letter to Fliess, Freud also stumbled when he unnecessarily attempted to reduce the perpetrator class to fathers. Initially, in the 1896 lecture, he was not so restrictive concerning the abusing classes, noting adults of both sexes (particularly male strangers, nurses and governesses) as well as other children who had themselves been abused. Limited as he was in trying to collect supporting data, Freud's own findings became narrowed and contradicted in this letter:

> Then the surprise that in all cases, the *father*, not excluding my own, had to be accused of being perverse — the realization of the unexpected frequency of hysteria, with precisely the same conditions prevailing in each, whereas surely such widespread perversions against children are not very probable. The [incidence] of perversion would have to be immeasurably more frequent than the [resulting] hysteria because the illness, after all, occurs only where there has been an accumulation of events and there is a contributory factor that weakens the defense. (*Letters*, 264)

This passage contains what looks like an epidemiological argument, but which in fact contains an unbearable idea for Freud. Because he is wedded to finding a single cause, which for him means a single and homogeneous class of perpetrators, he asserts here that, ergo, all cases of hysteria involve a perpetrating father. What is worse, since he considers himself, his brother and sister to be neurotic, then his own father must be implicated.

On the face of it, to base such a sweeping generalization on the basis of 18 cases is extremely weak methodologically. An approach designed to test this initial finding would simply involve looking at more and more cases to see what patterns turn up. Freud has at best a convenience sample, not even a cross-section of his quarter of Vienna, let alone a sample that could have any representative validity approaching a universal. The only way, in fact, to establish the frequency of the diagnosis would be population studies, and he is about as far from that, at 18 cases in his neighborhood, as he is from getting to the moon. And even if the father is implicated in all 18 cases he has seen so far, he does not know how their numbers would compare as a percent of population. In other words, all appendicitis cases involve the appendix; but at any given time, only a subset of the population suffers from appendicitis. A truly scientific mind at this juncture would wonder about what this group of essentially self-selected or referred patients means in relation to the asymptomatic population.

Next he remarks on the "unexpected frequency" of hysteria, whereas he finds it simply unbearable to think that so much perversion could be raging among the fatherly classes. In logic, this would be identified as one of the major premises both of his thinking and his argument. A very high percentage of the population suffers from colds each year, and yet despite that, physicians do not question the frequency of colds. On the other hand, if Freud had discovered that nursemaids were implicated in every case, rather than fathers, one wonders whether the shudder would have been so greatly felt. He finds himself on what he construes as shaky ground here — though he also narrows and extrematizes the epidemiological picture. Perhaps, following Fournier, he understands that his job as a physician includes a male and paternal class loyalty that he should be loathe to violate. Had the perpetrator class not included people more powerful than he, perhaps Freud would have been less ready to give up on his theory.

Finally, in his remarks on the numbers of attacks necessary in each case to have produced symptoms, it seems striking that Freud does not here simply hypothesize that some men do this and others do not. It would make sense that those perverse enough to engage in such behavior once or twice might make use of their opportunities for as long as they had them. As another methodological piece, however, he expresses no interest in asking, interviewing or attempting to treat these father perpetrators, or of gathering firsthand data from them.

When he becomes reluctant to imagine that so many fathers might be implicated, he rejects his own argument from the "Aetiology" lecture that a high prevalence should not be taken as a false sign. Here, two new developments intrude. I believe that because he narrowed his focus to the fathers' role, it became wedded to an unbearable idea in his mind.[4] Children were physically disciplined by their parents in this era. This was considered their biblical right and duty. Certainly, few people believed then that physical punishments were harmful to children. My suspicion is that Freud had to confront two unwelcome notions: that maybe adults took out their sexual aggression on children as much as they did their physical aggression, and that such actions were not only morally reprehensible but also palpably psychiatrically harmful. Second, the pivotal moment a few weeks from this time, when Freud turned away from his proto-database of father-related cases, occurred when he determined, though self-analysis, that his nurse and not his father molested him. Thus, Freud's own case confirmed the 1896 lecture at the same time that it gave him a straw to clutch at, to suggest that perhaps all these fathers were not perverse after all. By then, Freud was past the point of even considering how unrepresentative his own case was, against the backdrop of the cases he had already analyzed. One could say that, as a scientist, Freud was never the friend of statistics. His research on eels, where after hundreds of dissections he was able to find vestigial evidence of sex organs on a few subjects, was a worthy backdrop for his interpretation of these 18 cases he has at hand. Rejecting the weak conclusions he was willing to draw from 18 cases, he pounced on the universality of the Oedipal constellation based solely upon his own intimations about himself—a nonrepresentative sample of one.

That Freud faced constraints both internal and external to his early research has been well established. Marianne Krüll's interpretation of the admonition of Freud's father for his son to "close the eyes" and not look too deeply seems relevant here, as an internal constraint upon pursuing a hypothesis that would make many, if not all, fathers look bad.[5] Freud's scientific and investigatory conclusion, at the very outset of psychoanalysis, should not have become the final word on the experiences of all others, including his own patients, who were injured in diverse ways by a diverse group of perpetrators.

As for the "reality factor" in the unconscious, Freud had a simple alternative. He might have looked for independent confirmation and witnesses, or engaged the help of his colleagues to systematically do so. Freud seems to recuse himself from this task, however. He notes confirmations from time to time in letters to Fliess (for example, January 3, 1897). But he does not report any followup contacts with the

Viennese pediatricians he mentioned in the "Aetiology" lecture, nor any other attempt to find support in the medical or psychiatric literature. Surely this route would have offered some reassurance that he was on the right track.

Recanting, Horror and Method

When Freud renounced his theory to Fliess, he questioned the causal links that he could not sufficiently establish. And he also admitted that he had not been able to finish any analyses because patients broke off treatment. Freud's interpretation of this state of affairs, however, in retrospect, seems excessively catastrophic. While other critics have happily demonstrated shortcomings in Freud's procedures, generally they have not commented on the fact that subsequent studies in the twentieth century, both clinical and epidemiological, have confirmed Freud's initial concern, that child sexual abuse is indeed a widespread phenomenon, with a substantial number of survivors experiencing serious mental health and other sequelae.[6] The critics who scrutinize Freud's logic and data collection often seem oblivious to the fact that, like his French colleagues, Freud was on to something.

In other areas of scientific endeavor, we may reserve our criticism of the techniques used by pioneers, understanding that the first telescope or the first microscope will necessarily be more crude in design and less effective in operation than subsequent ones. Even at the distance of a century, it seems rare that anyone on either side is able to afford Freud the same sort of dispassionate assessment, which has also hampered our ability to look at Freud's self-assessment in 1897 and examine his reasoning in an epidemiological framework.

The question remains: Why was Freud not able to press on with the collection of additional data, which would either quiet or corroborate his misgivings, and potentially quiet his critics as well? In every data-driven undertaking, there comes the moment in the experiment when the researcher must decide whether he or she has the resources to continue. Freud obviously decided that he lacked them. I want to explore two lines of argument that previous critics have overlooked: the inadequacy of Freud's technique as a factor diminishing opportunities for data collection; and legal and financial constraints stemming from his patients' clinical revelations.

Freud's Technique circa 1897

In order for Freud to gain more certainty about his theory, and presumably to make it more persuasive to his colleagues, he needed additional data, which meant more patients, and enough time with each of them to complete the analysis.

Freud was really testing two questions. One was his etiological argument: are these hysterias caused by adult-initiated childhood sexual scenes? The other was whether his therapeutic technique, originally developed with Breuer, was effective.

It seems in the letter to Fliess of September 21, 1897, that Freud conflates the two in his mind, as if one has the power to invalidate the other. That is, he suggests that if he cannot cure his patients with his technique, then perhaps his theory about the etiology is wrong. Now, of course, Freud has a separate reservation about etiology, having to do with the indictment of a vast number of fathers. From a purely methodological standpoint, however, the question of technique stands on its own and needs to be explored as a factor contributing to patient flight from therapy. Freud gives his inventory to Fliess on this first point:

> So I will begin historically [and tell you] where the reasons for disbelief came from. The continual disappointment in my efforts to bring a single analysis to a real conclusion; the running away of people who for a time had been gripped [by analysis]; the absence of the complete successes on which I had counted; the possibility of explaining to myself the partial successes in other ways, in the usual fashion — this was the first group. (*Letters,* 264)

Freud stipulates disappointing outcomes and an inability to attribute his "partial successes" solely to his approach. But he does not question the possible limitations of the therapeutic approach itself as possibly contributing to the "failure" of analysis.

I will focus on the words "success" and "analysis." The index of success to which Freud seems to hold himself is the "complete and permanent" resolution of hysterical symptoms, which he claims in the

1896 lecture. The analogy is clearly to a medical procedure, such as a surgery, where, for example, once the appendix is removed the patient can be said to be successfully cured of appendicitis, provided there are no postsurgical complications. Freud's interest in hysteria, of course, may have been driven in part by the great potential payoff in finding a cause and a cure. In a malady so widespread, it would be the psychiatric equivalent (in his day) of curing influenza or polio.

But even given hysteria's notoriously multiplex symptomology and resistance to treatment, I think Freud is to be forgiven here for not completely understanding the tremendously difficult nature of trying to "cure" patients of the sequelae of childhood sexual abuse, especially in repressed cases. Researchers and clinicians in our own time would be as ecstatic as Freud must have been if they were able to achieve in every case a "cure" for their own sexually abused patients' psychological sequelae. Critics of Freud in essence adopt his own standard and comfortably show him falling short of it. To do so is simply a mark of ignorance, of how difficult though entirely possible it is to bring about therapeutic relief for survivors. It is not simple or easy for the patient, and neither is it for the clinician. But it is possible, and it does happen, in the contemporary setting. Faulting Freud for being unable to "cure" his patients' issues is like faulting Leonardo da Vinci for being unable to build a space shuttle.

What can we ascertain about the shortcomings of Freud's technique in the 1890s? Calling what he does "analysis" reveals Freud's focus: to unravel the puzzle, as one uncovers a mystery in a story. As the 1896 lecture and even the 1893 *Communication* reveal, Freud is very interested in unearthing causes and uncovering the most difficult repressed early memories in his patients. But there is no expression of concern on his part for the magnitude of the disturbance this new knowledge will have for patients.

Freud emphasizes the need to "get to the bottom" of the memories, as one excavates an archaeological site, and we hear much about his technique to achieve this. Oddly, he does not thematize or tout empathy or reassurance as therapeutic tools. In fact, he never discusses the provision of empathy to his patients as therapeutically significant for the emotional distress his uncovered information may cause them. And Freud's approach seems to afford patients no basis for a different kind of relationship to the revelation once the information is brought into consciousness, designed to provide emotional support as well as intellectual tools with which to face, process and eventually integrate the revelation. Instead, he offers them only "insight" into their symptoms.

No wonder they leave. How could they handle the information — so overwhelming in its power, so disintegrating of all the structures and expectations the person had previously held? How would they be able to regain a sense of being safe in the present, with knowledge of their violators so near? How could they grieve these shattering revelations — feel angry, sad, betrayed, violated, ashamed? or understand their fears, anxieties and symptoms which had resulted from the abuse? And how, given the magnitude of something so overwhelming and terrible the conscious mind had chosen to repress it because it could not otherwise sustain functioning, could patients then integrate knowledge of these crimes upon their persons into a normal mental state of affairs? This integration could not be done without tremendous emotional turmoil and effort. One should not fault the early researcher for not understanding the full magnitude of the therapeutic problem. But we can say, not unfairly, that Freud was emotionally oblivious to, or not culturally conditioned to notice, his patients' distress and attend to it as a legitimate emotional process necessary to their healing. As one contemporary group of incest survivors puts it, the courage to heal is really the carriage to hell. Such pain seems far beyond what Freud was prepared to imagine or deal with. As the saying goes, they don't care what you know until they know that you care. Without caring, knowing can be meaningless, offensive or simply indigestible.

Then there is the question of the patient's freedom and safety. In some cases, perpetrators were paying for the analysis (see, for example, *Letters*, 220–21). It seems obvious that the patient would feel enormous pressure and conflict regarding what she or he might reveal in sessions, or even allow herself or himself to remember. In some cases what Freud the doctor urged the patient to recover in analysis was presenting symptoms that were caused by sexual contact forced on the victim by the person paying for treatment. What abuse victim, without independent support, would be able to sustain an accusation against the person footing the bill for treatment? And what guilty party, when informed of the findings, would be interested in continuing a therapy that would provide ever more incriminating details?

This element is not dilated with Fliess. And Freud's obtuseness on this matter seems extraordinary with respect to the rate of flight from therapy. Yet it is matched by the obliviousness of subsequent commentators, who have failed to see this as the most basic kind of conflict for both patient and doctor. It is the ugly head of the forensic aspect of this work, and the legal implication of raising such information to consciousness rearing itself in the consulting room. Jose Brunner writes that "Freud's patients were mostly well-to-do women"; Freud himself later described his work as deriving from "private practice in an educated and literate class."[7] The famous Emmy von N. of the *Studies on Hysteria* was perhaps "the richest woman in Europe" (99).

And yet in his *Introductory Lectures,* Brunner comments on Freud's complaint that (unlike his French counterparts who engaged in hypnotism of poor patients),

> "Poor ourselves and socially powerless, and compelled to earn our livelihood from our medical activity, we are not even in a position to extend our efforts to people without means, as other doctors with other methods of treatment are after all able to do. Our therapy is too time-consuming and too laborious for that to be possible." In other words, since psychoanalysts are bourgeois professionals who need to make a living, they can do business only with members of their own class.[8]

At this earlier juncture, however, Freud does not thematize this huge conflict of interest between patients and payers. But he also does not discuss the possible stressors or dangers in his patients' situations which could bias their clinical transactions with him. On what neutral or objective ground does the patient stand in cases where a perpetrator pays the bill, or where the patient is still in regular contact with perpetrators? Where will she or he go after the therapeutic hour? Directly into the home of the perpetrator? Or a husband expecting a simple "cure" along medical lines? From a scientific viewpoint, it seems impossible to suggest that the experimental subject, the patient, is being protected from biasing forces in such a case. To extend Freud's smallpox analogy from the 1896 lecture (209), he seems to have little concern for the effects of reinfection or additional "viral loading" on the patient's ability to fight off ill mental health, despite the fact that he identifies repeated contact as one of the factors that produces hysteria.

Freud codes the patients' recalcitrance and reluctance as resistance, as frustrating to himself, and even as a character flaw. He minimizes or dismisses their embarrassment and mortification, while offering no means to alleviate it. We have suggested that the researcher himself is not protected from the biasing effects of billing. Freud, as he makes clear to Fliess on so many occasions, needs to make a living, and depends on his patients so that he may do so. In such a situation, Freud's theoretical pronouncements on his patients' "resistance" and his impatience with it represent less than the full story. He has thrown them into an emotionally untenable bind, and then seems surprised and even a little hurt that they leave therapy prematurely without having fully resolved their hysteria.

We must also try to imagine the magnitude of the purely emotional response to the discovery of suppressed memories. Freud's patients usually arrived in some state of suffering already, with sufficiently marked physical symptoms to be considered in need of medical attention. Freud focused on the intellectual content of the experiences; psychoanalysis was to figure out what happened versus what later associations the patient made with the event, and what symptoms have arose. He seems blinkered to the likely emotional cause of his patients' exodus from therapy: that intellectual understanding is insufficient for therapeutic completion or success. Making allowances for the limitations of the discovering scientist, when Freud speaks of the need to "abreact" the old feelings, he clearly misunderstands their significance. For the patient experiencing both the intellectual revelation and the release of previously unfelt and overwhelming negative feelings, which had been repressed and stored, the latter process of trying to deal with the flood of incredibly painful emotions becomes the more significant and primary therapeutic task. Freud's priority seems instead to be to establish in a short period of time an intellectual understanding of the antecedent of every symptom — the analysis. He believes that once the source of the symptom is uncovered, the symptom should simply re-solve. This assumes that the patient will have no other responses, moral, affective or otherwise, to understanding that he or she was indeed raped as a child, or sexually molested by a trusted adult.

The intellectual understanding and the immediate cessation of symptoms are critical for Freud as *doctor* and researcher, and they are sufficient. They represent the totality of his inquiry at this stage, operating as he does on the paradigm of physical medicine. The resolution of symptoms is also presumably what the parent or spouse or family member is paying for. Brunner points to Freud's own rationale for the economic efficiency of psychoanalysis in "On the Beginning of Treatment" in 1913:

> As far as the middle classes are concerned, the expense involved in psycho-analysis is excessive only in appearance. Quite apart from the fact that no comparison is possible between restored health and efficiency on the one hand and a moderate financial outlay on the other, when we add up the unceasing costs of nursing-homes and medical treatment and contrast them with the increase of efficiency and earning capacity which results from a successfully completed analysis, we are entitled to say that the patients have made a good bargain.[9]

In the early days, however, this was not necessarily a quick process, nor the primary agenda of the patient; as a result, the goals and needs of the patient, the doctor, and the person paying for analysis might be at complete loggerheads.

Thus, Freud seems unable to imagine or accept the possibility that his patients leave him because he is emotionally unsympathetic. His approach is insufficient in building a relationship with them to work through the emotional sequelae to the revelation. It is as if, once he has what he wants, that is, the causal factor he seeks, he impatiently wants the analysis to wrap up and the symptoms to end. Freud, the great Oedipedian, forgets in his own practice what Oedipus and Jocasta do when their incest is discovered. In Sophocles, Jocasta immediately kills herself by hanging. And Oedipus blinds and maims himself. Are these not the signs of overwhelming emotion — of mortification, of grief, of shame? of horror, anger, loss of the sense of one's self and one's sanity? These feelings and actions result, not from the violations themselves, but from their revelation. The revelation changes Oedipus's and Jocasta's condition in relation to their families, to each other, and to themselves, in the present. It should be surprising, if Oedipus is Freud's model for the revelation of incest, that he has no concept of living through a grieving process and returning to a life restored from shame. After all, Jocasta forecloses the possibility by suicide, while Oedipus spends the rest of his life wandering, mourning and suffering.

Strikingly, we see no sense of addressing the issue of injustice in the patient's life, especially where incest happens by the adult's design, and not unintentionally, as in Oedipus. Is there no wrong in raping a child, or forcing a child to perform fellatio, or demanding sexual acts from a child or sexual contact with a child, which the child cannot refuse without overwhelming and painful reprisal? Is there no wrong in such acts? We see no expression of it in Freud's letters. I think it is fair to say that Freud expresses no ironclad basis upon which he immediately recognizes that such acts are simply wrong and indefensible. We may therefore infer that it is not an issue he takes up in the therapeutic hour.

And yet, despite the operatic proportions of the tragedies being acted out in his consulting rooms, Freud's final and only goal seems to be getting rid of the physical symptoms of hysteria. Freud was unprepared for the emotional storms he unleashed in his patients. For the patient, however, the point of revelation marks but the beginning of the difficult emotional work that must be done. Judith Herman's psychotherapeutic techniques, which accept the reality of the patient's reported experiences of trauma, postulate three stages of recovery.[10] The first she calls the emergency stage, of remembering repressed experiences and the heretofore unfelt negative feelings associated with them, including rage, fear, helplessness, anxiety, the loss of personal safety and sovereignty, and betrayal. In the second stage, the patient works through grieving and experiencing the loss of formerly held relationships and realities. In the third stage, reintegration, receiving support from people who accept the reality and pain of the patient's experiences enables the patient to incorporate the knowledge of the abuse and what it means into the totality of the patient's present reality and sense of personal history. This process can take many years. The stages themselves are not chronologically exclusive or purely sequential. Herman makes clear, however, that the uncovering of the abuse or the sometimes spontaneous intrusions of fragmented memories into present life (hysterical symptoms could be thought of in this way) are certainly only the first steps in recovery. It has taken decades of therapies from many different approaches to arrive at this conclusion, decades of data from clinical work from which Freud certainly was unable to draw. Still, it seems clear that whatever intellectual strengths Freud possessed, he was not terribly, nor probably adequately, empathetic with his clients. Nor does he seem to have grasped the tremendous emotional and intellectual efforts that would be required for them to deal with the terribly difficult information he elicited.

Superficially, this suggests that he did not find the information in itself very troubling. He seems impatient, very often, for the patient to render up more and more material, oblivious to the pain the patient is experiencing in connection with the material that has already been uncovered. If the patient "resists" in giving him the more underlying scene he is seeking, he labels the patient problematic or intractable, even evil or naughty. But what is the patient supposed to be doing with the knowledge she or he is bringing into consciousness? What does Freud offer that will alleviate the pain this newfound material causes? When he states, years later, that he seeks only to turn patients' neurosis into ordinary suffering, he thereby offers very little incentive for anyone to truly face the pain that engendered their suffering in the first place. The revolutionary insights of Freud's early period will give way to the therapeutic preservation of the status quo. The patient is left with a lump she can now knowingly call a tumor.

Often in his letters, and even in the 1896 lecture on etiology, Freud gives the impression that his concern extends only as far as such sexual experiences result in symptoms that patients present to him for resolution. One might say this is where his powers of observation truly fail him. For he ceases to observe the affect of his patients, to notice the emotionally devastating effect his intellectual revelations have for them. I would argue, based on contemporary clinical evidence, that Freud's patients, in all likelihood, left analysis because of Freud's untenable pressure to resolve their symptoms postrevelation, and to resolve them posthaste.

Legal and Financial Constraints

I think it is reasonable to assume that most of Freud's patients were still having social contact with their perpetrators, and in some cases still living with them under the same roof. Benjamin Brody, analyzing the sociodemographic characteristics of patients Freud personally saw and referenced or wrote cases about between 1889 and 1924, concludes that in the period 1889 to 1900, Freud had six "major" cases and 70 "minor" ones.[11] Of the six major cases, three were single women. The oldest of the three was 24. Of the "minor" cases, for 42 of 70 there are no data regarding marital status, our best index of living with parents or not. Similarly, it is not possible to infer from Brody's table how many of the 34 women patients were single. We would assume, however, that in the case of unmarried women living at home, the father would be paying for therapy.

Additionally, in the nine cases for which data could be adduced, Brody concludes that all were "upper class" (10). Given that all patients, or those financially responsible for them, would have been paying for treatment out of pocket, it seems reasonable to accept Freud's own claim that his patients were generally not of the "lower class."

This may have influenced Freud, in terms of the Fournier thesis. He tells Fliess that the father, in all cases, "not excluding my own, had to be accused of being perverse" (*Letters*, 264). If his patients are primarily middle and upper class, that would mean their fathers would be Fournier's "men of substance." Brody finds not a single case of a lower-class person in Freud's practice in these years (or ever, for that matter, though the data are incomplete). Thus, Freud looked a substantial group of prosperous men in the face and had to believe they had sexually attacked and abused their own children.

Freud's overt argument to Fliess is one of numbers. All his patients have father perpetrators. From this he extrapolates that the numbers (assuming a singular etiology) would have to be too high to be valid. He has noted an "unexpectedly" high prevalence of hysteria. If hysterics represent only a subset of all persons who have experienced "infantile sexual scenes," the overall numbers of perpetrators become for Freud unimaginably high.

And yet Freud makes this leap without two significant epidemiological data. He has no numbers on the overall incidence of sexually based hysteria in the population (as distinct from hysterias induced by physical traumas such as work accidents). And he does not know the proportion of child sexual abuse cases that results in hysterical sequelae.

Freud's judgments here to justify recanting are based on less than sound epidemiological reasoning. Freud paints himself into a box by stating to Fliess that all the perpetrators are fathers. Of course this differs from his statement in the 1896 lecture, where strangers, governesses, maids, age-peer siblings and cousins are all included in the scope of violators, though the latter would not be paying his fees. He has made the narrower and more difficult-to-prove statement not to his professional audience, but to Fliess. Current studies on incidence put fathers in the mix with strangers, other children, stepfathers and other relatives as most frequent violators. Thus, Freud's first statement in 1896 proves more accurate historically than his second statement to Fliess in 1897, that "in *all* cases" the father is the wrongdoer. Even accepting that in all his current cases there is indeed a father-perpetrator, Freud must also know that a larger sample of cases would probably yield a wider range of perpetrators. His personal case, for example, would bear this out later. We know that he fears this possibility; for, based on the physical model of disease, he believes there must be one and only one causal factor. Why he is then unable or unwilling to put his known abusers into one class seems odd, except insofar as some members of that class strenuously or stonily object to being put there.

What he is saying here may also have something to do with a factor other than incidence or epidemiology. It may instead relate to his own mental condition, having worked so intensively with his (at least) 18 patients, all of whom seem to have had significant symptoms and infantile abuse. We would never expect a present-day clinician, working on trauma cases in professional isolation, without a supervising therapist or any professional or mental health support for him or herself, to be able to withstand the cumulative effects of vicariously witnessing tragic events without experiencing depression or other negative effects him or herself.[12]

In researching this book, I frequently came across writers and commentators in history who stated that incest was the most horrible and abominable crime. I have asked myself, given the long history of abominable human acts, why this one would be singled out, especially by men, for such odium. The conclusion I drew was that, of all the crimes men commit, including murder, adult rape, pillage, torture and destruction of all kinds, there are circumstances in each of those cases that may confer upon the man glory for committing them. Sometimes those circumstances are war; sometimes self-defense or defense of family or of nation. But I could not imagine or recall any circumstance in which a man's commission of incest with his own young daughter or son could be seen as conferring glory on that man. Incest is a crime whose benefits, mainly consisting of sexual pleasure and a sense of dominance and control, devolve only to the violator, without benefit to the home, the community, the nation or the race. It is not a crime men publicly boast about committing, even if their stated disgust with it has rarely led to actions to decrease or stop it. In fact, it has probably always been essential for men to believe that other men, whatever else they might do in the name of "satisfaction," do not do this. Those who do are seen by other men as utterly different, singular, freakish and rare. It is a commonplace that in prisons, hardly gardens of tender care and sentiment, the convicted men themselves put child abusers and incest committers at the bottom of the totem pole, and submit those men to the greatest abuses of any group within their ranks.

These are speculations, of course. But it seems both possible and probable that something of this nature affected Freud when he faced the tally of his caseload. I have never come across any awareness in the criticism of Esterson, Webster, Crews, Grünbaum or other recent anti-Freud partisans that, for a clinician or any person dealing with trauma in others, the process is not a game. It is not a logical or medical or legal mystery to be solved, which leaves the investigator unchanged. Freud hit a wall, which represented for him the moral unimaginable.

For cynics, let us remind ourselves that 1897 was decades before the Great War and the Holocaust. Freud existed in a moral universe that was still optimistic. He was committed to the idea of scientific progress and kept up a fighting spirit in the face of the setbacks and limitations his society imposed on him for being Jewish. Freud still had hope for a perfectable universe, or at least one he could conquer.

So two significant factors operated behind Freud's presentation of the father problem to Fliess. One was very likely his own unexpected inability to sustain his sense of a fundamentally moral universe in the face of so many father-criminals. The other may have been his vertigo when he realized the possible legal and financial implications of his findings. Freud was already outnumbered by eighteen to one, with no end in sight. The court of his colleagues' opinion had already turned him down once — so definitively that his paper was not even published for further debate.

Perhaps Freud experienced the same anxiety that Girard talks about in *Violence and the Sacred*.[13] Punishing the powerful perpetrator will set in motion a cycle of revenge killings whose end is unforeseeable. In *Oedipus Rex*, the men of ancient Athens demonstrate in the clearest possible terms that, for them, the rape of a citizen boy can unleash a cycle of violence that has the power to destroy an entire society. Perhaps Freud came to fear the same fate for himself.

Intersection of the Psychoanalytic and the Forensic

These matters distinctly narrowed and compromised the scope of Freud's early work. He conducted research in a funding framework that any professional scientific researcher would have to conclude was skewed. In essence, he had perpetrators funding his research and he depended on their continued patronage in order to carry on his research. And yet the results of that research necessarily alienated them, and could have resulted, if he pressed further, in lawsuits against him. Through his psychoanalytic sessions many slander cases could have arisen by alleged perpetrators. Of course, therapists have been sued in the United States within the last 15 years for precisely such kinds of claims.[14]

Freud can be likened to the tobacco company scientist who discovers cancer in his two-pack-a-day lab animals. His results are true, but the company cannot afford to publish them due to the liability. So the results are changed and the true findings suppressed. Subsequent research funded by other sources, however, repeatedly corroborates those original findings, now eschewed by the original researcher, who, unfortunately, still needs his job. In the case of Freud's own work, the conclusions shifted out of necessities both internal and external. Subsequent decades of clinical work, however, have given his original theses a solid measure of support.

And yet we must wonder about Freud's own reactions to the mountain of crimes that faced him. If he had personal feelings about the sadness or impropriety or even criminality of the kinds of experiences his patients related to him, we would expect him to convey them to Fliess, who was indeed his only and closest confidant. But there is no parallel text in the letters, where the public man of science carefully observes the symptoms, including the effect of their revelation on the patient, while privately expressing his grief to Fliess over the catastrophe he has unexpectedly uncovered. He speaks to Fliess about his findings with a certain distance. And while I disagree with much of Richard Webster's analysis of Freud's work, I do think there is some credible evidence for believing Freud was at times overly preoccupied with achieving the scientific breakthrough that would establish his reputation and give him a better income.

The passages concerning the sexual experiences of Freud's patients at the hands of older male relatives and others are handled with clinical nonchalance. Freud expresses no horror, no outrage, no sense that something wrong has been done to these patients as children. Rather, he reports that something has "happened" that has resulted in symptoms that are interrupting their otherwise productive lives. For example, in his letter of December 6, 1896, in describing the relationship between childhood sexual experiences and current symptoms, he writes: "Thus patients who have had something sexual done to them in sleep have attacks of sleep. They go to sleep again in order to experience the same thing and often provoke a hysterical fainting fit in the same way" (*Letters,* 213). This passage is significant insofar as it suggests the degree to which Freud himself ascribed to the male-defined sexual norms of his day. Children being sexually victimized *as they slept* represents merely another way in which such crimes were perpetrated in order to minimize the chances of detection. Freud, I think, grappled with the specificity of the material he was hearing. He was not more morally aware than his colleagues or other men of his time. He was exceptional in that, along with Breuer and some others, he noticed that there was a set of symptoms that patients presented with for which science at the time had no adequate explanation nor sufficient therapy for restoration to health and productivity. In a current setting, however, mandatory reporting rules would have been triggered and a legal investigation might have been required in such cases.

Some may object that, as a "man of science," it was not Freud's place to assess the rightness or wrongness of the acts, but value judgments are nevertheless embedded in Freud's terminology and discussions. The distinction among Freud's use of the terms "perversion," "hysteria" and "neurosis" suggests this. Namely, "pervert" is a term Freud uses often to refer to the prime originator of inappropriate sexual behavior. But he or she is considered "healthy" because of a lack of hysterical symptoms. In other words, indulging without restraint in the fulfillment of one's own desires, acting out on others regardless of the consequences for them, is a sign of health in Freud's world. No one is spared: not wives, not children, not servants, not even babies. At times he minimizes the suffering of his patients in favor of the "health" of their perpetrators, "perverts" who are not suffering because, merely by denying what they take care to ensure cannot be proved, they have had their pleasure and gotten away with it, too.[15] "Hysterics" and "neurotics" are in a sense merely those who are too delicate to take such abusive treatment without offense. Freud has no indignation about this, admitting in February 1897 to Fliess that his own father made both his brother and sisters hysterical/neurotic in just the same way:

> Hysterical cold shivers = being taken out of a warm bed. Hysterical headache with sensations of pressure on the top of the head, temples, and so forth is characteristic of the scenes where the head is held still for the purpose of actions in the mouth. . . .
>
> Unfortunately, my own father was one of these perverts and is responsible for the hysteria of my brother (all of whose symptoms are identifications) and those of several younger sisters. The frequency of this circumstance often makes me wonder. (*Letters,* 230–31)

So children were dragged out of bed for sexual purposes; their heads were held in place so that adult men could force them to provide oral gratification. None of this calls out any moral assessment from Freud. Acting without regard for others' feelings, then, becomes the highest dictum of psychic health. Freud will echo this sentiment much later in *Civilization and Its Discontents.*[16]

Judith Herman argues, in contrast, that while the therapist of such traumatized patients must strive for a "technical" neutrality in therapy, "Working with victimized people requires a committed moral stance. The therapist is called upon to bear witness to a crime. She must affirm a position of solidarity with the victim" (*Trauma,* 136). Herman emphasizes what Freud does not: The traumas committed upon persons such as he heard in his consulting room hour represented crimes.

Herman characterizes the therapeutic relationship and transference with traumatized patients:

> The alliance of therapy cannot be taken for granted; it must be painstakingly built by the effort of both patient and therapist. Therapy requires a collaborative working relationship in which both partners act on the basis of their implicit confidence in the value and efficacy of persuasion rather than coercion, ideas rather than force, mutuality rather than authoritarian control. These are precisely the beliefs that have been shattered by the traumatic experience. Trauma damages the patient's

> ability to enter into a trusting relationship; it also has an indirect but powerful impact on the therapist. As a result, both patient and therapist will have predictable difficulties coming to a working alliance. These difficulties must be understood and anticipated from the outset. (136)

One camp of Freud's recent critics has argued that Freud made up his conclusions; that he "led the witnesses," as it were, and suggested things to his patients that they had not experienced themselves. That his early patients usually left analysis without having what Freud considered a complete resolution of their symptoms is given as evidence that, in fact, they were rejecting his false pronouncements and voting with their feet. Herman's observations, based on her clinical work with trauma patients and the work of other researchers, provide a general basis for understanding why Freud's patients, if they had been traumatized, might also have difficulty establishing a workable relationship with Freud, and staying with him for the duration.

Herman also assumes that as a condition of successful therapy, the patient's safety must be secured. We have every reason to think Freud was in no case able to help his patients establish safe and sustainable living circumstances apart from their perpetrators, nor, as in the case of Dora later, that he would even have seen it as necessary.

Qua Herman, Freud in the letters does not entirely sidestep a moral posture with his patients. Rather, he absolves perpetrators, seemingly in awe of their asymptomatic condition. He reserves his moral perjoratives for his patients, and comments to Fliess about the "evil" tendencies of his patients who resist him and refuse his nostrums. Freud does not decline to make negative moral judgments; rather, he does so only with respect to his patients who are victims — not their perpetrators. Herman, writing with the benefit of her own practice as well as decades of clinical practice with traumatized patients accumulated by many other analysts and researchers, summarizes what is now understood about the "resistance" of such patients:

> Some of the most astute observations on the vicissitudes of traumatic transference appear in the classic accounts of the treatment of borderline personality disorder, written when the traumatic origin of the disorder was not yet known. In these accounts, a destructive force appears

> to intrude repeatedly into the relationship between therapist and patient. This force, which was traditionally attributed to the patient's innate aggression, can now be recognized as the violence of the perpetrator. The psychiatrist Eric Lister remarks that transference in traumatized patients does not reflect a simple dyadic relationship, but rather a triad: "The terror is as though the patient and therapist convene in the presence of yet another person. The third image is the victimizer, who . . . demanded silence and whose command is now being broken." (*Trauma,* 136–37)

Of course, as Freud stumbles onto the knowledge of the traumas of his patients, we can hardly expect that he would immediately grasp all of the dimensions of the phenomena he was experiencing with them, elements he subsequently recognized as transference. It also seems clear, however, that he was not able, at that early juncture, to fully understand or theorize the ways in which the damaged relationships experienced by his traumatized patients would affect the nature of his therapeutic relationships with them as well.

Many authors have questioned why Freud moved so precipitously forward with his 18 cases when he presented to the *Verein* in 1896, cases that in 1897 he admitted to Fliess were not, as he had claimed in his lecture, in any way "finished." He has been roundly criticized for this, and even characterized as having engaged in scientific fraud.[17] I believe Herman offers a more realistic and compassionate explanation for his behavior. In writing about the emotions experienced by clinicians working with traumatized people, she states:

> The patient enters the therapy relationship with severe damage to her capacity for appropriate trust. Since trust is not present at the outset of treatment, both therapist and patient should be prepared for repeated testing, disruption, and rebuilding of the therapeutic relationship. As the patient becomes involved, she inevitably reexperiences the intense longing for rescue that she felt at the time of the trauma. The therapist may also wish, consciously or unconsciously, to compensate for the atrocious experiences the patient has endured. Impossible expectations are inevitably aroused, and inevitably disappointed. (*Trauma,* 151)

In other words, the therapist, in identifying with the patient, may wish to act as the patient's rescuer. Certainly Freud's precipitous actions on behalf of his patients in the name of his sexual etiology theory may have been stimulated at least in part by his desire to act in a morally appropriate way, in the face of what he felt was the genuine, awful and undeserved suffering of his analysands. Herman writes that

> The therapist may experience the extremes of anger, from inarticulate fury through the intermediate ranges of frustration and irritability to abstract, righteous indignation. This anger may be directed not only at the perpetrator but also at bystanders who failed to intercede, at colleagues who fail to understand, and generally at the larger society. (143)

Certainly Freud's impatience with his *Verein* audience, his at times moving accounts in that speech about the degradation of his patients, and his subsequent statement to Fliess that his critics could all "go to hell," suggest that he was perhaps experiencing some of these feelings around the time of the lecture. Freud was unaware of the effects of this material from his patients on his own psyche. His rush to present may have been his attempt, premature by all scientific measures, to end his own sense of powerlessness in the face of his patients' sufferings. If he could find the source of their suffering, he presumed he could end their suffering. But he, too, was undergoing a process of traumatization, by bearing witness to their accounts.

None of Freud's recent critics, including Masson, seem to have considered the devastating effects of listening to such horrible stories, despite what we know clinically about the effects of even witnessing secondhand the recounting of traumatic events. I do not attribute this to the fact that many such critics are not analysts or therapists. Rather, I attribute it to a frightened response on their part to the third party in the consulting room, and the trauma that sits in all Freud's early work. The trauma that Freud is talking about scares them, I think. Their response is not to go after the source of their fear, as Freud did, but to attempt to expunge the words of the messenger from the discussion. I suspect that many critics of the veracity of Freud and his patients are terribly frightened that what he was talking about actually was true. Freud becomes the metonymic scapegoat for the disbelieved patients. But, at bottom, I wonder whether any of these critics believe in the stories and suffering of the patients.

Those who criticize Freud for not having done enough obviously believe the patients. But they, too, misdirect their anger. Who else was talking about this in Freud's day? Who was doing a better job? And how, in the face of the entire social and legal machinery of repression, do we expect one marginalized person to singlehandedly have brought about a perfect form of social change? We are all implicated in the trauma, as we idealize rescuers and then scorn them for being human after all.

Herman describes this phenomenon well, in ways that, I think, also explain Freud's behavior after the *Verein* lecture, when his colleagues shunned him and he began to doubt himself and the validity of his patients' stories. She observes that therapists "who work with survivors [inevitably] come into conflict with their colleagues." This is because the trauma enters the therapists' discussion, and generates its own countertransferences and conflicts:

> Some therapists find themselves drawn into vituperative intellectual debates over the credibility of the traumatic syndromes in general or of one patient's story in particular. Countertransference responses to traumatized patients often become fragmented and polarized, so that one therapist may take the position of the patient's rescuer, for example, while another may take a doubting, judgmental or punitive position toward the patient. In institutional settings the problem of "staff splitting," or intense conflict over the treatment of a difficult patient, frequently arises. Almost always the subject of the dispute turns out to have a history of trauma. The quarrel among colleagues reflects the unwitting reenactment of the dialectic of trauma.
>
> Intimidated or infuriated by such conflicts, many therapists treating survivors elect to withdraw rather than engage in what feels like fruitless debate. (*Trauma,* 152)

When we consider the social phenomenon of Freud-bashing, which has had quite a robust life in the past 20 years (and largely at the hands of men, interestingly), we could do worse than imagine that precisely such "splitting" of the critics has taken place, with various authors assuming the different roles Herman here describes. All, however, who disagree with Freud's approaches can be seen, at an underlying level, to be grappling with the same traumas Freud was witnessing in his patients. I believe the "false memory" crowd is not nearly as fearful of a false memory as it is of a true one. They feel safe, perhaps, as long as all memories can be called into question on some basis or another. All the anxiety about something that is not true, however, I take as an indicator of how unprepared or unwilling people are to witness the real horror of a truly traumatic event recalled in memory.

Similarly, I am astonished that recent critics of Freud have either ignored the work of Herman (Esterson, Sulloway) or criticized her (Webster) for accepting as valid some of Freud's insights in the early period. The fixation on the stories of Freud's early patients, as incomplete and problematic as they are, suggests this same inability to accept the truth of the story and all its horrors, regardless of the effects of doing so on those around the patient. Herman makes clear that the therapist must insist on honesty in the relationship between therapist and patient, and that he or she must take a clear moral position with respect to the crimes that have been committed on the patient. Some critics, on the basis of any false charges, would exile all patients with memories to a status of noncredibility. Others, angry at the failings of some clinicians and therapists, dismiss all therapies as useless and corrupt. Neither camp, in my view, has any defensible prescription for the truly hurt and the truly suffering.

Herman, who trains therapists to work with trauma survivors, has observed not only the therapeutic dynamics between doctor and patient, but also the effects of practice with such patients on the therapists themselves. The results of such conflicts over trauma patients, according to Herman, may take a therapist down a dangerous blind alley:

> Unless the therapist is able to find others who understand and support her work, she will eventually find her world narrowing, leaving her alone with the patient. The therapist may come to feel that she is the only one who really understands the patient, and she may become arrogant and adversarial with skeptical colleagues. As she feels increasingly isolated and helpless, the temptations of either grandiose action or flight become irresistible. Sooner or later she will indeed make serious errors. It cannot be reiterated too often: no one can face trauma alone. If a therapist finds herself isolated in her professional practice, she should dis-

> continue working with traumatized patients until she has secured an adequate support system. (152–53)

In this passage, I feel we see two important things. There is Freud's adversarial stance with his colleagues in the 1896 lecture, and his subsequent isolation. And there is in Herman's narrative something of what Freud himself did, in his flight from what I believe was his patients' real trauma, and his self-preserving instincts as a therapist. He did indeed stop treating traumatized patients, in some sense. He put a great distance, albeit in a problematic and dysfunctional way, between himself and such patients on the theoretical basis of the Oedipus complex. The legacy of psychoanalysis became, precisely, to treat "non-sick" patients. This may be the artifact of Freud's earliest experiences treating trauma patients. He lacked support for his support of his patients' truths.

Masson churlishly but predictably, in his assumed role as rescuer of the victimized, makes Freud's failing a personal one. In this I believe he misses entirely the critical social dimension of belief and support. Freud lived and worked in a society that did not share his early indignation and despair over the damaging effects *on the children* of adult sexual contact with children. As I have shown in earlier chapters, in Freud's day children suffered unto death with no acknowledgment. We should remind ourselves, lest we lose all perspective, that Freud died in exile on the eve of the Holocaust. Freud's society believed in the extermination of an entire people, of which he was a part. Four of his sisters died in death camps. To lambaste Freud as a moral failure for being unable, as a Jew in prewar Austria, to singlehandedly uphold a moral standard protecting all children from adult sexual depredations, is to act out one's own rage, not on the perpetrators of those crimes, but rather at the loss of one's own idealized image of who Freud was.

The intensity of critique against Freud during the 1980s and 1990s can be seen productively in the following light:

> At the moment of trauma the victim is utterly helpless. Unable to defend herself, she cries for help, but no one comes to her aid. She feels totally abandoned. The memory of this experience pervades all subsequent relationships. The greater the patient's emotional conviction of

> helplessness and abandonment, the more desperately she feels the need for an omnipotent rescuer. Often she casts the therapist in this role. She may develop intensely idealized expectations of the therapist. The idealization of the therapist protects the patient, in fantasy, against reliving the terror of the trauma. . . .
>
> When the therapist fails to live up to these idealized expectations — as she inevitably will fail — the patient is often overcome with fury. Because the patient feels as though her life depends upon her rescuer, she cannot afford to be tolerant; there is no room for human error. (*Trauma*, 137)

Herman then relates the story of a Vietnam veteran who experienced a "desperate rage at the rescuer who lapses even momentarily" from caring for his wounds (137–38). She writes: "This testimony reveals not only the helpless rage of the victim in terror of death but also the displacement of his rage from perpetrator to caregiver. He feels that the medic, not the enemy, almost killed him" (138). Here we see the echoes of, for example, Masson's rage at Freud, rather than at the patients' perpetrators.[18] Herman discusses the vengeful side of such reactions in traumatized patients to idealized caregivers:

> Further compounding his fury is his sense of humiliation and shame. Though he desperately needs the rescuer's help, he is mortified to be seen in his defiled physical condition. As his wounds heal in the hospital, he broods on a plan of revenge, not against the enemy, but against the inept rescuer. Many traumatized people feel similar rage at the caregivers who try to help them and harbor similar fantasies of revenge. In these fantasies they wish to reduce the disappointing, envied therapist to the same unbearable condition of terror, helplessness, and shame that they themselves have suffered. (138)

The vituperation against Freud — solid new scholarship on Freud notwithstanding — suggests a similar kind of crushed idealization and subsequent revenge fantasy against Freud, coupled with the critic's desire to substitute himself or herself as a better "rescuer" for Freud's abandoned women patients.

We have not yet begun to contemplate or fully assess the effects of individual traumas on society as a whole, nor on the contours and vicissitudes of academic discourse. But Judith Herman's work helps us to understand much more fully and compassionately our responses to trauma: as victims, as helpers, as witnesses and as critics. Child sexual abuse is not the kind of phenomenon one scientifically observes with the same emotional affect as phenomena in the physical world. It calls out a fundamental set of responses that have to do with feelings of vulnerability and the fear of our own traumatization, as well as the desire to manage and control the source of the originary event. In the case of a sacrificial therapy, the event is associated with the victim, rather than with the actions of the perpetrator. But from a psychoanalytic viewpoint, we should understand that all of us are, without training and support, liable to make unskilled, merely self-protective responses to trauma, which may even be dangerous or unhelpful for its victims.

The storied shift, then, from Freud believing in his own etiological theory and his subsequent abandonment of it, brings with it consequences for the future of psychoanalysis that Freud himself does not fully recognize. In setting the weight of agency for crimes firmly onto his patients and off of their perpetrators — who in a sense are the undiscussed mentally ill cases in the 1896 piece — Freud makes the same mistake as Oedipus. He places guilt onto the child without ever having asked why the father was cursed in the first place. It was not Oedipus, after all, who was originally marked, but his father.[19]

We should not equate the fact of a personally horrifying experience of violent trauma with the assumption that personal horrors will be validated and adjudicated by the public as a whole. Societies choose which such traumas they will hold as horrible. Consider the routine lashing of slaves in the American South. Then consider this from the point of view of slave narratives in which the person who experienced it tells what it was like to be beaten. For the ancient Greeks, in terms of public culture, which is to say largely men's culture, what was horrible was when someone other than a "weak" person suffered. As Thucydides has the Athenians tell the Melians, the strong do what they can and the weak put up with what they have to.[20] What is horrifying for the

Greek audience is not all rape, or all incest, but rather, the rape of a citizen boy, and incest between mother and son. Both have to do with diluting or eliminating the father's control over the bodies of his women and children. The horror for the Greeks occurs when not the weak but the strong must suffer.

FIVE

Freud Finds Oedipus

If the Oedipus complex is to be accepted as a powerful, mythically based hermeneutic system for understanding the human psyche, it seems worth examining, in light of all that we know about Oedipus and his father, Freud's grasp of the mythic structure he both adopts and adapts. What did Freud understand about Oedipus before he changed Oedipus into the Oedipus complex? How fully did he investigate? Did he plumb all that there was to find, in the complexity and pathos of the man trapped by fate? On this matter, certainly, turns the willingness of many scholars and members of the public to accept or not the whole of the validity of the Freudian enterprise.

I believe it is possible to show that the shift from the "seduction theory" to the Oedipus complex, which largely jettisons real sexual abuse of children as a phenomenon for consideration, is contained within the larger compass of the Oedipus myth. And so while Freud believed his Oedipus "complex" had solved the problems associated with his more radical "seduction" theory linking child sexual abuse and hysteria, the mythic context of Oedipus demonstrates that *real child sexual abuse is inseparable from the punitive legacy given Oedipus by his father.* And so I will begin with the classical scholarship, examining the mythic system first and then the versions of the myth that were apprehended in tragedy. This matter bears directly on the viability of Oedipus as a hermeneutic heuristic device. I will then explore some other episodes of parent-child incest in Greek myth in order to establish patterns of generalizability from Greek culture.

But before looking at the evidence available from classics scholarship, it is helpful to return to the primary sites in Freud's work where he reveals his understanding of Oedipus. A close examination of Freud's writing reveals not only the version of Oedipus that has become proverbially Freudian, it also reveals some of the rhetorical devices used by Freud to invite our adherence — to persuade us to accept his departure from the Oedipus people thought they knew. From there we will turn to the broader assemblage of classical texts and scholars on Laius, Oedipus and Jocasta.

There are strong reasons to return to Oedipus, to not see Oedipus as the "cooked" Freudian version of him, but in the more "raw," mythological form, even as it was used by Sophocles, Aeschylus and Euripides. Both Freud and the Greeks are concerned with the vexing question of who has sex with whom, under what circumstances and with what consequences. Early in Freud's career there is a concern about the noxious psychological sequelae for children who have had early sexual contact with adults and other children. Out of this early material, Freud ascertains, and I believe rightly, that it is possible for people to repress thoughts, feelings, and perhaps even experiences so that they drop below the level of consciousness but do not go away. These repressed thoughts, feelings and experiences can resurface and affect people in their present lives, just as Freud early on suggests hysterics are troubled by memories of painful experiences.

Those who consider his later work salient believe Freud resolved the issue of childhood sexual experiences through the development of the Oedipus complex, which shifted all accounts of experience into fantasy, and justified adult actions, as in the case of the (im)patient "Dora," because of the supposed desire for such contact on the part of the younger person. It is important in this connection, then, to query a salient aspect of the Oedipus myth. Freud does not treat the whole of the Oedipus story, and most importantly, the curse upon which it turns. Strangely, from the master of the depths, the curse is never questioned. This proves to be a substantial limitation for Freud's work, and this limitation looms large against the broader backdrop of Greek myths about incest.

We stand now at the watershed: the shift from Freud's early inductive work with hysterical patients, to the more literary-interpretive and nonfalsifiable work of his *The Interpretation of Dreams*. There are those who believe, by entering into "depth psychology" and turning toward the examination of intrapsychic structures, including the Oedipus complex, that Freud made possible a new understanding of the subtle, indirect and often contradictory nature of the human psyche. Freud left the "real," they would argue, to enable a full and complete exploration of the symbolic, as in dreams and jokes, and the imaginary, the great Lacanian extension. The idea of repression, for example, and the current debate over "false memories" certainly have to do with Freud's insights that experiences are not processed into memories as perfect copies, as it were, in the brain. Thus, they are not recalled as perfect memories and can be influenced by many factors, including suggestion. Freud's debatable conclusion is that all such memories should be treated as the products of the individual's instinct-based mental system, and not relatable to objective or observable experiences.

If this assertion is to be accepted, that the so-called "environmental factors" of experience are trumped or mooted in every case by the individual's endogenous psychological system, there should be good evidence for this conclusion in Oedipus. In *The Interpretation of Dreams* (1900), completed during and after Freud's self-analysis, Freud reveals his ambitions for his Oedipus idea and its dimensions:

> in their amorous or hostile attitude toward their parents, psychoneurotics do no more than reveal to us, by magnification, something that occurs less markedly and intensively in the minds of the majority of children. Antiquity has furnished us with legendary matter which corroborates this belief, and the profound and universal validity of the old legends is explicable only by an equally universal validity of the above-mentioned hypothesis of infantile psychology.
>
> I am referring to the legend of King Oedipus and the *Oedipus Rex* of Sophocles. Oedipus, the son of Laius, king of Thebes, and Jocasta, is exposed as a suckling, because an oracle had informed the father that his son, who was still unborn, would be his murderer. He is rescued, and grows up as a king's son at a foreign court, until, being uncertain of his origin, he, too, consults the oracle, and is warned to avoid his

> native place, for he is destined to become the murderer of his father and the husband of his mother. On the road leading away from his supposed home he meets King Laius, and in a sudden quarrel strikes him dead. He comes to Thebes, where he solves the riddle of the Sphinx, who is barring the way to the city, whereupon he is elected king by the grateful Thebans, and is rewarded with the hand of Jocasta. He reigns for many years in peace and honour, and begets two sons and two daughters upon his unknown mother, until at last the plague breaks out — which causes the Thebans to consult the oracle anew. Here Sophocles' tragedy begins. The messengers bring the reply that the plague will stop as soon as the murderer of Laius is driven from the country. But where is he?[1]

This passage has several terms that ask the reader to come along, and which attempt to rhetorically compel belief. First, Freud posits a relationship of magnitude among the thoughts, feelings and other mental processes of psychoneurotics (his patients), and "the majority of children." To a scientific eye, there is a kind of generalizing afoot here which, given the nature of the rest of Freud's book, is not regrounded in any actual survey or attempt at asking and counting up to verify the assertion. Those looking for an observational or scientific accounting will remain unsatisfied.

The next sentence, however, provides the warrant for the argument that Freud cannot supply "scientifically" due to methodological problems faced and unresolved by both himself and his French teachers. It is a crucial turn in the argument; for if it works, it enables Freud to reground his shaky but promising psychoanalytic enterprise upon a warrant which, he thinks, he can both prove, and which will be more acceptable to his public than the prior disaster of his "seduction" theory among his medical colleagues. Eliza Butler's 1925 *The Tyranny of Greece over Germany* suggests why this sentence would grant Freud's theory a provenance that might cause the public finally to accept his ideas: "Antiquity has furnished us with legendary matter which corroborates this belief, and the profound and universal validity of the old legends is explicable only by an equally universal validity of the above-mentioned hypothesis of infantile psychology."[2] The Greeks, whom the Germans idealized and with whom its intellectuals were thoroughly engrossed and engaged, had already formulated Freud's idea of father-hatred and mother-love. Sacred antiquity, the argument by authority, "corroborates" Freud's belief. In this gesture Freud aligns himself with the intellectuals of his day, saying in effect, I am one of you because my theory, like yours, is rooted in Greek thought. In this sentence, he attempts to establish the major premise of his argument, a premise that must be shared by his audience in order for the argument as a whole to succeed.

In such deductive argumentation, the procedure is as follows. The major premise is a general statement about a class of things the audience finds to be true. The next bit, the minor premise, represents a specific instance that the rhetor asserts belongs in the class of things described by the major premise. The rhetor's assertion is that the case being brought forward does indeed partake of the qualities and conditions of the stipulated class of things, such that we may conclude it is a member of that class. Here, in a generic sense, is Freud's argument:

> That which is Greek has a universal and timeless validity.
> My theory fits a Greek story.
> Therefore, my theory is universally and timelessly valid. (Implicit)

But Freud does not satisfy himself to play out his enthymeme in such a direct way. He adds an additional rhetorical flourish: "and *the profound and universal validity of the old legends* is explicable only by an equally universal validity of the above-mentioned hypothesis of infantile psychology" (italics added). Ironically, after using the accepted gravitas of the "old legends" to give ballast to what will indeed be a difficult theory for his audience to take seriously, he then attempts to say that the "old legends" are "only" valid because of the "equally universal" hypothesis of infantile psychology. In other words, in a kind of denial of paternity, Freud attempts to attribute the purchase of old Oedipus on modern readers because of the truth of his own theory! There is a kind of tautology here, which begs a question of logical fallacy. But on another level, there is Freud's self-assurance leaking through, that even when he seems to be standing under the protective cloak of the Germans' avowed intellectual ancestors, he is besting them, reading the present backward onto the past.

Masson has noted that Freud did not avail himself fully of the weight of evidence provided by well-regarded French forensic medical authorities in support of the points he tried unsuccessfully to establish to his medical audience in Vienna in 1895 and 1896 (*Assault,* 14–54). Masson suggests a Bloomian anxiety of influence, Freud wanting to take full credit for linking child sexual abuse and hysteria, and fearing to mention his French teachers, lest it appear that they had reached the head of the Nile first. Ironically again, his failure to bolster his arguments with the available sources may have undercut the persuasiveness of his arguments, delaying still further his quest for fame and notoriety. The possible hostility the Viennese may have felt toward the French, for nationalistic or patriotic reasons, has been given as another source of Freud's reticence about the French. Here, however, we see him again reluctant to give any real credit or to share the dais even with those whom the German-speaking intellectual world most highly esteemed, the Greeks.

In the second paragraph of this long passage, Freud reveals the provenance of his knowledge about Oedipus: the *Rex* of Sophocles. This is the same play that Freud had translated a portion of for a *gymnasium* examination.[3] It is also the stage version of Oedipus which he saw performed during his months in Paris in 1885–1886. The striking feature in this passage is the apparent satisfaction Freud expresses in "knowing" the whole of the story; his confident recitation is intended to show that he has mastered its principle features. But while he lacks an accounting of why Laius is cursed, he makes the most of the dramatized version of how the true murderer, Oedipus, is revealed: "The action of the play consists simply in the disclosure, approached step by step and artistically delayed (and comparable to the work of a psychoanalysis) that Oedipus is himself the murderer of Laius" (*Dreams,* 307).

Rudnytsky establishes Freud's close personal identification with Oedipus as a figure of history.[4] He also underscores this second relationship between the slow but irrevocable accumulation of evidence pointing at Oedipus and the process and method of psychoanalysis itself. And yet this is a curious analogy. If Freud identifies with Oedipus, as the man who will in the end "recognize" his "unconscious desire" to kill his father and marry his mother, then from the standpoint of the play the analyst himself is the obdurate one. In fact, Oedipus borders on impiety in threatening to kill Teiresias, the blind seer endowed with inner sight by Zeus, simply because he tells Oedipus a truth that Oedipus does not wish to hear. This hardly seems like a model of a simple but inexorable unfolding. Oedipus is seemingly frustrated by the difficulty of gaining relevant evidence, and yet he scorns it when it comes. Does Freud feel this way about himself, his patients, or both? And since Teiresias, not Oedipus, is the one who reveals the truth about Oedipus's terrible situation, ought not the transgendered and blind Teiresias be made the intellectual hero of the piece, rather than the arrogant and precipitous Oedipus?

And yet despite the absolute centrality of Teiresias's information to the denouement of the plot, Freud is not only silent about him in this important passage. There is not a single mention of Teiresias in the entirety of the *Standard Edition*, nor in Freud's complete published letters to Wilhelm Fliess. Curious, since Freud relies upon the Sophocles play as his primary source for the Oedipus story, and Teiresias is critical to the Sophoclean plot. In the same way that he claims the old legend has universal validity because of his new theory, Freud in effect claims that Oedipus solves the mystery by himself. There is a critical pruning, which eliminates all elements of the plot except those that have to do with the life of Oedipus and his own actions with respect to his mother and father. For Freud, there is no Laius before Oedipus, no Jocasta except as Oedipus knows her, and no helpers, including Teiresias, to aid Oedipus in solving the mystery of the crime. Freud moves from the wide end of the funnel of knowledge about Oedipus to the narrow end fairly quickly. And in that travel, what is lost is the "environment" of helpers and guides, so that the "instincts" of Oedipus seem to emerge as the sole motive sources for the action.

In the paragraphs following the passage cited above, Freud elaborates for the readers of his dream book his notion that "The Oedipus Rex is a tragedy of fate; its tragic effect depends upon the all-powerful will of the gods and the vain efforts of human beings threatened with disaster;

resignation to the divine will, and the perception of one's own impotence is the lesson which the deeply moved spectator is supposed to learn from the tragedy" (*Dreams,* 307). In a passage closely echoing the first letter Freud writes to Fliess mentioning Oedipus (October 15, 1897), Freud contends here that the failure of modern plays that attempt to imitate this "tragedy of fate" stems from the contrived nature of their plots. Oedipus, by contrast, speaks to us because of a "voice within us" that responds to the story's compelling power:

> And there actually is a motive in the story of King Oedipus which explains the verdict of this inner voice. His fate moves us only because it might have been our own, because the oracle laid upon us before our birth the very curse which rested upon him. It may be that we were all destined to direct our first sexual impulses toward our mothers, and our first impulses of hatred and violence toward our fathers; our dreams convince us that we were. King Oedipus, who slew his father Laius and wedded his mother Jocasta, is nothing more or less than a wish-fulfillment — the fulfillment of the wish of our childhood. But we, more fortunate than he, in so far as we have not become psychoneurotics, have since our childhood succeeded in withdrawing our sexual impulses from our mothers, and in forgetting our jealousy of our fathers. We recoil from the person for whom this primitive wish of our childhood has been fulfilled with all the force of the repression which these wishes have undergone in our minds since childhood. As the poet brings the guilt of Oedipus to light by his investigation, he forces us to become aware of our own inner selves, in which the same impulses are still extant, even though they are suppressed. (*Dreams,* 308)

This passage is critical to the entire Freudian project, post renunciation of the "seduction" theory. And again, we see the Freudian rhetorical machinery at work: moving in one sentence from the idea that it "may be" that we direct our first sexual impulses toward our mothers (is he referring here only to males?) and our first violent impulses toward our fathers, to the idea, following a semicolon and no additional evidence, that our dreams "convince us" that this is so. There is a running ahead to draw a conclusion that seems premature, unfounded. There is a world of difference between thinking something may be so and being convinced that it is so. The style of persuasion by suggestion here almost reminds one of a hypnotic technique — is Freud trying to persuade his readers by mesmerizing them?

Without offering any evidence for his position, in this paragraph Freud asserts two important pieces of interpretation. First, he presents a version of Oedipus unrecognizable to the Greeks and, for that matter, to most modern classicists. The disgusting feelings we have as children we have forgotten, repressed; the power of the play, and by extension the infantile psychology here proposed (or vice versa), reside in awakening in us the memory of those repressed feelings we once possessed. Freud needs to assert and convince us of the repression hypothesis, and he employs the tragic denouement of the *Rex* to accomplish his end. The question is, does *Oedipus* really serve his purpose? Let us set aside for the moment the matter of whether human beings repress feelings or memories. I accept the validity of that assertion. I believe it is one of Freud's most important contributions. At issue is how Freud attempts to persuade us of it here.

In his rehearsal of the plot, Freud correctly presents that Oedipus has no childhood or adolescent relationship to the people who gave birth to him. Hence Freud develops a problem for himself as he tries to make the departure into an overtly Freudian Oedipus. To suggest that the Greek Oedipus's motives stemmed from sexual and violent drives within himself in childhood toward Laius and Jocasta belies the précis he has just provided, or at least substantially complicates it. Does one have these feelings of hate and love only for one's birthparents, whether one knows them or not? Or does one have them for the woman and man who act as mother and father, without the necessity of consanguinity? In the first case, Freud ends up with a weird kind of dilemma, where these feelings of hate and love can lie dormant through a happy childhood with foster parents, but be immediately activated for no apparent reason except instinct at the first (though unrevealed) sight of one's biological parents. On the other hand, Oedipus shows no evidence of such feelings for the people who raise him as their son but who are in fact foster parents. He is so concerned about them, in fact, that on the basis of the oracle he leaves them and goes away so as to avoid unintentionally harming them. This, of course, does not prevent the oracle from being fulfilled.

Oedipus, for the record, loves his foster parents, and believes until very close to the time of the denouement that they are his birthparents. He does not confront them after speaking to the oracle. Apparently, despite receiving no answer about his lack of physical resemblance to them, which prompted his trip to Delphi in the first place, he is not motivated to even attempt to clarify this question with them before departing from them forever. Presumably, had he asked them on his return from Delphi, he might have become aware that his original parents were yet unknown and abroad, and that he might be a danger to them still. Let us be clear: Unlike the more intellectual heroes of Greek myth, including Odysseus, Oedipus is no great reality tester. In the solving of riddles, he is not very thorough.

However, the main difficulty is that Oedipus does not recall something he once knew about himself. Instead, the denouement is purely a dramatic revelation — not the recovery of a repressed memory. In the myth, Oedipus has no memory of his mother Jocasta, nor of sexual feelings about her. Likewise, he has no memory of being bound and exposed, in his father's hope that he would die in infancy. One could argue that the notion of repressed memory was not operative for the ancient Greeks.

Notably, Freud never explores the experiential reasons why Oedipus might have had repressed feelings of hatred for his birthfather. After all, Laius tried to kill him by exposure close to the time of his birth. Self-defense or even a desire for revenge, however, is never considered in the Freudian Oedipal kit of motives, perhaps because it requires us to acknowledge that Laius as a father has every intention of letting his infant son die. The aggressive, violent and sexual feelings parents have toward their children are a virtually undiscussed theme for Freud. Here we have instead a moment where Freud's romantic Hellensim gets in the way of understanding both the Greeks and ourselves. But scholars in Freud's lifetime did indeed consider those aspects of ancient Greek culture that offended Victorian sensibilities. Constans had published *La Légende d'Œdipe* in 1886. Bethe wrote his famous article "Dorische

Knabenliebe," regarding Spartan pederasty, in 1907. Robert wrote his two-volume *Oidipos* in 1915. Here, Freud's glossing over of Laius's leaving his son to die of exposure, a common practice among all Hellenistic peoples, especially in times of high population growth, denies simple reality. But it also misses an opportunity to explore potentially rich ground from the standpoint of psychoanalysis. Do aggressive and violent actions of parents toward their children have emotional and physical sequelae? Freud's French teachers certainly thought so.

The matter of boys directing their initial sexual drives toward their mothers is also complicated by the story. Oedipus grows up believing Merope, the woman to whose care he was eventually entrusted, is his birthmother. It is she whom he leaves, as he attempts to avoid fulfilling the prophecy. He believes Jocasta is a stranger to him; otherwise, armed with the knowledge of the oracle, he would shun her. Little boys, by contrast, who grow up with their natural mothers, know them and can have nonsexual nurturing relationships with them in ways that Oedipus does not with Jocasta. The development of marriage taboos among unrelated children of kibbutzim comes to mind here. In cases where children grow up closely together, an exogamous tendency even among nonconsanguinous people has been observed. Presumably the same possibility, with negative consequences, could happen in reverse: related people raised in isolation meeting as strangers might marry by mistake.[5] While Freud chooses the one story out of the hundreds of surviving Greek myths that depict this kind of tragic and mistaken incest, he is at a loss to explain, if challenged, why such a "universal" drive is in fact so rarely manifested in myth. By contrast, hostility between fathers and potential sons-in-law is a very frequent theme in many Greek myths. When a throne passes to a man by marriage, whoever marries the daughter dethrones the father. A woman, however, does not prolong her rule by marrying a younger man. But as Graves has shown quite thoroughly, Greek kings, because of matriliny, could prolong their term of kingship by marrying their own daughters.[6] So by that logic, *men had far greater motivation for committing incest with their daughters than women did with their sons.* Freud's contention, given the hundreds of Greek stories extant, or even the smaller breadth of material in surviving Greek drama, that the Oedipus situation is "universal" as he construes it is a difficult argument to establish. From the vantage point of Greek myth alone, the expected ubiquity of the Oedipus configuration is simply not in evidence.

The second point has to do with the basis upon which Freud calls for our adherence to his new theory. Freud shifts, in the paragraph discussing the superiority of *Oedipus Rex* to modern tragedies of fate such as *Die Ahnfrau,* from reference to a third-person-singular playgoer or spectator to a first-person-plural, which attempts to merge the author and the reader into an "us": "There must be a voice within us which is prepared to acknowledge the compelling power of fate in the Oedipus, while we are able to condemn the situations occurring in *Die Ahnfrau* or other tragedies of fate as arbitrary inventions" (*Dreams,* 308). This sentence immediately precedes the passage cited above which begins "And there actually is a motive." In this single paragraph in the original German text, beginning "Wenn der König" and ending "Szenen unserer Kindheit," first-person plural pronouns and forms are used 28 times. In the Brill translation, there are 37 such first-person usages; in the Standard Edition translation by Strachey, there are 39.[7]

This rhetorical technique exhorts the reader to find these very feelings in himself (nongeneric) as a means of verifying Freud's argument. This is Edelman's technique. There is almost a hypnotic quality to this paragraph in the repetitions of "we," "our," and "us." It is as if Freud believes that by repeating his idea enough times, in enough different configurations, the reader will accept the argument by force of repetition. Like an evangelical preacher, he indicts the reader for his base feelings and for his repression of those feelings; he reveals them, along with Sophocles; and then he crashes the reader's ego and his pride with baleful admonitions about man's ignorance regarding his true nature:

> The antithesis with which the chorus departs:
>
> Behold, this is Oedipus,
> Who unravelled the great riddle, and was first in power,
> Whose fortune all the townsmen praised and envied;
> See in what dread adversity he sank!

> This admonition touches us and our own pride, us who since the years of our childhood have grown so wise and so powerful in our own estimation. Like Oedipus, we live in ignorance of the desires that offend morality, the desires that nature has forced upon us and after their unveiling we may well prefer to avert our gaze from the scenes of our childhood. (*Dreams,* 308)

Factually, let us note here that Freud did not live in "ignorance of the desires which offend morality." If anything, his early practice had exposed him all too well to their despicable contours. He is positioning himself via projection, in this otherwise Burkean moment of identification, onto the reader, and hoping perhaps that this version of his story will stick in ways that the seduction theory did not. We are also put in mind of Freud's recollection of his times with his old nurse. She would take him to Catholic services, and he would return to preach to his family about God and hell. Perhaps this hortatory passage represents his own abreacting of that very early experience from the time of his nurse's abuse.

There is tremendous pathos in these lines. As always, when Freud says "we," I believe, with Christine Downing, that we are on the mark to read "I," especially since this is made so clear in the rhetoric of the 1897 letter to Fliess. [8] Here is the man who in 1895 and 1896 wrote to Fliess of his seduction theory, that he had found the head of the Nile with respect to the etiology of hysteria. After his time in Paris, after his many patients, after his work with Breuer, he grew wise and powerful in his own estimation. He dared to present his theory whole cloth to his Viennese medical colleagues. In their icy rejection of his ideas, Freud turned on himself, and relocated the source of hysterical or neurotic sexual delusions, not in the displaced fragments of remembered sexual traumas, but in the desires *within himself* that offend morality, the desire that "nature," not his molesting nurse, forced upon him, that caused him to avert his gaze from the scenes of his own childhood. He compares himself implicitly here with Oedipus, who so confidently believed the murderer was *out there* and had to be found. Oedipus, who solved the terrible riddle and ended the plague of the Sphinx, who grew wise and powerful in his own estimation, cannot avoid the terrible sentence over which he has no control: that he is, after all, the killer and the sexual monster. Freud asks, perhaps, for the same exculpation as Oedipus in this moment: that he knew not what he did. He hopes, perhaps, for some kind of professional rehabilitation; some kind of fame, or infamy, that will carry him on through his old age.

The parallels between Freud's life and the life of Oedipus do indeed begin to increase from this historical point. His daughter Anna, his Antigonal child, becomes his helper and the protector of his memory and, like Antigone, never marries. After his death, Freud's extended family of followers come to fight bitterly over the inheritance, with arguments that over time seem to have more to do with gaining the throne than with serving the people well, or solving any more plaguing riddles. One hopes there would be more to psychoanalysis than the fall of the house of Labdacus.

Freud closes this section by calling the reader's attention to a specific passage in Sophocles' *Oedipus Rex* regarding incestuous dreams. Licht has observed that ancient dream books seem to have been full of examples of incestuous dreams duly interpreted by their authors.[9] Freud directs the reader to an observation made by Jocasta shortly before the full revelation as proof of his own theories about dream content and its relationship to real wishes otherwise suppressed:

> In the very text of Sophocles' tragedy there is an unmistakable reference to the fact that the Oedipus legend had its source in dream-material of immemorial antiquity, the content of which was the painful disturbance of the child's relations to its parents caused by the first impulses of sexuality. Jocasta comforts Oedipus — who is not yet enlightened, but is troubled by the recollection of the oracle — by an allusion to a dream which is often dreamed, though it cannot, in her opinion, mean anything:
>
> For many a man hath seen himself in dreams
> His mother's mate, but he who gives no heed
> To suchlike matters bears the easier life.
>
> The dream of having sexual intercourse with one's mother was as common then as it is today with many people, who tell it with indignation and astonishment. As may well be imagined, it is the key to the tragedy and the complement to the dream of the death of the father. The Oedipus

> fable is the reaction of fantasy to these two typical dreams, and just as such a dream, when occurring to an adult, is experienced with feelings of aversion, so the content of the fable must include terror and self-chastisement. The form which it subsequently assumed was the result of an uncomprehending secondary elaboration of the material, which sought to make it serve a theological intention. The attempt to reconcile divine omnipotence with human responsibility must, of course, fail with this material as with any other. (*Dreams,* 309)

In this passage Freud draws several conclusions for the reader that require leaps of logic unsupported by evidence.

The notion that the Oedipus legend comes from "dream-material of immemorial antiquity" attributes a story with a specific cultural context to the vacuous cavern of the ahistorical past. It further confuses, in a gross way, a mythic *langue* or story with the very specific *parole* or discourse of Sophocles' *Oedipus Rex.* Certainly the myth precedes the writing of the play. What is extraordinary is that Freud takes an artifact of the playwright's craft, namely a short observation about dreams that does not appear in the myth (because there is no need to heighten dramatic tension in the telling of a myth), and attempts to make it the raison d'être for the play. It demonstrates a profound misunderstanding about the "timeless," recurring aspects of myth, and the specifically written dramatic versions of such stories, which tell the story differently depending upon the author.

The next line simply substitutes Freud's hypothesis for any other possible explanation for the motivation of the play: "the content of which was the painful disturbance of the child's relations to its parents caused by the first impulses of sexuality" (*Dreams,* 309). The painful contortions of logic have in part to do with the fact that Oedipus is a grown man, far from experiencing the "first impulses of sexuality." Freud gives no evidence here that links childhood and adult sexuality — though such proofs could be offered. Rather, the argument is simply made as an unsupported assertion.

The use of Jocasta's example of how men dream about sex with their mothers, and the triviality of such things, can mean many things. Alejandro Marcel has suggested that her words contain the pathos of a mother who tries to vainly offer comfort, the way one will say things in the face of doom to try to prevent the disintegration of the person one loves. He takes her words as a loving gesture, a holding gesture, guileless and full of the simple concern of a woman who is a mother to offer hope to her husband in torment.[10] Freud is unable to consider the gesture of psychological nurturance or holding here, perhaps because throughout his career he will contend that only love and death, and not nurture, exist as psychological forces.

These lines have also been taken by some critics as Jocasta trying to kick over the traces — for she may know, at this point, that her son actually has been sleeping with his mother.[11] She may have seen to it that her son was delivered and not exposed. As the net threatens finally to close around them, she now tries to buy some time by protesting a bit. Freud never considers that Jocasta might know more than she speaks. He does not examine her motivations: never asks if a woman whose legal husband forswore sex with her would ever want revenge; never asks if such a woman would be willing to use her son for such a task, and then eliminate herself when the clock ran out on her ruse. Freud may not have been able to imagine it. But the Greeks certainly could.[12]

Instead, Freud, the great master of suspicion, takes this piece of poet's art and turns it into proof positive for his hypothesis. He again asserts an unsupported claim: "The dream of having sexual intercourse with one's mother was as common then as it is today with many people, who tell it with indignation and astonishment" (*Dreams,* 309). It must be asked, given the gender tilt of Freud's caseload, how many male patients he had had by 1900 who might have revealed such a thing to him. How does he know how common such dreams are, or were in antiquity? The fact that this version of the Freudian hypothesis revolted many people argues against its simple presence as a facet of the culture. It is not self-evident. Oedipus himself never had such a dream, though in fact he lived the crime.

Freud gives no basis here to confidently conclude that he is right about the source of the dream, or that his infantile sexuality thesis can be the *only* source. He leaps to the suggestion that this dream "complements" the dream of the death of the father. But there is no such father dream in the play. It is an invention of Freud's own mind. Thus the "father dream" lacks the imprimatur of both immemorial antiquity and the ink of Sophocles.

But perhaps the most significant objection to Freud's interpretation of this passage is that he misapplies his own doctrine. Presumably only those who dream of such things without doing them are not neurotic. Their lives are easier, according to Jocasta, because they give no heed to such common dreams. But Oedipus never says he has had such a dream. However, as will be revealed, Oedipus has in fact killed his father and espoused his mother. He did not fantasize doing so, but did so in fact. Thus the dream may be common, though exactly how common we have no good way of judging, either from Jocasta or from Freud himself. But we do know, by the end of the play, that Oedipus did not dream. He actually committed the crimes foretold for him.

The final sentences show the clumsy means by which Freud attempts to tie up in one package several items that to this day draw objections. The dream, he says, "is the key to the tragedy and the complement to the dream of the death of the father." Freud lacks the key to the tragedy because he does not know, or at least does not acknowledge that he knows, the source of the curse. There is no dream about the father's death alluded to by Jocasta or anyone else in the play. Because he is seemingly ignorant of the antecedent material, Freud asserts confidently that "The Oedipus fable is the reaction of fantasy to these two typical dreams" (*Dreams,* 309). As I will discuss in the next chapter, the Greeks understood Oedipus's cursed life as a punishment for his father's crimes, specifically related to the abduction and rape of a young man. They have nothing to do with the son's fantasy life, and everything to do with how punishments were carried out in pre-judicial societies.

The latter portion of the final passage is intriguing, if read as a report of Freud's own inner life: "just as such a dream, when occurring to an adult, is experienced with feelings of aversion, so the content of the fable must include terror and self-chastisement." Freud's literary amateurism and intellectual arrogance surface in the closing lines: "The form which it subsequently assumed was the result of an uncomprehending secondary elaboration of the material, which sought to make it serve a theological intention. The attempt to reconcile divine omnipotence with human responsibility must, of course, fail with this material as with any other" (*Dreams,* 309). Here Freud attempts to make the literary act subordinate to what he elicits as an overarching psychological truth. Yet what he describes as "an uncomprehending secondary elaboration of the material" in reality is his own rendition of the play's meaning. The play in one sense is no more about divine omnipotence than is Cinderella. It is, as we shall see, simply about the punishment of acts that the Greeks felt were outside the prerogatives of mortals.

The epistemology of the Oedipus complex, then, is set around the one person who believes he gets to the bottom of the story and never does, even in exile. Oedipus is dramatically intriguing but intellectually very limited because he never really knows why he suffers. The ultimate privilege of the father is enacted here: to condemn one's child because of one's own sexual misdoing, and for the child to suffer and lose all, even believing himself a parricide as well as a committer of incest — and never to suspect it was all his father's fault. Even in punishment, Laius manages to deflect and extend his own guilt onto his son and wife. A clever move, which the conservative Sophocles will forever recommit upon the sympathies of the unsuspecting. Freud rushes in. Not like Sophocles, who knows the whole story, but like Oedipus. The curse is the key. And Oedipus never figures it out. Even in his enlightenment, he remains blinded to the truth. That, I will contend, has indeed been the lasting legacy of psychoanalysis, and its inherent limitation.

Six

Seducing Power

Laius and the Crisis over the Rape of a Citizen Boy

While Freud does not take up the business of Oedipus until 1897, in the chronology of his life, we know that by 1859 terrible deeds had already been perpetrated upon his young person. Freud's perpetrator was his nursemaid, and yet, in *The Interpretation of Dreams,* she drops out entirely from consideration. She is replaced by the mother, for whom the boy Sigmund felt inappropriate sexual arousal, after first having been abused by his other trusted female caregiver. What then will be the fate of the real perpetrator in Freud's consideration of the Oedipus myth?

In my own research I discovered what I thought to be a curious fact. In the entire *Standard Edition* of Freud's works, Freud mentions Oedipus's father Laius by name in only two places. This seems odd, given how important the father is in the Oedipal triangle, and that Laius is the original sexual perpetrator for whom the murder-incest curse is created. After a century that saw the acts of Oedipus become the representative anecdote for psychoanalysis in the broader culture, this chapter will carefully examine the acts of Laius, his father. The extant tragedies that constitute *Oedipus Rex, Oedipus at Colonus* and *Antigone* have a particular dramatic unity and have been critically treated by some as possessing a certain completeness. But ancient Greek audiences saw these plays as part of a fuller cycle of both myth and tragedy, which related to their social and intimate experience of life. Pederasty was a well-supported and well-regulated aspect of upper-class life for Greek men at the time these plays were written. Living under different social conditions that have officially prohibited man-boy sex for many centuries,[1] many modern critics have focused only on what the heterosexual Oedipus did, though others may have wished to.[2] The Greeks were deeply concerned with things Laius alone had done, though others also may have wished to. Just as Freud's response to his mother was conditioned by prior sexual abuse, the question here to be considered is the relation between Oedipus's crimes and the crimes of his father before him.

Psychoanalysis and the "Laius Complex"

In discussing Oedipus, modern literary critics and audiences, in deference until fairly recently to the heterosexual mores and expectations of Judeo-Christian audiences, have focused, *pace* Freud, primarily on the violence between father and son and the perverted relationship between son and mother. Freud's appropriation of the extant tragedy of Oedipus certainly placed the interpretation squarely within such confines. Even René Girard, who considers himself a critic of Freud, constructs nevertheless a triangle of desire in which Oedipus and his father Laius are locked in conflict because of their putatively colliding sexual desires for Jocasta.[3]

Discussions of Laius and Chrysippus have not been absent from the history of psychoanalysis, however. One could say, instead, that treatments of Laius's crimes, like those of daughter-raping fathers in myth, were not integrated into psychoanalytic theory as a whole, either by Freud or by his successors. Probably the earliest mention of Chrysippus within psychoanalysis is found in the work of Otto Rank, Freud's close adherent in the early years, who produced his opus *Das Inzestmotiv in Sage und Dichtung* in 1912.[4] While Rank insists on reading the presence of homosexual rape in the "background story" (220) in consonance with Freud's discussion of the phallic mother and the development of homosexuality (220–21), he nevertheless reproduces the tenets of the complete story, citing Bethe of 1891. He cites a variant of the legend that makes Oedipus also "originally" homosexual:

> Specifically, Pelops, the father of the abducted youth, curses Laius, wishing that he have no children, but that if he does, his son kill him. Considering Laius's homosexual inclinations, this curse of childlessness gains a deeper meaning. Indeed, Oedipus himself was considered to have been homosexual in his youth, as shown by fragments of Praxilla, a woman poet of the fifth century B.C. (cf. Schneidewin 1852). In her story, he was in love with the same youth (Chrysippus) as his unrecognized father; according to Euripides (*Phoenician Women,* 66), Laius is killed out of jealousy over Chrysippus, or in a fight over the youth — the complete opposite of jealousy over the mother. Just as Oedipus is the first and clearest example of incest among the Greeks, his father Laius is considered the original pederast. (221)

Thus, while Rank is eager to reweave the myth back into his own classificatory schemes which emphasize mistaken identity and triangular erotic struggles among the father, mother and son, it can also be said that Rank despite himself gives the *langue* of the story of Laius, his rape of Chrysippus, and either Pelops or Hera as the origin of the curse. Rank, immediately upon completing the passage above, states: "We may now disregard the completely impossible demand for a literal psychological translation, as it were, of the legend," citing his lack of knowledge regarding "the conscious factors leading to its creation" (221). In fact, as I will discuss later in this chapter, we do have some fairly solid inferences from modern scholarship regarding the "conscious factors." I include this passage as a demonstration that, even among Freud's closest followers, this additional knowledge about the Oedipus story was available to him, not later than 1912, if he had only been reading the work of his own followers and nothing else. But it seems Rank's additional material did not cause Freud to reconsider his uptake of Oedipus at all.

As early as the 1930s, however, more critical voices were emerging, and taking notice of the role played by Laius prior to the fateful meeting in the road. The Scottish psychoanalyst Ian Suttie considered that the

Oedipus complex and penis envy were far from the only "antisocial motives" or "jealousies" that could be identified as foundational. In *The Origins of Love and Hate,* Suttie details what he calls the "Laios [*sic*] jealousy," which the father feels toward his child:

> But man's jealousy of the woman with a child is supplemented also by his jealousy of the child who has arrived to take possession of the wife. The advent of the child enriches the woman's love-life; but, to begin with, impoverishes that of the man. Hence we find what I call the Laios jealousy, Laios who had his son Oedipus exposed and abandoned at his birth. Many other myths and a great deal of animal behaviour attest the resentment of the father at the child's advent, e.g. Kronos, Ouranos. As this jealousy is directed against boys and girls alike we must reject Freud's interpretation of it as merely a "timely provision" against the son's future challenge to the father's sexual possession of the mother.[5]

Suttie in general mounts a fairly trenchant critique of Freud, on grounds that we would see as highly amenable to an object relations view of psychoanalysis, with a wealth of anthropological and animal evidence knitted in. Here, his formulation of the "Laios jealousy" appears to take up a legitimate and recurrent theme in families, namely the hostile and even mortal feelings of the father toward his own and his wife's children. One thinks both of Agamemnon's killing of Clytemnestra's husband and infant before taking her as his wife, and of Miriam Johnson's argument in *Strong Mothers, Weak Wives,* that the primary bond in marriage for men is with their wives but for women is with their children.[6] As such, there is much to say about it as a central and gendered issue in childrearing within heterosexual relationships. However, we should also recall how much Laius was a reluctant father, due to his baseline homosexuality. All accounts suggest that his abstinence from his marriage to Jocasta was hard on her but not on him. Further, there is his apparent preference for young men and boys as partners (perhaps intensified by the fact that Athenian society had no provision for adult male homosexual relationships). I would simply say, against the backdrop of other strong myths of paternal and maternal killing of children, this story is hardly the most representative case — unless Freud believed all fathers were preferentially homosexual pederasts. Suttie does not take up Laius's previous crimes.

Patrick Mullahy, in his 1955 work synthesizing and comparing the theories of Freud and several of his followers, reads Rank as arguing that the Laius position resides in the desire to have no children — again, though, without acknowledging why. Mullahy quotes Rank: "The boy was immediately exposed after birth, because the father wanted no successor, but wanted to be his own immortal successor, a desire which the myth presents in the incest of Edipus [*sic*] with his mother. This concept makes Edipus himself a representative of the father who wants to have no children, yet tries to preserve himself indefinitely."[7] Rank touches upon an element of the mythic accounts that may deserve further attention. Laius is sometimes represented as emulating Zeus, who took the beautiful youth Ganymede and made him his lover on Mount Olympus, granting him eternal youth in exchange for his abduction from the otherwise expected heterosexual life course, including marriage to a woman and childbearing. But Laius may also have been asserting simply his core sexual desire for young men. His society made no allowance for men who did not wish to marry women and procreate. Zeus, of course, did procreate, and prodigiously. Laius's fault may simply have been viewed as not wishing to father boys but only to be sexually involved with them.

Eric Fromm views Oedipus as rebelling against the father's authority, rather than having primarily an incestuous motive.[8] Thus Laius becomes the representative of patriarchal power, which by then had triumphed, *pace* Bachofen, over earlier, matriarchal forms of society. This analysis suggests that the Oedipus plays attempt to work out a lingering tension between the older, egalitarian matriarchal forms and the newer, hierarchical patriarchal forms, a notion also supported by Robert Graves in the same time period of the 1950s. In such a light, Laius becomes a liminal case for how not to take patriarchy too far. Laius, in manifesting both his homosexual desire and his willingness to sexually neglect his wife, certainly could be said to be asserting the superiority of men over women as well. But in doing so to such an extreme degree, and by angering the father of the boy he abducts, Laius also becomes the poster boy, as it were, for what not to do with one's patriarchal privilege.

But without consideration of the play about Laius's rape of Chrysippus, Fromm's emphasis remains on the rebellion of Oedipus the son rather than on the crimes of Laius the father.

In the 1950s, however, the French psychoanalyst and anthropologist George Devereux discussed the salience of Laius's crimes in the Oedipal constellation. Of Freud's approach to adult "seductive" behavior toward children post theorization of the Oedipus complex, he writes:

> Unfortunately, from that time onward he [Freud] also began to ignore the genuinely seductive behavior of parents, perhaps because the theory of the Laius and Jocasta complexes was even more egodystonic and culturally objectionable than was the theory of the Oedipus complex which, in a sense, confirmed the nineteenth-century adult's low opinion of children in general. . . .
>
> The trend away from the recognition of the seductive behavior of adults, bolstered not only by Freud's prestige, but also by social pressure and by the analyst's need to scomotize this anxiety-arousing idea, was too strong to be reversed, even by the findings of Ferenczi and of certain of his students that, presumably by means of the "dialogue of the unconscious," children recognize the real instinctual roots of the tenderness which adults display towards them.
>
> Yet, it is a matter of common experience that in sexual relations between adults and children — which are far more common than is generally believed — it is usually the adult who takes the initiative. Only in rare instances are the children the actual seducers.[9]

Devereux backs his argument with research on the Mohave Indians.[10] Regarding Laius's acts of aggression against Chrysippus and the father Pelops's reaction to them, I think Devereux comes closest to emotional clarity when he imagines that young men may well have objected to such treatment — being abducted by an older man, with or without the father's consent, and then given a brief education in a few key manly arts, along with a sexual relationship with the man, on terms of propriety that the man may or may not have strictly observed. His notion that the myths "appear to express the Greeks' insight into the external and realistic sources of the male child's tendency to view his father as a homosexual ogre, and of his desire to exchange roles with the father also in this respect" seems to assume that fathers in general have homosexual desires that they direct towards their sons.[11] One might add "or son substitutes," as the Greek system of organized pederasty seemed designed to do. In short, Devereux does a better job of acknowledging the explicit and implicit issues of homosexual desire in adult men and the means and consequences of directing it toward male children, though he is less interested in thinking about the Greek system that placed older and younger men together sexually. Of course, one notes in such a connection that bad sexual behavior on the part of adult men toward boys is considered both a crime and a disgrace on the man, whereas such behavior directed at girls is often considered simply an unavoidable hazard of being born female, and therefore only disgraceful to the girl.

Marianne Krüll in the 1970s likewise acknowledges the fuller story, which sets the curse in motion, and asserts that Freud "probably" was familiar with the unabridged version from a collection of myths published by Gustav Schwab in 1838–1840, though she gives no additional evidence for her assertion. Her interesting conclusion as a biographer is that Freud "stripped" away the "Laius prelude" from the Oedipus story in alignment with "his relationship with his own father: his father's past must remain a closed book at all costs."[12] Krüll, then, should be counted as one who sees Freud's omission of the Laius-Chrysippus material as something of an act of bad faith.

In sum, while several psychoanalytic writers and critics have taken up the issue of Laius and the "Laius complex" heretofore, most have emphasized the generic elements of the father who resents the intrusion of children into his previously exclusive emotional relationship with his wife (with dire consequences for the children), or the issue of patriarchal and paternal dominance and the resulting rebellion of sons. This is more than can be said for Freud, who focused his attention on Oedipus and Jocasta, to the neglect of Laius and discussions of fathering as such.

To my mind, Devereux has most carefully and unflinchingly trod the truly "anxiety-arousing" ground of trying to imagine something about adult sexual (and violent) desires directed at children, and the possible reactions of children to such overtures and abuses. It is here, however, that I believe we find the Athenian playwrights attempting to mediate a path between the unbridled rape and abduction of boys (per Laius), and the population explosion they feared from unbridled reproduction among the citizen class (represented in Chrysippus being one child among many, and killed by his stepmother, according to one variant, so that her own sons would be heirs in his stead).

Laius and Man-Boy Rape

For the Greeks, whose society after the seventh century B.C.E. largely included institutionalized pederasty as a feature of which they boasted, the matrix of issues bearing on the family of Laius never had an exclusively heterosexual backdrop. Solon had commended pederasty, meaning ritualized sexual relationships between older men and younger boys, as a means of delaying the age of marriage for men until 30, thereby controlling the population explosion.[13] The citizen class, which controlled the poleis, were dependent upon property for their status and power. If families grew too large, estates had to be subdivided among heirs until they became too small to support their owners at the level necessary for their participation in political life. Likewise, while colonization and emigration eased the land crisis somewhat, after a time this too became unavailable as an outlet for excess population. So, along with infanticide, pederasty developed as a nonprocreative alternative sexual outlet for adult men before marriage, which enabled them to have sexual gratification while not reproducing themselves into penury. It also afforded them a means, as David Cohen has argued, to vie for honor in courtship, which arranged marriages and sexual gratification with their social inferiors otherwise largely foreclosed.[14] In a society in which reputation and glory figured so prominently, free men's opportunities for claiming such coups had to be cultivated and maintained.

There have been nonpsychoanalytic critics who have taken account of Laius's homosexual activity and attempted to bring it to bear on the myths as well as the tragedies. Classical scholars including Constans, Bethe, Licht, Sergent and others have drawn the connection between Laius's unlawful handling of the otherwise legal relationship between himself and Chrysippus as leading directly to the plague on Thebes and the curse on Laius and his family.[15] Importantly, the Greeks saw performed both a *Laius* by Aeschylus, and a *Chrysippus* by Euripides.

While these plays have not survived to us, they were well known to Greek audiences. They constituted the story of Laius, Oedipus and Jocasta as the Greeks had understood them mythically for centuries. Licht, for example, notes that Aeshylus wrote four plays that won him the first prize in 467 B.C.E.: *Laius, Oedipus, Seven against Thebes* and *Sphinx*. He writes:

> Of the *Laius* unfortunately only two unimportant glosses of words are preserved; yet we are in a position to state something in regard to the plot. There is much to be said for the conjecture that the love of Laius for the boy Chrysippus, the beautiful son on Pelops, formed the background for the further tragic destiny of the unhappy king. Indeed, according to many traditions, Laius was considered by the Greeks to be the founder of the love of boys. We may also add the information according to which Pelops, the father robbed of his boy, pronounced that fearful curse upon the robber, which then . . . found its end in the death of Oedipus, who after a long life full of sorrow was cleared from sin by the powers of heaven. Here one must avoid a grave error, into which in fact many, otherwise well acquainted with antiquity, have fallen. The father is not driven to the curse because Laius loved a boy and was intimate with him . . . as might be assumed considering the modern views upon pederasty; but simply and solely because Laius steals the boy, and abducts him against his father's wish.[16]

Similarly, Licht discusses what is known of Euripides' *Chrysippus,* attested to in the *Symposium,* Cicero's *Tusculan Disputations,* and in fragments from Euripides himself. The play was written and performed, it seems, to impress the beautiful young Agathon, over whom many Athenian men, including Euripides, apparently lusted. One surviving fragment has Laius saying that "one knows what is right, but does what is wrong." This apparently refers to the Greek idea of love "as a disease, since it disturbs the tranquillity of the mind and must therefore be combated with the weapons of understanding." Although it cannot be stated definitively, Licht infers that the drama must have ended with the death of Chrysippus in order to fulfill the genre requirements of tragedy.[17]

Thus Laius, whose acts were the subject of several legends and at least two tragedies, is to the ancients not the silent, invisible character Freud's two references would make him seem.[18] Several ancient sources that take up his life attest to some significant points. This conclusion is perhaps surprising or disturbing to the hetero-normative school: the history of Laius is inseparable from Greek pederasty. Bernard Sergent provides a concise account that can serve as a starting point. He observes that there are two common traditions among the ancient Greeks concerning the invention of pederasty. One, from Timaeus, reported by Athenaeus, credits the Cretans. One credits Laius, the "legendary king of Thebes." Apollodorus traces Laius's exploits in this way. Laius was the son of Labdacus, the king of Thebes. At the age of one, Laius's father was killed and his kingship usurped, "first by Lycus and then by his nephews Amphion and Zethus. They exiled Laius to the court of Pelops." There, Laius eventually fell in love with the young Chrysippus, Pelops's son, and abducted him. He took him, variously, to the Nemean Games or then also to Thebes.[19]

The abduction, however, was not the staged and consensual act that came to signify the onset of accepted pederastic relationships. Such normative "abductions" were understood as the act of the *erastes,* the adult male lover, taking his *eremenos,* the adolescent boy-beloved, away with him to his *andreia,* a living space restricted to men, after having gained the father's and the boy's permission.[20] There they would experience a period of seclusion from women, instruction for the boy in the manly arts of chariot driving, hunting and battle, and the completion of an intimate sexual relationship governed by strict rules prohibiting the penetration of the boy. The protection and strategic connections forged in this relationship would extend through the beloved's full initiation into manhood and into the rest of their lives.

William Percy notes several mythic "originators" of pederasty, including "Zeus, Laius, Orpheus, Posiedon, Minos, Tantalus (father of Pelops) and even Posiedon." He qualifies this list as follows:

> Why these individuals were specified is not always easy to explain. Beautiful Apollo and the heroic Heracles had the most eremenoi, but they are never said to have begun the custom. A close association with Crete may explain the choice of Zeus and Minos. The fact that Laius and Orpheus both for different reasons gave up sex with females and

> took up with boys as an alternative lends some credence to Marrou's theory that situational homosexuality prepared the Greeks for institutionalized pederasty.[21]

Percy suggests here that Laius "gave up sex with females," and the question is, when? That is to say, was he constitutionally gay, and after marrying a woman for political reasons chose to permanently and exclusively pursue boys? Is Percy referring to the injunction that Laius not have children with Jocasta? Sergent tries to establish that man-boy couples were formed for the purposes of initiation only. In the usual course of events, the *erastes* married a woman after the pederastic relationship. Cohen and Dover have shown that, outside Sparta, adult gay relationships were not universally approved of by the Greeks because of the perceived danger of sexual penetration, which would strip an adult male citizen of his political rights.[22] If Laius took the boy away and wished him to be his permanent lover, the story may be implying in indirect terms that, unlike men who entered into relationships with boys for initiatory purposes, Laius wanted Chrysippus to be with him forever, exclusively, and to the exclusion of marriage to (or at least sexual relations with) a woman.

Laius is noteworthy in this connection because founding myths sometimes contain the limiting conditions of a practice. They may specify both the way in which something is to be done, and the way it is never to be done. Given the Greeks' anxieties surrounding their rule that for male citizens certain sexual acts, such as receiving anal penetration, could cause the loss of citizenship,[23] there are several indications that part of Laius's *notoriety* as a pederast arises from precisely a felt need to sanction certain types of behaviors by adult men in pederastic relationships.

The credible grounds for this interpretation are as follows. Laius is given as the human inventor of pederasty. But he follows the tradition of Zeus, who takes the beautiful boy Ganymede to Mount Olympus to be his cupbearer forever. If Laius is the first mortal after Zeus to take a boy as his lover, we might expect there to be some mimicking of the behavior of the god. And yet the story gives us precisely the *limits* of human prerogatives in this matter. For while Zeus grants Ganymede eternal youth, and in essence prevents him from ever completing his "initiation" and entering his adult heterosexual phase (to live and have sex with his wife, never again with Zeus), this condition, were it granted to mortals, would prevent a potentially large number of citizen boys from being promoted into their roles as adult male citizens and leaders. The reproduction of pederasty, in other words, was dependent on the boys "graduating" from that state of being the *eremenos;* the boy had to be reborn as a heterosexual man through the completion of the initiation in order for pederasty to perpetuate itself. The gods, who were not confined by such limitations, could couple with whomever they chose for as long as they wished. But mortals faced their own social and legal limitations. Cohen, for example, argues cogently that Athenians generally would have repudiated a sexual relationship between "two middle-aged male citizens." His analysis of statutes prosecuting hubris shows the likelihood that they were applied to pederastic relationships, and that penetration of a boy under a certain age would entail a charge of hubris — that is, violent assault, outrage, rape or seduction — regardless of whether the boy gave his consent. In such a case, the man would be held liable as an offender.[24]

We do not know the age of Chrysippus, nor do we know whether he gave his consent to Laius, both crucial matters from the standpoint of Athenian law. What is indubitable, however, is that Laius violated the norm of gaining the father's consent prior to the onset of the pederastic relationship. Several sources attest that Laius's abduction of Chrysippus was carried out without his father Pelops's permission. This rashness and brutality were considered unnecessary and unseemly, even dangerous by the Greeks.[25] In all other ways Laius would have been a very suitable *erastes* for Chrysippus. His father Pelops, who had been abducted by Posiedon and had been his *eremenos,* would certainly have given his permission had he been asked. Licht suggests that it was Pelops himself who placed a curse on Laius. This version of the curse emphasizes the anger of a father over the rape of his son. Judith Herman and Linda Hirschman have suggested in their studies on incest that mother-son incest tends to be heavily punished while father-daughter incest is proverbially glossed over,[26] because in patriarchy, it is the fathers who punish. Fathers who perpetrate are not available to prosecute themselves, and fathers as a class are less than willing to prosecute other fathers for these acts. In the case of Pelops, a similar logic arguably holds. The father remains the final arbiter of who will sexually interact with his children, and the final authority on who will mete out punishment, or not, on those who do.

Others, however, have imputed the curse to Hera, the goddess of heterosexual marriage.[27] She is regularly associated with the Sphinx descending on Thebes. Her complaints are conjectured on a few key points. First, pederasty threatened the prerogatives and power of married women even further; it was a means for both delaying marriage and limiting the number of children in a relationship.[28] The timing of a pederastic relationship in a man's life was intended to make it a means of honorable sexual outlet in the years after adolescence but before men's marriages at the now delayed age of 30. There was an age, however, after which it was not considered honorable for an adult man to still be interested in beautiful youths.[29] If Laius was intended by the post-Solonic poets as a bad example not to be followed, it could be that when Laius brings Chrysippus home to Thebes, he is already married to Jocasta and is using the boy postnuptially to avoid or sexually put off his lawful wife, a boon Sergent attributes to the misogynistic Apollo.[30] This would obviously be upsetting to Hera, the goddess of marriage and long-suffering wife of philandering and pederastic Zeus.

A second concern of Hera might be revenge. It is proverbial that Hera takes out her anger about Zeus's unfaithfulness on the women and boys with whom he is intimate, and not her more powerful husband directly.[31] Chrysippus is the son of Pelops, the beloved of Poseidon. Depending on the source, Zeus may have fallen in love with the beautiful Ganymede first, or he may have followed Poseidon's example after the sea god brings Pelops to Olympus as his lover. In either case, Ganymede replaces Hebe, Hera's daughter, as cupbearer to the gods. This, of course, is an insult to Hera since Zeus thereby places a boy lover before his own daughter. Hera may have been keen to find a mortal *erastes* to punish for such disrespect and insensitivity on the part of her newly pederastic husband Zeus. If Pelops is mythically made to represent the anxiety and rage of fathers over misdeeds committed by adult lovers on their sons, it makes sense that there would also be some kind of mythic representation of the anxiety and rage of wives over this new practice. For while pederasty as practiced by Sparta, Athens and other Greek states had specific social and economic justifications and benefits, it also created new kinds of violations and new social tensions, including its impact on women. Every solution, as the saying goes, has its problems.[32]

If Laius were the inventor of pederasty, on what basis could he have been seen as violating an established norm? Some authors have observed a homology between the rite of heterosexual marital abduction as practiced by "primitive" societies, and the kidnapping scene in Greek pederasty, which in its earlier, "Cretan" style involved both an abduction and a two-month "honeymoon."[33] The kidnapping itself, however, according to proponents of this view, was always ever only to be an apparent one, its details and extensive gift and alliance agreements having been worked out mutually between the parties in advance. A second possibility is that Laius was the "inventor," and that the rape of Chrysippus does indeed represent some kind of foundational myth. However, as the story was told and retold while pederasty became more systematized and spread to regions outside of Crete, the legal and customary practices surrounding it became more specific and detailed and bore more severe consequences when violated.[34] Thus, the story of Laius, retold in the fifth century context of well-developed legal codes, becomes a cautionary tale for overeager *erastes,* who might contemplate rash and glory-seeking acts in competition for their beloved.

There seem, out of all the versions I have read, two strong reasons for Laius's actions being seen as wrong. One is the violation of the rules of hospitality (Laius was the guest of Pelops) and the etiquette of pederasty (ask permission of the father; give gifts and recompense, as Zeus gives horses and a golden vine to Tros for stealing his son Ganymede). In this view, Laius breaks the rules because he cannot control himself — he is rash and arrogant and simply takes what he wants, which happens to be the beautiful Chrysippus. He offers neither apology nor recompense. "One knows what is right, but does what is wrong," as Euripides' Laius tells us. Those who follow the hubris school of thought see the echo of his actions in Oedipus's character, where Oedipus acts rashly and capriciously, killing his father on the road for a minor insult, and later threatening to kill those who tell him he did so. Sergent does much to minimize the sting of the "curse" on Laius, rationalizing it away as a normal injunction against having marital relations while serving in the military. For him, it seems important to argue that Laius does nothing worth punishing. He emphasizes the version of the story that Chrysippus is killed by his brothers, not that he commits suicide out of shame over Laius abducting him.[35]

I am unconvinced of Sergent's reasoning on this occasion. If Euripides has Chrysippus committing suicide, I am still not certain this makes the story "moralistic," by reflecting badly on man-boy love in general. Laius offends the practice on at least two clear grounds. He abducts without permission, and presumably also rapes a male fellow Greek, a godly prerogative not regarded as a human right by the misogynist and reputation-minded Greeks.[36] And, he gives no recompense to Pelops and seemingly no gifts to Chrysippus. This violates the expectation of gifts and, parallel to the case of Zeus and Ganymede, restitution to the father for the loss of his son.

The second possibility is that Laius does not ask permission, not simply (or only) because he is a sociopath with impulse control problems, but because he wants to be with Chrysippus permanently. In a time of institutionalized pederasty, this must surely have been a temptation for men with strong constitutional homosexuality. Finding a beautiful boy with whom one is supposed to form an intimate but finite sexual relationship in which manhood is taught — how many men fell deeply in love with their *eremenoi* and did not want the predetermined time to end? Zeus, after all, granted Ganymede eternal youth and life, surely a metaphor for Zeus's unending sexual interest in him. Ganymede is brought to Olympus by Zeus to spend eternity with his divine lover, and never to "finish" his initiation into manhood by heterosexual marriage. Why, perhaps thinks Laius, may I not do the same?

The sexual aspect of pederasty among mortal Greeks was an active affair of a few months. Legislators made clear that it was not intended to replace or displace heterosexual marriage, which, for reasons of citizen-class procreation and political alliance, would remain crucial in the Greek mind.[37] Percy, however, points out that many men, after its institutionalization, chose to remain bachelors all their lives, meaning that they could continue to serve as *erastes*, at least until a certain age. This became a particular problem in Sparta.[38] So this may indeed have been an issue for some *erastes*. Same-sex relationships between adult Greek men were not encouraged. The Greeks had a very difficult time with the notion of equality in relationships. One partner had to be on top, as it were. And, in a misogynist and heterosexist economy of sexual positionings, it was assumed that one partner or both might, sometimes or always, allow himself to be sexually penetrated. Greek law rendered the penetrated man politically a woman, and he lost all his rights of citizenship in becoming so. In a political system that had eliminated the political rights of women, any man who took on even the appearance of being a woman, as woman was there defined — most especially in sex, where being penetrated was considered by the Greeks to be an exclusively "feminine" situation — was socially and politically debilitated. Undone.

If Laius truly loves Chrysippus and wants to stay with him, the difficulties of this situation make themselves immediately clear. If Laius expects Chrysippus to be with him, then because he is the older partner, it invariably will be assumed that Chrysippus is taking the "woman's" role. Ganymede's name, in parallel, becomes the Latin *catamite*, the receiving partner in a male homosexual relationship.[39] Outside of pederastic relationships between two citizens, where strict rules about sexual technique allow the adult man to have an orgasm between the boy's thighs, the assumption will be that the younger man is being penetrated.[40] This would be disastrous for his career; it would literally render him a noncitizen.

Let us also try to imagine what might be going on for Chrysippus, whose voice, with the loss of Euripides' tragedy about him, is lost to us. If Laius is in love with him, but he does not return the feeling, then the "abduction" would be experienced as a rape — immensely violating and humiliating. In the normal procedure, the boy could turn down a potential *erastes.* A boy badly treated could return home and demand satisfaction, and would be free to publicly vilify the *erastes.* Pelops certainly seems angry at Laius, and in one version cited by Graves comes marching with soldiers on Thebes to take back his son.[41] Chrysippus might, therefore, expect support. But after a violent abduction, the question would always remain as to whether he had been penetrated. It would be an unrecoverable blow to the reputation of a citizen.

On the other hand, if Chrysippus loved Laius, and realized that Laius was "only interested in sex," or even simply that their time together had to end, such a situation would also be emotionally devastating. Boys were not supposed to act as if they really "wanted" their *erastes;* they were supposed to be coy and placid.[42] And they certainly were not supposed to enjoy the sex. Suppose Chrysippus were terribly in love with Laius and *offered* himself to be penetrated — perhaps he wanted to be with Laius after the initiation as well. Running away and experiencing the intensity of a first intimate relationship with someone he really loved might have caused Chrysippus and Laius to forget for a while the rules that would bind them once they returned. Perhaps Laius revealed that he intended to marry Jocasta, or was married to her, even as he professed his desire for Chrysippus. He needed Jocasta to gain a throne. How devastating for Chrysippus, to know that this great romantic idyll would certainly come to an end! If his feelings for Laius were not reciprocated, on the other hand, one can also imagine a disastrous emotional outcome for Chrysippus. To have been raped with no emotional recompense would have been an unrecoverable humiliation as well as his political undoing.

In trying to account for Chrysippus's death in Euripides' play, these several possibilities suggest themselves. If he did not love Laius and Laius forced penetration; if he loved Laius and wanted to stay with him and realized he could not; if Laius raped him, and he knew his reputation would never recover from this blow, and that he was now as good as a prostitute or slave — these seem to me to be cogent reasons for why Chrysippus might kill himself, in the context of Greek mores.

Greek myth is replete with tales of both women and youths who find or choose death as an escape from sexual assault. By the same token, in any society that enjoins relationships that people deeply desire, the possibility that in their despair they will commit suicide must always be before us.

In the myths, however, Chrysippus is killed by his stepmother.[43] She asks his half-brothers Atreus and Thyestes, two characters with their own vicious careers ahead of them, to do the killing. But they demur, unwilling to violate the hospitality of Laius. She then kills the boy so that one of her own sons will get the throne. Then she commits suicide. The myths may have been less romantic about such things where power and inheritance were concerned — the other side of the pederasty coin. Myth is less concerned about the emotional lives of individual people, which become the very stuff of tragedy.

Laius as Husband

The chronology of events surrounding the abduction of Chrysippus and Laius's marriage to Jocasta is extremely ambiguous from the sources. Licht reconstructs the paradoxes of Laius's situation:

> Thus we may say that the tragedy of Aeschylus found its special theme in the fact that the royal hero Laius became a curse-laden man in consequence of an offense against conventional form; he thought he might be allowed to abduct the boy, when he could have sued for the beautiful prize freely and openly. The curse pronounced over his head contains a fearful irony: what in his youth formed his greatest delight, a lovely boy, is denied to him, the married man; his marriage remains childless, and when he nevertheless forces a son from fate, he is destined to fall, through disastrous links in the chain of destiny, by the hand of the son he so eagerly longed for.[44]

One could weakly infer that Licht supposes Laius was already married when he sought Chrysippus, or at least hoped to retain his relationship with him after marriage. The latter notion is supported by the mythic version that has Laius taking Chrysippus back to Thebes, his home and castle.[45] And he implies that Laius had a desire for beautiful boys from the time he himself was a youth. We may infer that for Laius, acting as an *erastes* was not merely the fulfillment of a duty, but something that he sought to do and did eagerly. Licht cites a fragment from Euripides, wherein Laius complains that "one knows what is right but does what is wrong" (frag. 841; 139). This may be taken to mean that Laius had an innate desire for boys; that he was too weak to control himself with regard to the oracle and Jocasta; or on a larger philosophical level, as that against which all humans struggle. Aristophanes describes such men as Laius, who marry women by force of custom only, in Plato's *Symposium*.

Jean-Pierre Vernant, responding to Levi-Strauss's structuralist interpretation of the Oedipus story, produces a slightly different reconstruction, emphasizing Laius's "homosexuality" and the genealogical predisposition to "deviance" as his inheritance from his father Labdacus:

> Labdacus, the lame one, dies when his son is still a baby, only one year old. The legitimate lineage is broken as the normal link between father and son is cut. The throne is occupied by a stranger, Lucus. Young Laius is not only pushed aside from the throne but is sent away, expelled from Thebes. He takes refuge with Pelops.
>
> When Laius, the left-hander, grows up, he proves to be unbalanced and one-sided both in his sexual relations and in his relations with his host. His erotic behavior is rendered deviant by his excessive homosexuality and by the violence to which he subjects the young Chrysippus, Pelops's son, thereby breaking the rules of symmetry and reciprocity that should obtain between lovers and between guest and host. Chrysippus kills himself. Pelops announces a curse against Laius, condemning his race to infertility: The *genos* of the Labdacids is not to be perpetuated.
>
> Laius returns to Thebes, is reestablished on the throne and marries Iocasta (or Epicasta). Then he receives a warning from an oracle. He must not have a child. His lineage is condemned to sterility and his race bound to disappear. If he disobeys and engenders a son, this "legitimate" son, instead of resembling his father and carrying on the direct line, will destroy it and sleep with his mother. The *gnesios*, the well-born son, will turn out to be worse than a *nothos*, beyond even bastardy: He will be a monster.
>
> Laius's sexual relations with his wife are deviant, in the homosexual manner, to avoid producing children. But on one evening of drunkenness, he forgets to take care: He plants a child in the furrow of his wife. This son, at once legitimate yet cursed, is expelled at birth from Thebes.[46]

Keeping in mind that his characterizations of deviance accord with Greek views, Vernant, who does not cite any sources for his version of the Laius myth (though his discussion of Oedipus does cite specific sources and passages), asserts several interesting ideas. Laius is sent away from his own birthplace at the age of one and is raised by Pelops, the father of his future beloved and victim. The rape takes place prior to Laius's marriage. Laius receives the injunction regarding procreation after he is married and attempts to comply with it by putting his wife in the position of being a homosexual partner, namely, by employing anal intercourse as a means of avoiding pregnancy. But through his own weakness, he succeeds at what he has been avoiding and impregnates his wife.

Vernant's interpolation that Laius was buggering his wife is also interesting. Does he imply, as does Licht, that the punishment for raping Chrysippus was to have boys also put off-limits to him? Is his supposed buggery of his wife evidence of his "excessive homosexuality"? Vernant does not supply any motive for why Laius, who legally could have sex however he wanted to with both male and female slaves, prostitutes and concubines, would resort to buggering his citizen wife for sexual release, especially with the stakes so high. Finally, it is important to note that Vernant refers to attestations that put the curse in the mouth of Pelops, the outraged father.

Bernard Sergent provides yet another construction from the ancient sources. If we accept, from Licht and Sergent, that Laius became enamored of Chrysippus while he was at the court of Pelops, this implies that the rape took place prior to Laius's marriage to Jocasta after returning to Thebes. Sergent traces the oracle to a broader tradition within the military life of Greek men:

> The taboo on reproduction was thus common to the Aegidae of Sparta and Thera, yet it never prevented them from producing offspring. What we see here is a kind of ritual, in which each male member of the Aegidae clan was for a time forbidden to engage in sexual relations with women. Subsequently, these same males participated in some sort of cult act associated with the sanctuary of the Furies of Laius and Oedipus. Then and only then were they allowed to procreate. The founding myth of

> this taboo can be traced back beyond Oedipus to Laius: Aeschylus and later Euripides showed how all the misfortunes of the royal family of Thebes can be traced to Laius's failure to obey the order given him by Apollo (or by Hera, goddess of marriage!) not to have a child. So it was that Laius and Oedipus both committed, against the advice of the oracle, the egregious sin of having normal sexual relations with their legitimate wives: Laius because his son would eventually kill him, as a result of which Thebes suffered incalculable ills, and Oedipus because his legitimate wife happened to be his mother.
>
> But what was the reason for Laius's initial sin? In what respect was it a crime to have sexual relations with his wife? The taboo originally related to procreation. It was institutionalized among the Aegidae, descended from the Thebans of heroic times, and it involved a ritual. We know that homosexual relations were commended by the Greeks as a means to avoid producing children. And we also know that Laius's sin was linked (as early as the fifth century, hence from its inception) to his behavior with Chrysippus. It follows that Laius's real original sin — a sin that, being sexual in nature and producing no children, was transformed into a prohibition of sexual relations, and hence reproduction, between the hero and his wife — was homosexuality, of which Laius was the paradigmatic founder. In truth the notion of "sin" is surely secondary: Pederasty was sufficiently official in Thebes that the relationship between Laius and Chrysippus would not have been considered monstrous. Furthermore, Aeschylus and his successors do not say that the oracle forbidding Laius to have children was a punishment. The advice is given for no apparent reason, largely as prior justification for the dramas that will follow.[47]

Sergent, I find, is a bit disingenuous here with respect to the reason for the curse. Mythically, several possible reasons are alleged on the parts of both Pelops and Hera. And both have the weight of probability, namely, that actions like Laius's would very likely upset the father and the wife involved.

Conclusions

The view of Oedipus's father as held by the Greeks puts a very significant Freudian tenet to the test. Despite Freud's attempt, in abandoning the "seduction" theory, to protect the fathers and exculpate them from sexual wrongdoing, in the context of the Oedipus myth, he fails to do so. In his attempt to find a story that could make his difficult idea persuasive, Freud ironically happens upon a story that is all about how a father's sexual crimes with a child condemn his son and his wife to further crimes of their own. Like Oedipus, however, Freud writes confidently about what he has "discovered," never knowing, or at least never acknowledging, that the curse and Oedipus's suffering are first activated by the *father's* sexual and violent misdeeds.

Freud's accounts of Oedipus, which were created for publication, suffer from what I would call a certain classical and literary amateurism. That is to say, he makes several errors of interpretation and fact. He reads a single text of a single author as the timeless and uniform telling of a story known in many versions and in more completeness to its original audiences. Thus, he substitutes the particular *parole* or discourse of stage drama for the *langue* or story of myth, attributing timeless authority to words composed for a specific historical audience and for a specific dramatic purpose. In narratological terms, he conflates story and discourse.[48] He then attempts to argue as a major premise from "timeless" myth what is in fact an artifact of Sophoclean stagecraft. Even Jocasta's remarks about dreams, which Freud seized upon, can be taken as a false comfort to her husband and a dramatic irony, since the audience knows, as perhaps she knows as well, that Oedipus is *living* what others may only dream.

Second, Freud is unaware, according to his publications, that plays lost to him were well established in the consciousness of the Greek audience. Like a hasty archaeologist who reconstructs the entire history of humankind from a single bone found at a single site, Freud fails to ask himself what he does not know about the story. He does not attempt to verify his version, asking if there could be any other explanations, any other sources that might need to be checked. He writes to Fliess that he must read up on the Oedipus legend (March 15, 1898; *Letters,* 304), but it seems he never does.

That he forms no hypotheses about the provenance of the story that becomes so crucial to him seems odd, coming out of a culture almost obsessed with classical philology and textual redaction. It was known that Sophocles had written 125 plays, of which only 7 had survived, Aeschylus 90, with 7 surviving, and Euripides 92, with 18 surviving to the present day.[49] The scholarship on Oedipus was pretty well established even by the late 1880s. At Maresfield Garden, Freud's library contained an 1886 full-length work on the Oedipus legend by the Frenchman Leopold Constans (*Letters,* 304). Constans does indeed treat the matter of Laius and his crimes. The few pages containing Freud's notations, however, begin only after the pages containing the material on Laius.[50] I have tried to show the leaps and false connections in Freud's analysis of the Oedipus he knows. The fuller sources of his linchpin story, however, break down completely his argument about the motivations of Oedipus.

The absence of discussion about the root of the curse in Sophocles' *Oedipus Rex* serves as what I will call a "poetic enthymeme," a suppressed dramatic premise upon which the remainder of the play hinges nevertheless. The Greek, or the informed, audience participates in the pathos of the play because it is able to supply this unstated premise, and to understand the deepest irony of all: that even at the moment of his blinding, and the moment when he believes himself to have been fully enlightened about the source of his sad fate, Oedipus is still ignorant of his father's role in condemning his life to ruin. The audience may feel pity for Oedipus, both because he did not know what he was doing, and because he did not know why he was doing it. They may have condemned Laius, with the play serving as a kind of fearful warning for what happens to men who neglect their wives for their boy lovers. Especially offered as it was in a tetralogy by Aeschylus, including a *Laius* and an *Oedipus,* it seems both reasonable and logical to assume audiences connected the deeds of the father and son. Sophocles, in choosing not to emphasize Laius's deeds, may have done so as a dramatic challenge, or to give a fresh approach to material quite familiar in both dramatic and mythic form to his audience. Or, perhaps, as a confirmed lover of boys, he wished to separate fully Laius's crimes from Oedipus's punishments.[51] What might have been created as an ideological defense of pederasty in his own day becomes the distorted basis for victim- and child-blaming in our own.

Thus, while Freud never writes about the father of Oedipus in specific terms, Laius was well known and well understood by the Greeks to have abducted a beautiful young boy Chrysippus from his father Pelops's house, without having obtained Pelops's permission. Enamored, and unwilling to control himself as men (but not gods) in his condition were expected to do, he kidnaps Chrysippus rather than fulfilling his ritual obligations as a pederastic lover. This exposes the boy to numerous dangers, including the implication of rape, and, in the end, subjects the house of Laius to numerous punishments.

The mythic versions and glosses I explored do not discuss whether Laius sexually uses the boy in ways that would have been proscribed by Greek law. The social shame, however, of being kidnapped — overpowered — by a man stems in part from the assumption that abductions always imply rape.[52] One's choice has been removed, and therefore one can never, as Helen cannot, regain one's lost honor. If the boy *wanted* to go with Laius, that would be considered a form of weakness on Chrysippus's part, since boys were supposed to chastely resist their male suitors. Giving in so easily, without getting the requisite permission from the father, would be tantamount to saying that the boy wanted to be mounted by the man. Such feelings, if carried out, would result in the boy losing his citizenship, for no citizen male was ever to be sexually penetrated by any other citizen male. If, by contrast, Chrysippus did not want to go, there would be the shame of being overpowered — not being strong or wily enough to escape the man, his father's protection too weak to ensure his safety and protect his wishes. There is also the breaking of the very strong Greek injunction against abusing a host's hospitality. As a guest of Pelops, Laius clearly does this when he abducts his son. These are extreme cultural violations.

And then there would be the personal feelings of the abducted boy. In Euripides' lost tragedy of this story, Chrysippus kills himself. In some versions, Pelops puts the curse on Laius and then throws himself off a cliff in protest against Laius's crimes. In this way Laius earns both infamy and the reputation for being a man not in control of himself, a supreme fault for a Greek man. He acts prematurely; he acts based on his desire alone, not taking into account the feelings or welfare of others nor his obligations to them. If Chrysippus had not killed himself, Laius might merely have been a pervert: not for having sex with a boy, which the Greeks permitted, but for having it in the wrong way. The pervert takes care of his own feelings and utterly disregards the feelings of the other person. For restraint comes, after all, from consideration for others, as well as from the fear of being punished. In this case, Laius shows disregard for both sources of self-management. Instead, he is a pervert who pursues his own pleasure principle above all else and thus becomes a sociopath. In modern terms, the whole family, from Laius to Oedipus to Antigone, Eteocles and Polyneices, suffers from poor impulse control. And they suffer ill ends as a result.

Like Oedipus, Freud at first is content to have solved the riddle of the Sphinx and become a hero. The dream book, after all, with its code-breaking appeal, is something like the riddle-solving of Oedipus at the gates of Thebes. Freudians mostly have been not sufficiently curious, as Odysseus surely would have been, to ask why the Sphinx is there in the first place. Constans, whose *La Légende d'Œdipe* Freud had in his last library at Maresfield Garden, makes it clear that the ancients saw the Sphinx as the plague sent by Hera to punish Laius for Chrysippus's death.[53] The plague, in short, the *symptoms,* are there because of the father's sexual misconduct with a child. But rather than hold onto the why of the Sphinx's presence, which he had done in the early and mid-1890s, Freud shifts his ground. *The Interpretation of Dreams,* which contains the first offerings of the Oedipus complex, is about breaking a code — solving a riddle, as Oedipus is at first content with solving the Sphinx's irrelevant riddle. She dies, but the plague comes back. Freud, like Oedipus, fails to see that the Sphinx is the trap. She is sent by Hera, and tailor-made to catch a clever fellow who seeks most of all to triumph over a woman. In abandoning his early techniques without attempting to improve or refine them, Freud condemns himself and psychoanalysis to an ever-returning plague of psychological pain and ineffective therapeutic nostrums. The wounded healer proves unable to heal himself. Thus he loses his ability to heal others.

Seven

Seducing the Scapegoat

Greek Mythology and Father-Daughter Incest

The world of drama is sometimes like the world of journalism. The story that gets dramatized is the man-bites-dog story. We are struck by people doing things we do not expect them to: Willy Loman the optimistic salesman killing himself; Hamlet mourning his father too long; Antigone defying her uncle Creon; Clytemnestra killing her husband Agamemnon at the moment of his triumphant return from the Trojan War.

What dramatists choose to dramatize also reveals a great deal about the mores of the society they live in, and perhaps something about themselves. If tragedy is defined by Aristotle as entailing both pity and fear, we must be prepared to feel pity for the hero, fear for ourselves were we in the same situation, and cathartic relief that it was indeed not we who suffered the ultimate fate of the play's hero or heroine. Euripides wrote a tragedy called *Chrysippus*, about the boy that Laius abducted and probably raped, who may have committed suicide as a result. The play does not survive to us, perhaps a casualty of cultures subsequent to Athens, whose homophobia and antipathy for pederasty became increasingly pronounced.[1] But what we know of this play in fragments and references by other writers suggests that, for the Greeks, to be a young boy abducted by an enamored adult man is a fate capable of engendering fear and pity. Plutarch, observing pederasty when it had become a well-established practice, writes:

> There is no class of men for whom they [youths] have more persistent suspicion and hatred than their pederasts and when the opportunity offers they exact terrible vengeance. Archelaus was killed by Crateas who had been made a minion and Alexander of Pherae by Pytholaus. Periander, the tyrant of Ambracia, asked his minion whether or not he was with child and the lad was so infuriated that he killed him.[2]

The passage, parenthetically, casts a shadow over Dover's suggestion that all pederastic sex was intercrural.

Oedipus is surely a man-bites-dog story from the beginning. Zeus rapes a lot of women, but those are stories told, not played. It's Zeus's nature. He is not expected to behave otherwise, though occasionally Hera gets fed up enough to do something in retaliation, usually to the woman he has taken up with. But when Laius rapes a boy, that is news. A strict code of conduct surrounds man-boy pedophilia in ancient Greek cultures, as Cohen, Sergent, Dover and others have discussed. Such a breach as Laius makes cannot go unpunished. So he is told not to have children, even though he is a married man. Strange enough. And, when his day comes and he is slain by his son on the road, the resulting smash-up is that the mother ends up married to her son. Now that's pretty unique. Not Electra, not Orestes, not even Hamlet comes close to that much actually incestuous mess. It might also account for why it made such an impression on Freud when he saw a production of *Oedipus Rex* in Paris in the 1880s. How very unlike every other story is that of Oedipus.

On the other hand, how very common, how everyday and even usual is the rape of a woman or of a girl in the world of the Greeks.[3] With Zeus as the great role model, few maidens or nubile women could be considered safe wandering freely about or even sequestered. There is something alluring, at least to the male involved, to these tales of what sometimes is characterized as consensual if adulterous sex. It affirms the man's virility, attractiveness and power, especially if the woman is nubile, beautiful, young, noble or divine. And if the sex is not consensual, how much more is the man's power confirmed. Cohen discusses the need among Greek men for opportunities for gaining fame through courtship. Certainly myth describes scores of contests for the maiden's hand, winning eternal glory for the man who outwits his father-in-law or gets past some other obstacle to king-making matrimony.

How much less edifying, then, to dramatize the stories of fathers who have sex with their daughters or, even worse, of daughters who instigate sex with their fathers, in defiance of their prescribed social and sexual passivity. Freud chose Oedipus specifically because his story is about incest. Freud's language reads oddly to us now, however, as he urges out of whole cloth the universality of the Oedipus triangle:

> His [Oedipus's] fate moves us only because it might have been our own, because the oracle laid upon us before our birth the very curse which rested upon him. It might be said that we [*sic*] were all destined to direct our first sexual impulses toward our mothers, and our first impulses of hatred and violence toward our fathers; our dreams convince us that we were. King Oedipus, who slew his father Laius and wedded his mother Jocasta, is nothing more or less than a wish-fulfillment — the fulfillment of the wish of our childhood.[4]

It is odd now, as a woman, to read this passage, where the implied reader is clearly and strictly male. Unless Freud is implying here that *all* children have sexual desires for their mothers and hate their fathers, his universalizing must be questioned on its face — unless he means to say that all girls start their lives as lesbians. But his use of "our" might more accurately be read as "my." For certainly the Greeks did not understand Oedipus as acting to fulfill an erotic wish. The rehabilitation of Oedipus depends, in fact, upon his innocence — not his seduction of a woman known to be his mother.

Feminist scholars have long been troubled by Freud's cavalier extrapolation of the Oedipus story to suit both mother-son incest, relatively rare, and father-daughter incest, overwhelmingly more common.[5] Little consideration by mainstream theorists has been given until recently to man-boy and woman-girl incest or molestation, which we discover to be clinically represented as well.[6] Judith Herman and Linda Hirschman suggest that father-daughter incest gets relatively little interest because "there is no avenging father" to punish the perpetrator.[7] As the initial reception of Freud's lecture on the sexual the etiology of hysteria and his own later writing suggest, men are loathe to prosecute one of their own powerful number for such crimes. But an interloping son, or an errant wife, will always and surely be punished.

This is the economy of psychoanalysis which is most roundly criticized: the punishment of mother-son relations, and the wink at father-daughter incest. But Freud does change Oedipus in this respect. Freud accomplishes his primary theoretical move by shifting sexual agency from adulthood to childhood. Oedipus and his mother are both adults, after all, although their fate remains tragic for that fact. But children for Freud are the repository of the motive desire for incest. It is their wish, and not the desire of the parent or adult, which brings about the terrible crime. The son, in Freud's version, triumphantly takes his mother in marriage. All is well, in his view, with this picture of "wish-fulfillment," until the sin is discovered: "Like Oedipus, we live in ignorance of the desires that offend morality, the desires that nature has forced upon us and after their unveiling we may well prefer to avert our gaze from the scenes of our childhood."[8] Boys, at least, are trapped by "nature" into having these offensive desires, though Oedipus presumably ennobles them through his suffering.

It is striking to consider that Freud never discusses Phaedra, who falls in love with her stepson Hippolytus and manipulates his innocence into damnation when he rejects her. The index to the *Standard Edition* references neither name in the entire 23-volume work. Of course, Phaedra runs counter in every way to the economy of agency and desire that Freud attempts to write. She, the mother figure, falls in love with her stepson and declares her love to him. When he rejects her, she cries rape and hangs herself. It is clearly her desire as the female parent that instigates the trouble. So she is neither sexually passive nor the "victim" of the overtures of her male child. She is a powerful woman with a powerful sex drive, and she is a parent willing to cross the lines of conventionally understood incest. For reasons to which I have already referred, this is precisely the kind of woman Freud had to theoretically hide and make over into the sexually passive and masochistic female type he characterizes as universal.

We should mark it significant, too, that despite the many *female* patients abused by men whom he has treated by the time he writes *The Interpretation of Dreams*, when it comes to clinching his theory of infantile psychology and sexuality, he turns to a story that depicts incest between a grown *son* and his mother. Clearly Sophocles' *Oedipus Rex* gave Freud a crucial opening for attempting to graft his theories of repression onto some larger kind of cultural construct that would be recognized and accepted by his audience. And in a sense, for all his errors, I believe we should be thankful that he succeeded in making persuasive his arguments about the function of repression in psychic life.

My investigation remains, however, concerned with what exactly Freud says we are to have repressed. For there is clearly a shift in his work from the early 1890s until the dream book, which moves from arguments about real molestation, howsoever imprecisely and indirectly it may be recalled, and supposed childhood sexual fantasies not preconditioned by abuse. What he leaves behind constitutes one of the persistent sources of criticism for Freud, especially by those who believe he had documented real cases of abuse, and backed away from supporting them publicly for a variety of reasons, ranging from the scientific to the opportunistic.

If, however, Freud had applied same yardstick of credibility to the rest of Greek myth that he applied to Oedipus, his early position supporting the reality of his patients' testimony might have been bolstered. For apart from the dozens of cases of outright rape of girls by gods and strangers in Greek myth, there are also stories of young women who, like Oedipus, had sexual contact with their opposite-sex parent. Like Freud's early patients, whose suffering was palpable, one sees evidence of great torment and great suffering among these mythic figures as well. Some of these women become pregnant by their fathers. The choices they make about the fate of those children are the unfolding of psychological disasters for each one.

It is possible that their stories were dramatized and the plays lost. In the male-dominant and frequently misogynistic world of later Greece, their stories perhaps did not entail what was considered heroic (which might be the same as saying male) suffering. To observe fathers with great power in a society as they debase their daughters who have little power seems debasing to everyone, including the observers. Such actions may not even have seemed excessive in a society of men obsessed with the phallus and untrammeled in their legal ability to have sex with their wives, prostitutes, slaves, concubines, boys and prisoners of war.[9] But unlike Freud's case studies, which characterize his patients' stories of unwanted sexual contact with adult men and male relatives as fantasies, or something they wanted, the Greeks record perpetrators' actions and the attendant suffering with a much less averted gaze. Because there is no countervailing force to censure them, like white lynch mobs in the post-Civil War South, they feel free to publish their accounts in detail. There is no need to cover anything up, for they are sure that everyone agrees with their morals.[10]

The Greeks, too, are much less prudish about women's sexual agency, desire and frustration. They easily imagine Phaedra's passion for her stepson, for example, while Freud cannot bring himself to consider it. But Freud opens himself to other sexual non sequiturs. If toddler boys without active hormonal equipment fantasize about sex with their mothers, how much more likely is it that adult men fantasize about sex with their daughters? The difference is that adult men, according to Freud, usually threaten their sons into not acting on their unrealizable impulses (Freud overlooks the fact that prepubescent boys do not ejaculate). If the father is the lawgiver, however, there is no one else to keep the selfsame father from acting on his fully hormone-powered and developmentally realizable desires.[11] Here we should understand the father in both his individual and larger socio-legal mantle.

Three Greek stories of father-daughter incest survive. The women figures involved, though filtered by male authors recording their stories, do not have anyone on the scene telling them how to feel about what has happened, in contrast to a case study written by the psychoanalyst. We do not know for certain what from among this material was ever turned into a play by a Greek dramatist. Thyestes' story is treated dramatically in extant works, but in those works his daughter Pelopia's portion of the story is absent. However, Sophocles is believed to have written a *Thyestes* that covers the story at least as far as the rape of the daughter.[12]

But the myths themselves tell us a great deal. They possess a power that René Girard would ascribe to the earlier versions of sacrificial rituals, in which the participants do not understand that what they are doing may be seen by others as shameful.[13] They are not self-aware, in the sense that Freud believes Oedipus becomes self-aware; they are not self-conscious. But in another sense they are more aware: they are aware that they are at the scene of the crime.

Oedipus never figured out that his father had committed an offense that he would have to pay for. That may be why Derrida believes at the source that there is simply another supplement. No one can "get to the bottom" of anything, because in truth Oedipus never understands that his fate comes from his father's sins. For Freudians, Derrida's reading is true. It is as if Freud and Oedipus simply cannot believe that such a bad thing has happened to them. They are, after all, men! Oedipus, after whom Freud models himself, does not see himself as belonging to a scapegoatable class. When bad fate comes, it is a shock. The irony never captured by either Freud or Derrida is that the Greek audience always knew better. Oedipus was such a sad case, not because he knew everything, but because he was foolish enough to think he did.

For women in incest situations, the message was more clear. Father-daughter incest in Greek myth was expectable, not punished, because the law and the perpetrator were one in the same, and therefore the offense was not even noteworthy. It was not serious or *unusual* enough for them to become heroines in a play. For unmarried girls, sexual attack by their fathers did not constitute a sacrificial crisis. It did not upset the order of things. As we shall see, it *was* the order of things. Thus, their suffering was not considered tragic by the men who raped them because it was simply the death rattle of the expended sacrificial victim. Still, Greek myth records their plights, and Greeks heard at least some of their stories told. If Oedipus has "universal" validity according to Freud, because of the myth's antiquity, then surely these stories must also.

Father-Daughter Incest in Greek Myth

The versions of the three myths I will examine concerning father-daughter incest come from Robert Graves's 1955 collection. Rank's chapter on the father-daughter relationship in *The Incest Theme* is commendable for the range and variety of "Myths, Legends, Literature, Life and Neurosis" that he discusses. He includes Norse, Cypriot, biblical, Indic, Italian, Shakespearean, Persian, German, Norman, Babylonian, Scottish, Armenian, Russian, French, Dutch, Danish, Swedish, Icelandic, English, Lithuanian, Gaelic and Norwegian examples, as well as classical Greek. He also mentions examples from newspapers of court cases involving fathers and their incestuous relationships with (older) daughters. Rank in general concludes that the motivating agency for sexual contact in these relationships is invariably the father — contra Freud, it would seem. However, all the cases he cites involve teenaged girls or young women, not the very young girls of the "Oedipal" age phase. Rank emphasizes stories of mistaken identity as covers for paternal desire, also paralleling the mistaken identity problem in Oedipus. It is worthwhile reading, but driven with a preordained conclusion in mind. Rank also makes some factual errors, such as asserting that the rape of Pelopia was a case of mistaken identity.[14]

I consider here only Greek myths, since it is reasonable to assume that the parade of nationalities Rank assembles would not have served so nearly nor so completely Freud's wish to identify a myth of high prestige (in the eyes of his audience) that encapsulated a device representing repression. However, as Freud did aver that Oedipus was the incest case nonpareil in Greek literature, and therefore the base from which "variations" such as the daughter's experience or the gay son's experience would have to be extrapolated, it seems fair to examine the basis for his claims.

I have also tried to avoid Freud's mistaken confusion of *langue* and *parole* by looking at the myths as primary sources, rather than the plays. Graves drew on Apollodorus (*Epitome*), Hyginus (*Fabulae*), Servius, Athenaeus, Sophocles (*Thyestes*), Aeschylus, Eustathius, Pausanias and Parthenius as his sources, and offers a far more comprehensive compilation of sources than Freud's reliance on Sophocles.

The three cases I consider here show the limitations of Freud's views of incest. They also ask us to consider Freud's views on the direction of incestuous desire. Freud's Oedipal theories rest on the notion that the child (or initially at least, only the son) is the source of incestuous desire, and that adults play only the part of preventing the fulfillment of the child's wishes. If we accept, as Freud asks, the "immemorial antiquity" and truth of Greek myth, the following cases offer several elements that bear reconsideration of that formulation.

Pelopia and Thyestes

Atreus and Thyestes, sons of Pelops, were set against each other as rivals for the same throne in Mycenae. Having quarreled over the golden fleece, the signifier of who would rule, Atreus wins with the help of Zeus. Thyestes had committed adultery with Atreus's wife Aerope in order to get the fleece. When Atreus finds out, subsequent to his ascension to the throne, he vows revenge on his brother, who has been banished. Atreus's children with Aerope include Agamemnon, Menelaus and Anaxibia, the first two of whom are the chief Argive prosecutors of the Trojan War. Menelaus is the husband of Helen.

The text from Graves is included from here in full, as I must assume that readers are less familiar with this story than with the myth of Oedipus.

> [g] Atreus now sent a herald to lure Thyestes back to Mycenae, with the offer of an amnesty and a half-share in the kingdom; but, as soon as Thyestes accepted this, slaughtered Aglaus, Orchomenus, and Callileon, Thyestes' three sons by one of the Naiads, on the very altar of Zeus where they had taken refuge; and then sought out and killed the infant Pleisthenes the Second, and Tantalus the Second, his twin. He hacked them all limb from limb, and set chosen morsels of their flesh, boiled in a cauldron, before Thyestes, to welcome him on his return. When Thyestes had eaten heartily, Atreus sent in their bloody heads and feet and hands, laid out on another dish, to show him what was now inside his belly. Thyestes fell back, vomiting, and laid an ineluctable curse on the seed of Atreus.
>
> [h] Exiled once more, Thyestes fled first to King Thesprotus at Sicyon, where his own daughter Pelopia, or Pelopeia ["muddy face"], was a priestess. For, desiring revenge at whatever cost, *he had consulted the Delphic Oracle and had been advised to beget a son on his own daughter.* Thyestes found Pelopia sacrificing by night to Athene Colocasia and, being loth [*sic*] to profane the rites, concealed himself in a nearby grove.

Presently Pelopia, who was leading the solemn dance, slipped in a pool of blood that had flowed from the throat of a black ewe, the victim, and stained her tunic. She ran at once to the temple fish-pond, removed her tunic, and was washing out the stain, when Thyestes sprang from the grove and ravished her. Pelopia did not recognize him, because he was wearing a mask, but contrived to steal his sword and carry it back to the temple, where she hid it under the pedestal of Athene's image; and Thyestes, finding the scabbard empty and fearing detection, escaped to Lydia, the land of his fathers.

[i] Meanwhile, fearing the consequences of his crime, Atreus consulted the Delphic Oracle, and was told: "Recall Thyestes from Sicyon!" He reached Sicyon too late to meet Thyestes and, falling in love with Pelopia, whom he assumed to be King Thesprotus's daughter, asked leave to make her his third wife; having by this time executed Aerope. Eager for an alliance with so powerful a king, and wishing at the same time to do Pelopia a service, Thesprotus did not undeceive Atreus, and the wedding took place at once. In due course she bore him a son begotten on her by Thyestes, whom she exposed on a mountain; but goatherds rescued him and gave him to a she-goat for suckling — hence his name, Aegisthus, or "goat-strength." Atreus believed that Thyestes had fled from Sicyon at news of his approach; that the child was his own; and that Pelopia had been affected by the temporary madness which sometimes overtakes women after childbirth. He therefore recovered Aegisthus from the goatherds and reared him as his heir.

[j] A succession of bad harvests then plagued Mycenae, and Atreus sent Agamemnon and Menelaus to Delphi for news of Thyestes, whom they met by chance on his return from a further visit to the Oracle. They haled him back to Mycenae, where Atreus, having thrown him into prison, ordered Aegisthus, then seven years of age, to kill him as he slept.

[k] Thyestes awoke suddenly to find Aegisthus standing over him, sword in hand; he quickly rolled sideways and escaped death. Then he rose, disarmed the boy with a shrewd kick at his wrist, and sprang to recover the sword. But it was his own, lost years before in Sicyon! He seized Aegisthus by the shoulder and cried: "Tell me instantly how this came into your possession?" Aegisthus stammered: "Alas, my mother Pelopia gave it me." "I will spare your life, boy," said Thyestes, "if you carry out the three orders I now give you." "I am your servant in all things," wept Aegisthus, who had expected no mercy. "My first order is to bring your mother here," Thyestes told him.

> [l] Aegisthus thereupon brought Pelopia to the dungeon and, recognizing Thyestes, she wept on his neck, called him her dearest father, and commiserated with his sufferings. "'How did you come by this sword, daughter?" Thyestes asked. "I took it from the scabbard of an unknown stranger who ravished me one night at Sicyon," she replied. "It is mine," said Thyestes. *Pelopia, stricken with horror, seized the sword, and plunged it into her breast. Aegisthus stood aghast, not understanding what had been said.* "Now take this sword to Atreus," was Thyestes' second order, "and tell him that you have carried out your commission. Then return!" Dumbly Aegisthus took the bloody thing to Atreus, who went joyfully down to the seashore, where he offered a sacrifice of thanksgiving to Zeus, convinced he was rid of Thyestes at last.
>
> [m] When Aegisthus returned to the dungeon, Thyestes revealed himself as his father, and issued his third order: "Kill Atreus, my son Aegisthus, and this time do not falter!" Aegisthus did as he was told, and Thyestes reigned once more in Mycenae.
>
> [n] . . . others [say], that it cannot have been Aegisthus who killed Atreus, because he was only an infant in swaddling clothes when Agamemnon drove his father Thyestes from Mycenae, wresting the sceptre from him.[15]

On its face, this story is both horrifying and extraordinary, in the level of cruelty shown by Thyestes to everyone: his brother, his daughter and to his son by her. Atreus, who is slain in the end by Aegisthus and does indeed become the means by which his brother ascends the throne, is no less cruel in his instrumentality of the nephews he kills and feeds to his brother, and the son he commands to commit murder. But this story is no less Greek than Oedipus. The wiliness and self-serving cleverness of the brothers are no less culturally applauded than Pelops's, who with his lover Poseidon's help replaced the king's axle pin with a bolt of wax, sending his future father-in-law to his death in a chariot race. Lest we recoil from Thyestes, remember that these are the same Greeks as Freud's Greeks.

What of the daughter of the piece, Pelopia? Her father rapes and impregnates her and then flees. She then suffers incest by her uncle, via the agent of the knowing king, Thesprotus, whose personal mores are seemingly not compromised by giving to a friend in marriage and certain intercourse a woman whom he knows to be the man's niece.

So there is a double incest. The father's is commanded by the oracle in order to extract revenge and regain political power. The uncle's is simply engineered for personal gain by a calculating third party, undeterred by the knowledge of what he is doing.

Pelopia's suffering is shown to us by her actions. She chooses to subject her son to exposure rather than raise him. She has apparently told no one about the rape, since Atreus assumes the baby is his. How devastating, to have been raped by a seeming stranger, within the temple precincts. With perhaps days to recover in secret, she is wed without her consent or dissent, her husband exercising his right to have sex with her almost immediately. We would expect any woman in modern Western cultures subjected to such violence and forced marriage to be outraged, and thousands of lawyers and district attorneys would spring to the task of prosecuting her case. What authority would be defensible, were it to call for a man to have a child by his own daughter, simply to avenge himself on his brother? In the contemporary world, such an action would be considered a violation of the woman's human rights as well as a felony by the father. Mark the distinction, though, for Freud and for the Greeks. Mother-son incest is a curse and ends the power of the man involved in it. Father-daughter incest is a means to an end, and enhances the power of the man involved in it. The same oracle prescribes both courses of action.

Freud would be shocked at the idea that Jocasta, for example, knowingly seduced her husband, and then contrived to save the resulting child so as to activate a curse that would eliminate her neglectful and unfaithful husband from her life. But no one, including the Greeks, seems especially shocked at the notion that this young woman's father would rape and brutalize her for the sole purpose of creating an avenging son to kill his brother and gain him the throne. No one, that is, except Pelopia herself: her response to her father's revelation of his identity is a far cry from the triumphant scenes of unmasking in *The Libation Bearers* or *Electra*. Pelopia's response to her father's revelation that he raped her is to immediately kill herself. Rank tries to minimize the effects of Thyestes' rape by calling it a case of mistaken identity, making a parallel to Jocasta and Oedipus.[16] Thyestes, however, is entirely clear about his prey. And their encounter is not a triumphant wedding but a rape premeditated by the father, who flees as soon as his crime is completed. The criminal's identity is hidden, not mistaken.

In her death, Pelopia unwittingly provides her evil father the necessary tool to carry out the next step of his ruse: a freshly bloodied sword. He puts it to use posthaste. He has no tears for his daughter. Indeed, we must wonder whether in fact he calculated the effect of his revelation on her, knowing what a terrible and unrecoverable disgrace he had inflicted. Pelopia was so distraught by the rape that she had tried to kill the baby that it produced. She had experienced the intense violation and devastating aftermath of the rape itself. She had been forced to accept a hasty marriage to a man she may or may not have known was her uncle. She had borne a child conceived by rape. But when she tries to rid herself of the baby — surely a sign of her grave discomposure — he is rescued, and she is forced despite her intentions to raise him. The rescue of the child sets the stage for the mother's complete emotional demise.

Oedipus gets an entire play devoted wholly to his survival after the revelation that he had been married to his mother. He, in short, survives the crash. Pelopia, the female victim of paternal incest, does not survive. But her father-perpetrator does. His act of rape is rewarded by a son, whom he coerces into killing his rival. The son of incestuous rape enables the perpetrator Thyestes to triumphantly ascend the throne. The life of Pelopia — and her shock, her suffering, her torment, her words, her thoughts, her tears — simply vanish.

Murder and incest resulted in Oedipus's removal from the throne. They are the selfsame and durable means by which Thyestes ascends to it. His daughter is his baby machine and his son by incestuous rape is his killing machine. And once they have done his will, he is rewarded by being made king.

Harpalyce and Clymenus

> Thyestes was not the last hero to find his own child served up to him on a dish. This happened some years later to Clymenus, the Arcadian son of Schoenus, who conceived an incestuous passion for Harpalyce, his

> daughter by Epicaste. Having debauched Harpalyce, he married her to Alastor, but afterwards took her away again. Harpalyce, to revenge herself, murdered the son she bore him — who was also her brother — cooked the corpse, and laid it before Clymenus. She was transformed into a bird of prey, and Clymenus hanged himself.[17]

Graves bases his account on Parthenius, *Erotica* and Hyginus' *Fabulae*. While Thyestes and the saga of the throne of Mycenae have been treated by both Greek and Latin dramatists, we have no record that the story of Clymenus and Harpalyce was.

Here, the sources make even more clear that the wellspring of the "incestuous passion" is the father and not the daughter. Clymenus develops a passion for his daughter Harpalyce and "debauches her," by which Graves seems to mean that he repeatedly rapes her. He marries her to another man, but then takes her back again. This suggests that he reached a point where he allowed his incestuous desire for his daughter to completely overtake him.

The story does not include a plague, which is elsewhere associated with offensive sex between adults and (their) children. But Harpalyce, like Pelopia, does not want the child who is created from the incest. She does succeed in killing him. Unlike Pelopia, who did not know her rapist until well after the birth of the child, Harpalyce is clear about her perpetrator, so revenge seems viable. Strikingly, while Harpalyce dies by being transformed into a bird of prey, her father hangs himself, much as Jocasta did. This is the single case I am aware of in Greek mythology where the male perpetrator of a sexual crime commits suicide. We must wonder, from the standpoint of Greek mores, why.

A few important questions stand out in this account. Where is Epicaste, Harpalyce's mother? Is she still alive, estranged from her husband, ill, deceased or away from the household? There is no recorded reaction from Epicaste. Did she object? Was she in the home while the incest was taking place? Had she died? She is not present to confront her husband, nor to comfort, castigate or attack her daughter, all maternal responses noted in modern father-daughter incest situations.[18] Epicaste is another version of the name Jocasta, but we presume that this is not Jocasta the mother of Oedipus.

Then there is the question of the public's reaction. Is it possible that no one would know that Clymenus had taken his daughter back from her husband? Or that no one would think it was strange? The lack of a plague, a publicly felt sign that something is amiss, suggests one of two things. Perhaps Clymenus had been able to keep his actions a secret, so his daughter would be unable to enlist the help of Alastor, her husband. Why, after all, would a husband not be outraged to have his bride taken back from him by her father? Or, it may suggest that culturally, father-daughter incest was only an outrage to the parties involved, if to anyone — not to the community as a whole. Mother-son incest, accidental or not, is a matter of public concern and consequence. But the sexual violation of the daughter by the father is treated here as a purely private affair with no public consequences or repercussions.

The following scenario might fill in some of the "missing" details that Greek audiences would be presumed to understand but a modern one would not. If Clymenus "debauches" Harpalyce prior to her marriage, he will have broken her hymen. On her wedding night she will not appear to be a virgin, because she will be unable to bleed from her broken hymen as she is expected to at the time of first intercourse with her spouse. When she is discovered, the husband would have the right to demand satisfaction from the father, who in this case is willing to supply it by dissolving the marriage and forcing his daughter to come home to him in disgrace. The father, however, need not acknowledge that he is the man who took his daughter's virginity. He is free to cast aspersions on his daughter's sexual honor. This would compromise both her ability to gain public sympathy, and her ability to make allies, with her husband or anyone else in the community powerful enough to repudiate her father for his actions. Harpalyce has no way of securely proving her father's crime. So the father "ruins" his daughter. Then, because she is no longer a virgin and therefore not "fit" for a husband, he is able to reclaim her from her marriage and sexually use her for himself. He creates the bounds of her prison by socially damaging her, thereby foreclosing any public sympathy or attention to her case.

Harpalyce clearly believes she must take revenge into her own hands.

This suggests that she has no faith that anyone will come to her aid. According to Herman, there is no avenging father available, because the father is in fact the perpetrator. Nor does there seem to be an agentic mother. Indeed, Harpalyce seems unable to convince even her husband to help her. In the same way that Clytemnestra knows that no man will punish her husband for killing her daughter Iphigenia, Harpalyce becomes a self-appointed agent of justice because no other is forthcoming.

When justice is served *indirectly* in Greek myth, it is my observation that the agent of justice conceives of that single thing that will most arouse a response in the target, that she or he will take the desired action as a result. Thus Artemis, angry at Agamemnon for the impending war, requires him to publicly sacrifice his first-born daughter Iphigenia. He thinks little of this. But it infuriates his wife. So when he returns from the war, she deceives and kills him. Athena may have picked the winner of the war. But Artemis sees to it that his triumph has no glory.

Strikingly, Graves notes that Harpalyce kills her brother, that is, the son she bears by her father. Perhaps she realizes that this is the one thing she can do that will make her father despair enough to kill himself. He has no shame for raping her, for ruining her marriage, for impregnating her and forcing her to bear his child. Only when she kills the son of his incest does he react, in terms of having experienced an unrecoverable shame. Namely, he had a son whose life he could not defend. He had allowed a citizen son of his to be killed, and by a mere woman. Perhaps it is the social shaming of this act, finally, that proves sufficient cause for him to kill himself. We should notice here that he self-punishes. There is no legal system or even avenging neighbors to invoke punishment for his offenses.

The significance of this story is several-fold. First, there is no plague, no taboo, no announced curse or punishment for what Clymenus has done. Oedipus was cursed before he was even born. And yet Clymenus, were it not for Harpalyce's horrible revenge, sounds as if he would have lived to old age, and perhaps impregnated her again and again. We see that, while sexual relations between mothers and sons are highly sanctioned and heavily punished, sexual contact between fathers and daughters, where the father initiates it, are at best commanded by the gods, and at worst ignored by them. It is Harpalyce who is punished for her crime by being turned into a bird of prey.[19]

Clymenus kills himself. This is an unusual turn of events. Normally it is the female and/or the sexual victim who commits suicide. The questions concern why in his mind he would do so. Would his social position have been untenable after the incest was revealed? That was not the case for Thyestes, who, unlike Oedipus, ascended the throne *after* the incest. Father-daughter incest was rewarded with kingship for Thyestes, who ruled his kingdom after having committed incest with his daughter. Clymenus thus should not be considered, on the face of things, to have felt remorse for the incest, or to have expected social sanction. What may have been the deciding factor was that his *son* was killed. Graves writes that Harpalyce killed the son, cooked him, and laid the "corpse" before her father. Thyestes ate a stew that had been cooked from pieces of his children's flesh, and thus ate them unknowingly. Clymenus, however, seems to have been presented with a body he would recognize as his son's, prepared with the express intention of inflicting pain with this awareness. Harpalyce was not attempting to deceive her father, but deliberately to undeceive him: to make known to him in completely clear terms what she thought of him and what he had done to her. The dead child would also be found by others. His cooked body might be a sign to servants, to townspeople or anyone else of something terribly awry in this household.

Smyrna and Cinyras

Graves also records a case of a daughter deciding to have sex with and becoming impregnated by her father.

> One day, the wife of King Cinyras the Cyprian — but some call him King Phoenix of Byblus, and some King Theias the Assyrian — foolishly boasted that her daughter Smyrna was more beautiful even than Aphrodite. The goddess avenged this insult by making Smyrna fall in love with her father and climb into his bed one dark night, when her nurse had made him too drunk to realize what he was doing. Later,

> Cinyras discovered that he was both the father and the grandfather of Smyrna's unborn child and, wild with wrath, seized a sword and chased her from the palace. He overtook her on the brow of a hill, but Aphrodite hurriedly changed Smyrna into a myrrh-tree, which the descending sword split in halves. Out tumbled the infant Adonis. Aphrodite, already repenting of the mischief that she had made, concealed Adonis in a chest, which she entrusted to Persephone, Queen of the Dead, asking her to stow it away in a dark place.

Graves cites Apollodorus, Hyginus's *Poetic Astronomy* and *Fabulae*, and Fulgentius's *Mythology* as sources for the story.[20]

This story is the single instance which at any level accords with the Freudian account — though Rank reads the tale as a screen for the father's desire.[21] Namely, the daughter "falls in love" with her father and climbs into his bed, has sex with him, and becomes pregnant. Here, the father is the punisher of his daughter. In a patriarchal society the power to punish incest ultimately resides with the father or ruling males. The father is the unknowing party to the crime, and thus can righteously attempt to carry out just punishment.

However, unlike the Freudian scenario, it is the mother who incites the incest between father and daughter. She boasts of her daughter's beauty, and this pride, according to the story, causes Aphrodite to be angry at the insult and her daughter to fall in love with her father. In a certain way, there is a parallel with Oedipus. Laius is arguably uninterested in women because he is attracted to boys. This creates an opening, as it were, in the marital constellation which the son will errantly fill. The son is punished through incest for the father's neglect of his wife. Smyrna's passion for her father is also a punishment for a boastful remark by her mother and results in her mother losing her daughter. It may be that the mother is not interested in her husband, and errantly pushes her daughter toward him to take her place sexually.

This story contains the indirection so frequent in Greek justice: the daughter, not the mother, is punished for what the mother said. That is probably a more honest depiction of how life generally goes. The weaker party ends up bearing the blame for the transgressions of the stronger.

Setting aside the deus ex machina of Aphrodite's curse, the situation on its own must be considered. In Greek society, it would have been considered improper to boast about the beauty of one's unmarried daughter, in the sense that daughters of the citizen class were sequestered, and their chastity well looked after. To boast of one's daughter's beauty would be like sexually advertising her, and the question would be, to whom. Was this a story about a mother improperly sexualizing her daughter? Aphrodite is the goddess of sexual love, as well as being considered the most beautiful goddess. Beauty in a woman and sexuality are bound tightly together in Greek mythology. A woman's beauty is useful in that it makes her attractive to men.

Graves observes that in matrilineal societies, a king could extend his term as king by marrying the young priestess who was designated to become queen in the next term. This woman was usually his daughter. By marrying her himself, he prevented a young "princeling" from coming along and taking away his own office through matrimony.[22]

This idea certainly throws an interesting light on Jocasta's actions. Jocasta, too, was the owner of the throne; kingship passed through marriage to her and her daughters. By marrying her own son, she, too, wittingly or not, prolonged her stay on the throne. Who would have become queen, and king for that matter, had Jocasta not had children? We wonder with Graves if this is the source of the curse in part; namely, that Jocasta would have been trying to extend her own reign by marrying her son, much as matrilineal kings extended their kingship by remaining attached to their daughters. Graves explicitly argues for the likelihood that Oedipus sought to displace the matrilineal descent of the throne, and Jocasta (here Iocaste) kills herself in protest. The city of Thebes rejects Oedipus's attempt at the overthrow of their traditions and is banished, dying ignobly after years of hounding by the Harpies.[23] In the case of Smyrna, there is also a son involved, and divine intervention to save him, even as the mother is rent in two by her father's sword. We should compare him with other children of incest.

Adonis, a beautiful man, is the result of incest between a daughter and her father. He goes on to have an illustrious life little hurt by his problematic parentage. His father apparently had no difficulty in engaging in sexual relations with the woman in his bed; at least we have no indication that Smyrna forced her father. We wonder whom she portrayed herself as — his wife? A concubine? A servant? That Adonis, who is associated with romantic love and sexual desire, is the son of father-daughter incest, tells us once again that the gods both ordained and condoned such relations. Otherwise, we would expect Adonis to have been born crippled and ugly, like Vulcan. This myth, however, *pace* Rank, might also have been an attempt to suggest that father-daughter incest, when it occurs, is the fault of the women involved — the goddess, the mother and her daughter. The father's indiscriminate sexual behavior is never called into question.

Pelopia's son Aegisthus, born of the rape of a daughter by her father, has a more difficult life, and in the end is killed by Orestes. He sides, however, with Clytemnestra, the losing party in the sororal conflict over wife (Helen) versus mother (Clytemnestra) known as the Trojan War.[24] So his alliances as much as his parentage may have doomed him. We wonder why he did not remain to ascend to the throne his father won because of his precocious act of murder.

Eteocles, Polyneices, Antigone and Ismene, the children of mother-son incest, fared not so well as Adonis. Two died in battle with each other. One died for protesting the nonburial edict for the losing brother. The fourth, Ismene, is almost unknown to us, but it seems unlikely she lived happily.

Analysis

Having examined three father-daughter incest myths from Greek antiquity, their existence calls into question the use of Oedipus as a representative anecdote for "incest" in psychoanalysis. Thinking synecdochically, perhaps his strongest kind of logic, Freud raises the Sophoclean Oedipus to paradigmatic status for parent-child incest. But for the Greeks, there were many variants in the theatrical versions' outcomes which modern writers outside classics have acknowledged only very slowly. There is the Sophoclean drama, which makes possible to the uninitiated the idea that everything that happened—the breaking of the injunction against having a child, the saving of baby Oedipus from exposure, the return of the adult Oedipus, the murder of Laius and the marriage with Jocasta — is cosmic error, mistakes born of the hubris of the humans involved. However, Euripides produced a play covering the post-revelation period in which Jocasta did not kill herself, but lived on to comfort her husband and even mourn his death. What is general to the theatrical versions, however, is that incest between mother and son is a thing to be loathed, something that is monstrous, catastrophic and accidental, and no less destructive for all that. Even Freud's version of Oedipus, tendentious and limited as it is, essentially attributes the "desire" of Oedipus for his mother to his unconscious. The effects of unconscious desire remain painful, and "incest" (though we really mean here "mother-son incest") is something humans must avoid. We read the oracle as damning the family of Laius and Jocasta for experiencing it — not raising or rewarding them for it. This is a version of events that retains a sense of right order. It is a morality which, even if in its outlines only, modern society finds congruent with its own ideals. However, the very same culture produced myths of explicit and god-ordained father-daughter incest, which can be read as the culture accepting it as creative, and even rewarding it with high office.

Freud's letters and numerous Freud biographies have revealed that Freud had an attachment to the Oedipus myth beginning in his high school years.[25] He saw Oedipus as a hero. And when in the period just preceding the development of the seduction theory he casts about for ways of understanding this material, he considers only two dramatic pieces, *Hamlet* and the trilogy of *Oedipus Rex, Oedipus at Colonus* and *Antigone*. Unlike Jung, Freud seems to have been an amateur classicist, content with the low-hanging fruit of the Oedipus available to him from youth in its Sophoclean form. Freud is an industrious Victorian, and yet he seems remarkably uninterested in the complete history and mythic attestation of the Oedipus story. Likewise, he is uninterested in other Greek myths or plays which might also contain material of psychoanalytic import regarding incest. For example, he rejects Jung's suggestion that the Electra story might be useful to explain the workings of the "female Oedipus" complex, even as he struggles with the intractability of his data regarding girls' early childhood feelings.[26] He rejects Electra, preferring to keep the notion of the Oedipus complex as essentially valid for both sexes. Freud is right, insofar as there is no unequivocal physical incest between Electra and her father, and because there are variant versions as to whether it was her brother alone or the two of them together who kill her mother. But surely Freud's silence concerning these other three instances of explicit father-daughter incest cannot stand unchallenged.

There may be some intrinsic value for psychoanalytic method in the way the Oedipus play slowly causes "repressed" material to be uncovered and revealed to the inquirer, though as I have pointed out, such material was consciously *suppressed* by the shepherd, Jocasta and others — not known and then forgotten by Oedipus. We must consider separately this matter of psychoanalytic technique in *Oedipus Rex* from the content and context of incest in Greek myth as a whole. The Greeks were well aware of and ready to admit that the immortal, universally valid Greek fathers had intercourse with their mortal (but we also hope "universally" valid) Greek daughters, and produced children with them. It is only Freud, the Victorians or ourselves who refuse to acknowledge such things.

Strikingly, in the case of Harpalyce, there is no preceding crime that dooms or opportunes her father's actions. He is compelled neither by the gods nor by circumstance to rape and impregnate his daughter. But he does so anyway. And there is no plague, no general outcry, no attempt even by the husband to protect the stolen honor of his wife. In all three cases, there are fewer veils of repression on the material because such fathers saw no need to hide their crimes. Smyrna dies. But her mother and father do not.

EIGHT

Freud as Twentieth Century Patient

Judith Herman has written that after the rejection of his seduction theory by the Viennese establishment, the only source of support that could have enabled Freud to sustain his theory was the nascent feminist movement. This, of course, he rejected.[1] The subsequent development of psychoanalysis was certainly shaped by Freud's desire to reinstantiate himself within the prevailing views of his times, which granted him certain privileges by virtue of being a man. It was also formed, though, by his primordial experience with his female nurse, a wound that remained unhealed for the rest of his life. Freud's great imagination remained boxed up, just as he feared his mother had been. He would never be able to generalize past his own experience. Like the Viennese journalists of his day, Freud sought, in the face of real tragedy, an immediate literary gloss to overtake and domesticate the facts.[2] The Oedipus complex arguably kept Freud from experiencing the kind of complete posttraumatic breakdown that he had witnessed in his own patients. It did not prevent him from dying a painful death from an addiction. But then, existentially, he saw himself as alone, especially after the break with Fliess. And as Herman has observed, no one recovers from trauma alone.

So we come to an answer, after considering both the external and internal reasons, for why Freud turned away from the seduction theory and created the Oedipus complex and psychoanalysis. Freud did not only turn blame away from perpetrators and onto generations of anonymous victims; he created the Oedipus complex to turn blame away from his own perpetrator and onto himself. He stopped his pain by cutting himself. Blunted in his efforts to convince his colleagues that victims deserved care and compassion, he regressed in his own self-analysis to the reasoning of children: it must be my fault. Even as he remembered his molestation by his nurse, and the recriminations for his infantile sexual "incompetence," he remembered the secondary result of the molestation: a precocious sexual arousal response at the sight of his nude mother, whom he no doubt expected to treat him as his nurse (now incarcerated) had treated him. Instead, while he experienced the physical reaction he had been conditioned to by abuse, his mother did not behave as his nurse had. Thus, he was left with an unbearable shame and embarrassment. What kind of terrible little son gets sexually aroused at the sight of his mother? In Freud's mind, of course, the answer was waiting close by. Oedipus, of course: King Oedipus, who unknowingly slept with his mother after unknowingly killing his father. The terrible shame of Oedipus Freud immediately universalized to all men (and then all children regardless of sex), thereby diluting its particular power to damn him by instantaneously making all men such tiny criminals.

In fact, it was not the baby Freud who had first attached his illicit desire to his mother, but his aged nurse who had attached hers to him. Freud never makes literary his abuse by his nurse. Instead, he, like Oedipus, focuses on the triumphs of his adult life, and the trauma at one remove, which he *can* talk about. As Oedipus never knows that his father Laius's act of raping a boy doomed him to crime and social demise, Freud likewise never publicly writes about his own rape by his nurse as the true foundation for his shame before his mother. Instead, like Oedipus, who blinds himself at the moment of discovery of the incest, Freud, too, at the moment of remembering his arousal before his nude mother, blinds his public self. He turns away from the incomprehensible pain of the nursemaid's abuse, a scenario in which he is a helpless child-victim betrayed by a most trusted adult and mother-figure. He regains his sense of agency by taking the blame for arousal at *matrem nudam*. He purifies himself through self-mortification before the mother. The difference is that Oedipus never knew about his father's crimes. Freud knew about his nurse's.

The strategy, however, is created out of an attempt to tame the trauma. The Oedipus complex becomes Freud's posttraumatic symptomology. If he desires his mother, he is King Oedipus. If he is raped by his aged female nurse, he is merely an abused, helpless and betrayed little boy. There is no Greek legend to sanctify or heroize the truth for him.[3] The very notion of female sexual desire was taboo to patriarchal Victorians, who saw women as passive and lacking sexual drive. It was also anathema to the defensive imagination of Freud, who summoned all his considerable powers to develop theories that could prove to himself that his female nurse could not possibly have raped him, and he could not possibly have been damaged or made "hysterical" as a result of it. And if not he, then not others. Simple. He had only his friend Fliess to write to, and Fliess was not enough to save his career. There was no supportive body of therapists, colleagues, friends or family members, no infrastructure or ideological climate to help him process his feelings as he recalled his actual abuse. To be a Jewish boy abused by a Catholic woman — in some sense, in Freud's own worldview, he must have felt he was the lowest of the low. The strongest of the Jews, because a male and firstborn, toppled by the weakest of the Catholics, because a female; the least protected by his father, the most humiliated of all. Freud was psychologically unable to integrate this reality into his sense of self.

It is the Greek King Oedipus who rescues Freud's ego and restores his sense of safety and invulnerability. If his father was not there to protect him from the ravages of his Catholic nurse, it must be because he, Freud/Oedipus, had already "killed him." If he can re-repress the memories of the nurse and focus on his arousal before his mother, then he is no longer the pathetic, precociously conditioned object of a female abuser's work. He is instead a powerful king brought down by ancient and universal forces in his unconscious, over which he and all men can only struggle to inadequately control.

The truth is indeed a much more frightening and shattering psychological picture. If generations of therapists, family members and society as a whole rejected such violent and ugly truths in the lives of children, we may perhaps pause to consider Sigmund Freud, a victim, a patient without a physician, unable, alone, to face it for himself.

In a real sense, the courts, the mental health system and public opinion in the west by now have rendered the Oedipus complex largely obsolete. We no longer judicially or socially accept the rape or molestation of girls or boys, though we have not extirpated entirely its incidence. The testimony of women and children is no longer held to be legally suspect on its face. In less than 150 years, the United States has transformed itself from a society with close resemblances to ancient Greek society to one in which many of those parallels — slavery, the political disenfranchisement of women and unpropertied men, legalized child murder — no longer hold. The tragedy of Oedipus occurs in a society that lacks a judicial system, and which therefore relies upon sacrificial scapegoating mechanisms when it needs to rid itself of the pollution associated with certain categories of wrongdoing. The rape of a noble boy by an adult man was clearly an instance of a legal category of action to which the ultimate punishment was attached. Not only were the children and spouse punished; Laius himself, through the mechanism of the curse, also had to die. The genius of the curse from the Greek point of view was in a mechanism of punishment that did not open the way to revenge killings and a cycle of violence that could go out of control. No nonfamily member is implicated by having to partake in judicial punishment of Laius. Instead, the curse turns all violence inward, against the family itself, until all its vestiges are burned out and removed from society, to survive only in a cautionary legend. Such, we might add, was the case of Harpalyce and her father.

We can see the particularity of the case in the Greek view by contrasting Thyestes with Laius. The same oracle that condemns mother-son incest as the most disastrous punishment against Laius and his family commends father-daughter incest to Thyestes as a means of making whole his claim to a throne. Father-daughter incest for Thyestes is an instrument of his ascent to power with full religious sanction, whereas mother-son incest between Oedipus and Jocasta is part of a divinely ordained scheme of demise.

If considered as a ritual of initiation to adulthood, it becomes clear that, in post-Solonic Greece prior to the end of Alexander's reign, the sexual initiation of a boy by a woman is considered a humiliation. Oedipus is not properly made a king because he lacks the support of an *erastes* and the experience of a pederastic initiation. His father has been made unavailable to the social network of pederastic fathers who initiate each other's sons because of disqualification over the rape of Chrysippus. He went too far. As a result, his own son will not have a proper initiation into manhood and the holding of power, and, in due course, will lose his power because of it. Oedipus becomes king because of his *mother*. Graves speculates that this reflects the change from matriarchal to patriarchal control of power in historical Greece. Howsoever it is, we see that, despite the law regarding outrage that Cohen describes, which would include sexual assaults on women, father-daughter incest at the mythic level was a noncriminal category of action.[4] The pure case of Harpalyce, where the father initiates and sustains the rape of his daughter unto pregnancy, requires her to avenge the situation herself. There is no generalized plague to mark the wrong, as there is in Oedipus. There is no social or exterior sign that anything is wrong that might stir up concern on the part of the men or the women of her community. She is completely at her father's mercy. As Herman and Hirschman so aptly point out, there is no avenging father.[5] Freud, when he got the chance, played the same part with respect to such cases. The sexual initiation of girls by their fathers was a shame only to the girls themselves in Victorian times, a notion repeated over and over in the historical literature. Having failed in his attempt to be the avenging angel, Freud reverted to the timeworn formulation of blaming women victims.

In the myths, the social break for a woman once incest is publicly revealed is total. Her only option is suicide or murder by the gods. Women are the perfect scapegoats in these Greeks myths, as we see from the fact that no one ever appears to protest their deaths or demand satisfaction from their violators. It took two millennia and the women's movement to make changes in that patriarchal sacrificial economy.

If the tragedy of Oedipus, his mother Jocasta and their children was designed to punish his father for raping a boy, we should ask ourselves whether in a judicial society we should be embracing the same mechanism for understanding sexual abuse of children. If the stories of Pelopia and Harpalyce, who were raped and impregnated by their fathers for the most self-serving reasons imaginable, are *not* seen as tragedies, we should ask the same questions. And we should appreciate the work of those who have created the beginnings of a new consensus about what is criminal as well as traumatizing in the sexual abuse of children.

One way of understanding the extreme controversies that psychoanalysis has always generated from its inception is to compare them to Girard's discussion of the sacrificial mechanism that wears out. Over time, the same rituals of blame, violence and purgation cease to produce the dependable result. At that point, new mechanisms must be designed to cleanse a society polluted by sins, crimes, offenses against tribal mores. Here, blaming the recipients of childhood sexual abuse declined in its effectiveness as a social purgative as feminism developed in the twentieth century. As concern for children's welfare increased, along with a focus on the earliest years of life as particularly vulnerable and formative, engendered partly by psychoanalysis itself, the ability to blame children for actions that knowing adults carried out became more difficult. In this area, legal protections have moved ahead of Freudian formulations, even as Freud pointed a way forward out of dying rituals. The International Declaration of Human Rights no longer enshrines and protects the kinds of abuses that the Greeks, who considered themselves the most highly civilized people of their known world, would have thought customary. Nor does it accept that the lives and bodily sovereignty of girls and women are less valuable or more expendable than those of boys and men.

Freud himself, the great psychoanalytic lawgiver of the twentieth century, could not escape the plague of childhood sexual abuse. In his earliest career, he attempted to make the leap, from the history of child rape which was creating an epidemic of hysteria, to a future in which those abused would be treated with compassion and support. To his critics, this has often been construed as quite a modest enterprise. And yet the rejection and isolation he experienced for even attempting a single step in that direction were enough to lead him, in his own implicated state, to create the Oedipus complex, to rid himself of his own sense of pollution for the nurse's crimes and then for all such crimes.

In identifying with Oedipus, Freud placed himself on the stage, as a character. He became a figure who attempted to explicate in theoretical and systematic form the tenets of an "Oedipal" worldview. Thus, he lost the ability to see and discuss all that the audience was seeing and had seen. Most importantly, he missed the first play, about the rape of Chrysippus, which would always reveal the true source of Oedipus's torment. And, as the character Oedipus, he missed the stories of Pelopia, Harpalyce and Smyrna, which belied an equivalent taboo on father-daughter incest. And yet in so doing, Freud brought to us that liminal point, the gasps of a sacrificial system that we may hope will, within perhaps fewer than 25 more centuries, be extirpated altogether, and not replaced with anything worse.

To those whose anger at Freud fueled the controversies of the bellicose 1990s, let us remind ourselves of these traumatic wounds, and the deep and infuriated disappointment that is transferred from the enemy to the orderly, who cannot seem to get the victim to the stretcher, the ambulance, the hospital, fast enough. Freud, too, was angry at those who failed him. Many people had. Let us not, therefore, make the mistake of the disappointed patient who is now being carried off the field. Although he believes he is the doctor, he will require the same care as all the other patients wounded that day. Although he denies he is wounded, his untreated hemorrhages require immediate attention. Such is the power of shock, of an unbearable, overwhelming traumatic memory.

Notes

Notes to Introduction

1. Ian Suttie, *The Origins of Love and Hate* (1935; reprint, London: Free Association Books, 1988). With new prefaces by John Bowlby and Dorothy Heard.

2. Erich Fromm, *Sigmund Freud's Mission: An Analysis of His Personality and Influence* (New York: Harper and Brothers, 1959).

3. Morton Schatzman, *Soul Murder: Persecution in the Family* (New York: Random House, 1973).

4. Marianne Krüll, *Freud and His Father*, trans. Arnold Pomerans (New York: W.W. Norton, 1986); Marie Balmary, *Psychoanalyzing Psychoanalysis: Freud and the Hidden Fault of the Father*, trans. Ned Lukacher (Baltimore: Johns Hopkins University Press, 1982).

5. Frank J. Sulloway, *Freud: Biologist of the Mind: Beyond the Psychoanalytic Legend* (Cambridge, Mass.: Harvard University Press, 1979); Adolf Grünbaum, *The Foundations of Psychoanalysis: A Philosophical Critique* (Berkeley and Los Angeles: University of California Press, 1984); Alan Esterson, *Seductive Mirage: An Exploration of the Work of Sigmund Freud* (Chicago: Open Court Publishing, 1993).

6. Bennett Simon and Rachel Blass, "The Development and Vicissitudes of Freud's Ideas on the Oedipus Complex," in *The Cambridge Companion to Freud*, ed. Jerome Neu (Cambridge: Cambridge University Press, 1991), 161–74; Judith Herman, *Trauma and Recovery* (New York: Basic Books, 1992), 96–114.

7. Sachs cites Freud in a lecture of 1917: "[a patient's] conflicts will only be successfully solved and his resistances overcome if the anticipatory ideas he is given [by his analyst] tally with what is real in him." Quoted in "In Fairness to Freud: A Critical Notice of *The Foundations of Psychoanalysis*, by Adolph Grünbaum," in *The Cambridge Companion to Freud*, ed. Jerome Neu (Cambridge: Cambridge University Press, 1991), 311. Marshall Edelson, *Psychoanalysis: A Theory in Crisis* (Chicago: University of Chicago Press, 1988).

8. See Jeffrey Masson, *A Dark Science: Women, Sexuality and Psychiatry in the Nineteenth Century* (New York: Farrar, Straus and Giroux, 1986); *The Assault on the Truth: Freud's Suppression of the Seduction Theory* (New York: Farrar, Straus and Giroux, 1984).

9. The question remains when. Schatzman, *Soul Murder*, writes, "Freud

almost certainly knew this part of the myth [concerning Chrysippus and Laius]; Rank, his close disciple for many years, reported it (1912)" (115). It seems less clear that Freud knew about Chrysippus at the time of his letter to Fliess, unless he was being entirely disingenuous, or had repressed his own knowledge of it from previous reading.

10. A good example of such a view is Martha C. Nussbaum, "The Oedipus Rex and the Ancient Unconscious," *in Freud and Forbidden Knowledge*, ed. Peter Rudnytsky and Ellen Handler Spitz (New York: New York University, 1994), who argues that the Greek sense of Oedipus exonerates him because he is presumed innocent.

11. For example, George Devereux, "Why Oedipus Killed Laius: A Note on the Complementary Oedipus Complex in Greek Drama," in *Oedipus: A Folklore Casebook*, ed. Lowell Edmunds and Alan Dundes (New York: Garland Publishing, 1983), 215–33.

12. D. W. Winnicott, *The Child, the Family, and the Outside World* (Reading, Mass.: Addison-Wesley Publishing, 1987), 88.

Notes to Chapter One

1. Sigmund Freud, *The Complete Letters of Sigmund Freud to Wilhelm Fliess 1887–1904*, ed. and trans. Jeffrey M. Masson (Cambridge, Mass.: Belknap Press of Harvard University Press, 1985), 268–69. Hereafter cited in the text as *Letters*.

2. Ernest Jones, of course, followed up Freud's speculations regarding Hamlet and attempted to present a credible account of Hamlet as an Oedipal figure in *Hamlet and Oedipus* (New York: Norton, 1949). However, Jones's reading of Hamlet is even more tendentious and filled with *a priori*-isms than Freud's reading of Oedipus, if one cares for the story at all. It is a convincing account to those who have already accepted Freud's major premises regarding Oedipus, but adds little to our understanding of Hamlet if one does not.

3. Ernest Jones, *The Life and Work of Sigmund Freud*, vol. 1 (New York: Basic Books, 1953); Peter Gay, *Freud: A Life for Our Time* (New York: W. W. Norton, 1988), 7, 94–104; Marianne Krüll, *Freud and His Father*, trans. Arnold J. Pomerans (New York: Norton, 1979); Sulloway, *Freud*, 206–16; Gerald Izenberg, "Seduced and Abandoned: The Rise and Fall of Freud's Seduction Theory," in *The Cambridge Companion to Freud*, ed. Jerome Neu (Cambridge: Cambridge University Press, 1991), 25–43; Peter Newton, *Freud: From Youthful Dream to Mid-Life Crisis* (New York: Guilford Press, 1995), 38–41; Esterson, *Seductive Mirage*, 138–39; Richard Webster, *Why Freud Was Wrong: Sin, Science and Psychoanalysis* (New York: Basic Books, 1995), 241–58; Sander Gilman, *The Case of Sigmund Freud: Medicine and Identity at the Fin de Siècle* (Baltimore: Johns Hopkins University Press, 1993), 69–79, 169–215.

4. Josef Sajner, "Sigmund Freuds Beziehungen zu seinem Geburtsort Freiberg und zu Mähren," *Clio Medica* 3 (1968): 167–80.

5. Gay, *Freud*, opposite page 106.

6. Josef Sajner, "Drei dokumentarische Beiträge zur Sigmund Freud-Biographik aus Böhmen und Mähren," *Jahrbuch der Psychanalyse* 13, 143–52.

7. Sigmund Freud, "The Aetiology of Hysteria," in *Standard Edition of the Works of Sigmund Freud,* vol. 3, trans. Alix Strachey (London: The Hogarth Press and the Institute of Psycho-analysis, 1962), 214–15.

8. See, for example, Ellen Bass and Laura Davis, *The Courage to Heal* (New York: Harper and Row, 1988); David Finkelhor, *Sexually Victimized Children* (New York: Free Press, 1979); Sister Vera Gallagher, *Speaking Out, Fighting Back: Women Who Have Survived Child Sexual Abuse in the Home* (Seattle: Madrona Publishers, 1985); Toni McNaron and Yarrow Morgan, eds., *Voices in the Night: Women Speaking about Incest* (Minneapolis: Cleis Press, 1982); Michelle Morris, *If I Should Die Before I Wake* (New York: Dell, 1982); Elizabeth Ward, *Father-Daughter Rape* (New York: Grove Press, 1985).

9. Jeffrey Masson makes this observation in a note in the Freud-Fliess *Letters* (304).

10. Leopold Constans, *La Légends d'Œdipe: Étudiée dans l'antiquite au moyen age et dans les temps modernes en particulier dans le roman de Thèbes* (Geneva: Slatkine Reprints, 1974).

11. See, for example, Bass and Davis, *The Courage to Heal,* 104–5; Jill Duerr Berrick and Neil Gilbert, *With the Best of Intentions: The Child Sexual Abuse Prevention Movement* (New York: Guilford Press, 1991), 41, 55; P. C. Kendall, "Social Cognition and Problem Solving: A Developmental and Child-Clinical Interface," in B. Gholson and T. C. Rosenthal, *Applications of Cognitive-Developmental Theory* (New York: Academic Press, 1984); J. S. Wallerstein and J. B. Kelly, *Surviving the Breakup: How Children and Parents Cope with Divorce* (New York: Basic Books, 1980); S. C. Anderson, C. M. Bach and S. Griffith, *Psychosocial Sequelae in Intrafamilial Victims of Sexual Assault and Abuse* (paper presented at the Third International Conference on Child Abuse and Neglect, Amsterdam, The Netherlands, 1981); V. DeFrancis, *Protecting the Child Victim of Sex Crimes Committed by Adults* (Denver: American Humane Association, 1969); W. N. Friedrich, A. J. Urquiza and R. Beilke, "Behavioral Problems in Sexually Abused Young Children," *Journal of Pediatric Psychology* 11 (1986): 47–57.

12. I am not unsympathetic to the historical research on such threats of castration in German child-rearing in the nineteenth century. Schatzman, *Soul Murder,* for example, gives quite a good disquisition, 118–27. I simply mean to add this additional and personal level to Freud's experience, and the possibility that a child as bright and reflective as Freud would take even so commonplace a threat and reendow it with his own meanings.

13. Gilman, *The Case of Sigmund Freud,* 76; Krüll, *Freud and His Father,* 119.

14. Siegfried Bernfield and Suzanne Cassirer Bernfield, "Freud's Early Childhood," *Bulletin of the Menninger Clinic* 8 (1964): 107–15.

15. Sigmund Freud, "Screen Memories," in *The Standard Edition of the Complete Psychological Works of Sigmund Freud,* vol. 3, trans. James Strachey et al. (London: Hogarth Press, 1962), 312.

16. Louis Breger, *Freud: Darkness in the Midst of Vision* (New York: John Wiley and Sons, 2000).

17. See, for example, Madelon Sprengnether, *The Spectral Mother: Freud, Feminism and Psychoanalysis* (Ithaca, N.Y.: Cornell University Press, 1990), and "Mourning Freud," in *Psychoanalyses/Feminisms*, ed. Peter Rudnytsky and Andrew M. Gordon (Albany: SUNY Press, 2000), 11–37.

Notes to Chapter Two

1. Much of what is known about what Freud studied in Paris has been unearthed by Jeffrey Masson. Masson rightly has been criticized for the motives he attributes to Freud and the aggressiveness of his charges against Freud. I have, however, validated much of his archival research on Freud's Parisian teachers. See Masson, *Assault*, 27.

2. Jose Brunner, *Freud and the Politics of Psychoanalysis* (New Brunswick, N.J.: Transaction Publishers, 2001), 93–105.

3. Sigmund Freud, "The Aetiology of Hysteria," in *Standard Edition of the Works of Sigmund Freud*, vol. 3, trans. Alix Strachey (London: The Hogarth Press and the Institute of Psycho-analysis, 1962), 191–221.

4. *Letters*, 44.

5. The study is outlined to Fliess in a draft postmarked February 3, 1893. He tells Fliess, "If it should turn out that the same disturbances of functions of the nervous system which are acquired through sexual abuse also come about on a purely hereditary basis, it would give rise to the most significant speculations which are today only beginning to dawn on me" (*Letters*, 44).

6. "When I first made enquiries about what was known on the subject, I learnt from colleagues that there are several publications by paediatricians which stigmatize the frequency of sexual practices by nurses and nursery maids, carried out even on infants in arms; and in the last few weeks I have come across a discussion of 'Coitus in Childhood' by Dr. Stekel (1895) in Vienna. I have not had time to collect the published evidence; but even if it were only scanty, it is to be expected that increased attention to the subject will very soon confirm the great frequency of sexual experiences and sexual activity in childhood." ("Aetiology of Hysteria," 207). One wonders why, in such an important talk, he had not waited until he had been able to "collect the published evidence," especially since it so materially corroborates his claims.

7. Quoted by Masson, 25, from the first volume of Lacassagne's journal, *Archives d'anthropologie criminelle et des sciences pénales* (1886), 67. Lacassagne held the chair in legal (forensic) medicine at the University of Lyon.

8. As Masson points out but does not fairly construe, Freud's problems were in one sense not unique. At the time Freud was working on the seduction theory, the testimony of women and children was often considered legally suspect on its face. Masson discusses French sources (40–51). See, for example, Alfred Fournier, "Simulation d'attentats veneriens sur jeunes enfants," *Annales d'hygiène publique*

et de médécine légale, ed. Paul Broardel, 4, no. 6 (1880): 498–519: L. Thoinot, *Medicolegal Aspects of Moral Offenses,* trans. Arthur Weysse (Philadelphia: F. A. Davis, 1916). Many others attest to the history of such legal incredulity, especially in cases charging sexual abuse or rape, in England, Holland and the United States, including into the twentieth century. For England, see Anthony E. Simpson, "Vulnerability and the Age of Female Consent: Legal Innovation and Its Effect on Prosecutions for Rape in Eighteenth-Century London," in *Sexual Underworlds of the Enlightenment,* ed. G. S. Rousseau and Roy Porter (Manchester: Manchester University Press, 1987), 181–205. Simpson also, importantly, predates the so-called Wigmore doctrine of the later 1930s and early 1940s, cited by Ashby, 118–19, which among other things stipulated that the accused man was usually the actual victim in such cases, by recognizing the origins of Wigmore's doctrine in the work of Lord Hale. Anthony E. Simpson, "Criminal Law: The 'Blackmail Myth' and the Prosecution of Rape and Its Attempt in Eighteenth Century London: The Creation of a Legal Tradition," *Northwestern School of Law Journal of Criminal Law and Criminology* 77: 101, accessed via Lexis June 7, 2001, 40 pages. See also Carol-Ann Hooper, "Child Sexual Abuse and the Regulation of Women: Variations on a Theme," in *Regulating Motherhood: Historical Essays on Marriage, Motherhood and Sexuality,* ed. Carol Smart (New York: Routledge, 1992), 53–77. Louise Jackson, *Child Sexual Abuse in Victorian England* (London: Routledge, 2002), shows that, while the number of sexual assault cases involving child victims rose dramatically in three major English jurisdictions throughout the nineteenth century, most were either thrown out entirely, or resulted in conviction for misdemeanor assault. A tiny proportion resulted in conviction for sexual assault. See also Charles Behlmer, *Child Abuse and Reform in England,* 1870–1908 (Stanford: Stanford University Press, 1982), 70–75. For Holland, see Manon van der Heijden, "Women as Victims of Sexual and Domestic Violence in Seventeenth-Century Holland: Criminal Cases of Rape, Incest and Maltreatment in Rotterdam and Delft, *Journal of Social History* 33 (Spring 2000): 3, 623–44. For Canada, see Joan Sangster, "Masking and Unmasking the Sexual Abuse of Children: Perceptions of Violence against Children in 'The Badlands' of Ontario, 1916–1930," *Journal of Family History* 25, no. 4 (October 2000): 504–26. For the United States, see Linda Gordon, *Heroes of Their Own Lives: The Politics and History of Family Violence* (New York: Penguin, 1988); Clifford Dorne, *Crimes against Children* (New York: Harrow and Heston, 1989); LeRoy Ashby, *Dependency, Neglect and Abuse in American History* (New York: Twayne Publishers, 1997). For Germany, Switzerland and Austria as well as a general review of incest historically and its legal treatment, see Hans von Hentig and Theodor Viernstein, *Untersuchungen über den Inzest* (Heidelberg: Carl Winters Universitätsbuchhandlung, 1925); Alfred Eber, *Die Blutschande: Eine kriminilogische Untersuchung unter besonderer Berucksichtigung der Tatsituation* (Liepzig: E. Wiegandt Verlagsbuchhandlung, 1937); Hans-Ulrich Gebhart, *Der Inzest im Schweiz. Strafrecht mit einem Verblick über seine strafrechtliche Behandlung in der Vergangenheit* (Zurich: Buchdruckerei Stampfenbach AG, 1947).

9. Freud writes to Fliess on May 4, 1896, that "Word was given out to aban-

don me, for a void is forming all around me" (*Letters,* 185). This, after writing Fliess on April 26, that his lecture had been given "an icy reception," that Krafft-Ebing had likened the theory to "a scientific fairy tale"; and that "They can go to hell, euphemistically speaking" (184). Peter Gay suggests things weren't as bad as Freud seemed determined to make them out; see Gay, *Freud,* 138–40. But business did indeed seem to contract into the following fall, when Freud had enough time on his hands to work on his self-analysis, due to lack of other patients (*Letters,* 264–73).

10. This occurs on page 502 of "Simulation." *Assault,* 41.

11. And men; Linda Gordon and others have shown that lower-class men were much more likely to be prosecuted for such crimes than "men of substance."

12. See, for example, Fournier, "Simulation," 499, 506, 509–12; Gordon, *Heroes,* 223–25, 244; and Ashby, *Dependency,* 20–21, 76–77, 118–19.

13. Defenders of psychoanalysis have pointed out in recent years that, while Freud gave up his seduction etiology theory, he never stopped accepting the reality that sexual abuse of children occurred. Lloyd deMause and the psychohistorical school tend to hold this view; see, for example, Brett Kahr, "The Sexual Molestation of Children: Historical Perspectives," *The Journal of Psychohistory* 19, no. 2 (Fall 1991): 191–214, 205. However, I think it is fair to say that affirming this truth was not, after 1897, any important part of the work associated with him. That the psychiatric and legal communities took his disavowal of the seduction theory as establishing that all complainants were fantasizing or lying is the standard understanding of twentieth century practice prior to the 1970s and the rise of the feminist movement. See for example Gordon, *Heroes,* 208 and Ashby, *Dependency,* 118–19. If the actual sexual abuse of children had been of concern to Freud, we surely might have expected either his public avowal of its seriousness, or some evidence of his support for others working in this area. Even Freud's defenders have been unable to muster evidence for either point. On the other hand, Freud's assumptions on this point were, as I have suggested above, much of a piece with the views predominating in European and U.S. cultures at least as early as the seventeenth century. See, for example, Hooper, "Child Sexual Abuse," 59.

14. René Girard, *Violence and the Sacred,* trans. Patrick Gregory (Baltimore: Johns Hopkins University Press, 1977), 89–118.

15. See Gebhart's review of incest laws in the post-Enlightenment period (*Der Inzest,* 54–75).

16. Gebhart reviews Indian, Persian, Egyptian, Hebrew, Islamic, Greek, Roman and Incan laws, for example (ibid., 28–46), as well as European canon law (49–53), which included such punishments.

17. René Girard, *Violence and the Sacred;* Kenneth Burke, *The Rhetoric of Religion* (Berkeley and Los Angeles: University of California Press, 1968).

18. See, for example, Lloyd deMause, *The Evolution of Childhood,* ed. Lloyd deMause (New York: Psychohistory Press, 1974), 47–49; Gebhart, *Der Inzest,* 59.

19. Elizabeth Wilson, "Not in This House: Incest, Denial and Doubt in the White Middle Class Family," *Yale Journal of Criticism* 8 (1995): 35–58, provides a good discussion of the range of professional and clinical opinion on repressed

memories and their verifiability, including the work of Loftus. Frederick Crewes's recent work also supports this line of thinking.

20. Gordon, *Heroes,* documents the extent to which poor and working-class men were netted by social service agencies in Boston. Recent high-profile prosecutions in Massachusetts have focused on stranger/youth worker molestations and priest-child abuses.

21. Hans Joachim Schneider, "Sexual Abuse of Children: Strengths and Weaknesses of Current Criminology," *International Journal of Offender Therapy and Comparative Criminology* 41, no. 4 (1997): 317. The studies cited are G. Davies, "Research on Children's Testimony: Implications for Interviewing Practice," in *Clinical Approaches to Sex Offenders and Their Victims* (Chichester, N.Y.: John Wiley, 1991), 93–115; and K. Coullborn Faller, *Understanding Child Sexual Maltreatment* (Newbury Park: Sage, 1990).

22. Judith Herman, "Crime and Memory," in *Trauma and Self,* ed. Charles Strozier and Michael Flynn (Lanham, Md.: Rowman and Littlefield, 1996), 3–17; Mary Harvey and Judith Herman, "Amnesia, Partial Amnesia and Delayed Recall among Adult Survivors of Childhood Trauma," *Consciousness and Cognition* 3 (1994): 295–306.

23. Judith Herman, *Trauma and Recovery: The Aftermath of Violence from Domestic Abuse to Political Terror* (New York: Basic Books, 1992), 11.

24. Brunner, *Freud,* 38.

25. Ibid., 35.

26. Ibid., 39, quoting the SE, 16, 367–70.

27. Charles Rycroft, *Viewpoints* (London: The Hogarth Press, 1991), 77–78.

28. Ibid., 78.

29. Simpson, "The 'Blackmail Myth."

Notes to Chapter Three

1. *Standard Edition of the Complete Works of Sigmund Freud,* vol. 3, trans. Alix Strachey (London: Hogarth Press and the Institute of Psychoanalysis, 1962), 27–39.

2. *Standard Edition of the Complete Works of Sigmund Freud,* vol. 2, trans. James Strachey et al. (London: Hogarth Press and the Institute of Psychoanalysis, 1955), 3–17.

3. "Charcot," in *Standard Edition of the Works of Sigmund Freud,* vol. 3, trans. Alix Strachey (London: The Hogarth Press and the Institute of Psychoanalysis, 1962), 21–23. This is significant because it represents the opening stage of the arguments concerning the extent to which environmental versus inherited factors are salient in the etiology of neurosis. As Winnicott would later point out, Freud and his followers ultimately rejected almost wholly the significance of environmental factors as contributing to mental illnesses. See, for example, D. W. Winnicott, *The Maturational Processes and the Facilitating Enviroment: Studies in the Theory of Emotional Development* (Madison: International Universities Press, 1965), 176. The development of the drive theory sealed off the impact of actual events and

experiences in the child's life and pushed responsibility for psychic disturbance back on the newly theoretically sexualized child. For where patients claimed that they had been sexualized by their attackers, Freud would later claim, as a substitution, that they were sexualized *by nature* as children. Therefore, nothing that actually happened to them — no event that took place in their lives — was more important than the effect of their own instinctual lives upon their mental — symbolic, imaginary — lives.

4. Freud, and Breuer, quoted by Freud in "The Psychotherapy of Hysteria," in *Standard Edition of the Complete Works of Sigmund Freud,* vol. 2, 255.

5. Masson, *Assault* (37–38), gives good evidence that Freud owned the three central works by French authors on sexual abuse of young children: Ambroise Tardieu, *Étude médico-légale sur les Attentats aux Moeurs* (1878); Paul Bernard, *Des Attentats à la Pudeur sur les petites Filles* (1886); and Paul Brourdel, *Les Attentats aux Moeurs* (1909). Masson gives in the notes a fuller summary of the work of Brourdel and Tardieu and others on the issues of child rape and child physical abuse (195–204). Masson mentions the work of Adolphe Toulmouche (197), which Tardieu cites in "Étude médico-légale sur les sévices et mauvais traitements exercés sur des enfants" (A forensic study of cruelty and brutal treatment inflicted on children), *Annales d'hygiène publique et de médecine légale,* 2nd ser., 13 (1860): 361–98, as establishing the fact that children may be molested without leaving physical traces. A later work by Charles Samson Féré, which Masson reports was owned by Freud (199), does make a connection between traumatic experiences and their psychological sequelae: *L'Instinct sexuelle: évolution et dissolution* (Paris: Felix Alcan, 1899).

6. Adolf Grünbaum, *The Foundations of Psychoanalysis,* 95–159.

7. See Judith Herman's discussion in *Trauma and Recovery,* 7–50.

Notes to Chapter Four

1. Herman describes these stages in *Trauma and Recovery,* 115–236.

2. See, for example, deMause, "The Universality of Incest," 28 pages with citations.

3. Out of an enormous literature, see, for example, James A. Chu, *Rebuilding Shattered Lives: The Responsible Treatment of Complex Post-Traumatic and Dissociative Disorders* (New York: John Wiley and Sons, 1998); Herman, *Trauma and Recovery,* 133–54; Susan Reviere, *Memory of Childhood Trauma: A Clinician's Guide to the Literature* (New York: Guilford Press, 1996); John Briere, *Child Abuse Trauma: Theory and Treatment of the Lasting Effects* (Newbury Park, Calif.: Sage, 1992).

4. Ironically, while on September 21, 1897, he cannot bring himself to imagine that so many fathers, with full hormonal complements, superior physical and verbal powers, and the sole support of their dependent charges, would force or coerce those children into a variety of sexual relations with them, he has no trouble at all imagining, on October 27, 1897, that all children possess an aggressive and jealous animus against their fathers and a sexual and seductive posture toward their fathers.

For the first contention, he has the evidence of 18 cases. For the second, he has himself, and notably, a case where he discovers that the "prime originator" of his illness is *not* his father, but his old nursemaid. And whereas he is unwilling to trust the reality principle of the material brought from unconsciousness into consciousness in his patients, through rigorous analytic procedure, he is willing to trust the reality of material from the dream material of his own unconscious.

5. Krüll, *Freud and His Father,* 42–43, 176–81.

6. For the United States see Diane E. H. Russell, *The Secret Trauma: Incest in the Lives of Girls and Women* (New York: Basic Books: 1986); Dante Cicchetti and Vicki Carlson, eds., *Child Maltreatment: Theory and Practice on the Causes and Consequences of Child Abuse and Neglect* (Cambridge: Cambridge University Press, 1989); Mildred Daly Pagelow and Lloyd Pagelow, *Family Violence* (New York: Praeger, 1984); Chu; Briere, *Child Abuse Trauma;* Herman, *Trauma and Recovery*; Judith Herman, Diana Russell and Karen Trocki, "Long-Term Effects of Incestuous Abuse in Childhood," *American Journal of Psychiatry* 143 (October 1986): 1293–96; Daniel Finkelhor, Richard Gelles, Gerald Hotaling and Murray Straus, eds., *The Dark Side of Families: Current Family Violence Research* (Beverly Hills: Sage, 1983). For Germany, see Schneider, "Sexual Abuse of Children," 310–24. For Austria, see Irmgard Kretz, Ricki Reichel and Marguerite Zoechling, *Sexual Abuse of Children in Austria* (Vienna: Federal Ministry for Environment, Youth and Family, 1988).

7. Brunner, *Freud and the Politics of Psychoanalysis,* 98.

8. Ibid., 105.

9. Ibid., 103.

10. Herman, *Trauma and Recovery,* 133–213.

11. Benjamin Brody, "Freud's Caseload," *Psychotherapy: Theory, Research and Practice 7,* no. 1 (Spring 1970): 8–12.

12. Herman, *Trauma and Recovery,* 143–47.

13. Girard, *Violence and the Sacred,* 39–67.

14. See, for example, Moira Johnston, *Spectral Evidence — The Ramona Case: Incest, Memory and Truth on Trial in Napa Valley* (Boston: Houghton Mifflin, 1997).

15. See Freud, *Letters,* 212, for perversion (asymptomatic) as the alternative sequel to neurosis resulting from childhood sexual trauma.

16. Freud puts in tension the individually oriented pleasure principle with the constraints humans agree to in order to form a community. Thus it requires people to forego the gratification of all their instinctual drives, which necessarily results in a limitation on happiness and hostility to civilization. He argues that sexual acts are the model for all other forms of happiness. See especially *Civilization and Its Discontents,* 97, 101, 103–7, 134.

17. For example, Esterson, *Seductive Mirage.*

18. We might first point to the title of Masson's book in which he makes the case that the seduction theory was supported by facts: *The Assault on Truth.* Masson calls Freud's recanting of the seduction theory a "failure of courage" (*Assault,* xxi). Masson rightly holds psychoanalysts responsible for harming their patients

by denying the reality of their experiences and subsequent suffering, and demonstrates instances, such as the well-known case of Emmy Eckstein, where Freud did real damage to a patient. In these cases, psychoanalysts may be considered perpetrators of therapeutic malfeasance. However, by undervaluing the context and constraints under which Freud worked and overestimating Freud's powers in the situation, Masson himself creates something of a distortion. For example, Masson points out that during Freud's early career, the most cited German work that discussed the sexual abuse of children in a forensic context, *Clinical Stories from Forensic Medicine*, by Johann Ludwig Casper (1863), was even more dismissive of children's allegations than the most corrosive French critic of the time, Fournier (*Assault*, 137). A later book, *Against Therapy: Emotional Tyranny and the Myth of Psychological Healing* (New York: Atheneum, 1988), rejects "the very idea" of psychotherapy as wrong (ix). Interestingly, *The Courage to Heal* appeared in the same year, with a much more optimistic view regarding the help that sympathetic psychotherapy could afford incest survivors.

19. In this Freud not only follows the structural and dramatic lead of Sophocles. He follows the sacrificial logic which demands that guilt be kept away from the powerful and deflected onto the expendable.

20. Thucydides, *The History of the Peloponnesian War*, trans. Rex Warner (London: Penguin Books, 1954), 401–2.

Notes to Chapter Five

1. Sigmund Freud, *The Interpretation of Dreams* (1900), reprinted in *The Basic Writings of Sigmund Freud*, trans. and ed. A. A. Brill (New York: Random House, 1938), 306–7. Although I have elsewhere used the translation of the *Standard Edition*, the deviation between the two translations here is minimal in tone and substance.

2. Eliza Butler, *The Tyranny of Greece over Germany: A Study of the Influence Exercised by Greek Art and Poetry over the Great German Writers of the Eighteenth, Nineteenth, and Twentieth Centuries* (Boston: Beacon Press, 1925).

3. Peter Rudnytsky, *Freud and Oedipus* (New York: NYU Press, 1987), 11–12.

4. Ibid., 4–89.

5. This, in fact, is one of Rank's main themes in *The Incest Theme in Literature and Legend* (1912).

6. Robert Graves, *The Greek Myths*, vol. 2 (London: Penguin, 1955), 9–15.

7. Sigmund Freud, *Die Traumdeutung*, 8th rev. ed. (Leipzig: Franz Deuticke, 1930), 181; Freud, *Dreams*, 308; Sigmund Freud, *The Interpretation of Dreams*, in *Standard Edition of the Works of Sigmund Freud*, trans. James Strachey et al. (London: The Hogarth Press and the Institute of Psychoanalysis, 1953), 4:262–63.

8. Christine Downing, *Myths and Mysteries of Same-Sex Love* (New York: Continuum, 1989).

9. Hans Licht, *Sexual Life in Ancient Greece*, trans. J. H. Freese (London: Constable, 1994).

10. Alejandro Marcel, personal communication.

11. Harold Stewart, for example, suggests this possibility. See "Jocasta's Crimes," *International Journal of Psychoanalysis* 42 (1961): 424–30.

12. George Devereux argues that much of the mythical fighting between Zeus and Hera may reflect the combative adjustments that occurred when patrilineal conquerors entered matrilineal Greece, with a resulting loss of status and power for women, both materially and symbolically. See "Why Oedipus Killed Laius," 215–33.

Notes to Chapter Six

1. Lloyd deMause, "The Universality of Incest," 28 pages with citations.

2. See, for example, Girard, *Violence and the Sacred,* 68–88.

3. See ibid., and also by Girard, *Deceit* and *Desire and the Novel: Self and Other in Literary Structure,* trans. Yvonne Freccero (Baltimore: Johns Hopkins University Press, 1965).

4. *Das Inzest motiv in Dichtung und Sage,* trans. Gregory Richter (Baltimore: John Hopkins University Press, 1992).

5. Suttie, *The Origins of Love and Hate,* 109–10.

6. The details regarding Agamemnon's child-murder are summarized in Clytemnestra's speech in Iphigenia at Aulis:

> First — to make this the first shame
> I charge you with — you married me against my will,
> Took me by force, killing my first husband Tantalus;
> You grabbed my baby from my breast, and broke its head
> On the hard ground. My brothers, the two sons of Zeus,
> Mounted their gleaming horses and made war on you.
> You knelt as suppliant to my old father Tyndareos;
> He saved your life, and you became my next husband.

Euripides, *Iphigenia in Aulis,* in *Orestes and Other Plays,* trans. Philip Vellacott (Middlesex: Penguin, 1972), 409. Miriam Johnson, *Strong Mothers, Weak Wives: The Search for Gender Equality* (Berkeley and Los Angeles: University of California Press, 1988), argues that men primarily have a sexual connection to their wives but no inherent connection to their children. Women, on the other hand, bind to their children, once born, and the sexual tie to the husband becomes secondary.

7. Patrick Mullahy, *Oedipus, Myth and Complex: A Review of Psychoanalytic Theory* (New York: Grove Press, 1955), 202. The quote is from *Modern Education.*

8. Erich Fromm, *The Forgotten Language: An Introduction to the Language of Dreams, Fairy Tales and Myths* (New York: Grove Weidenfeld, 1951), 196–231.

9. Deverux, "Why Oedipus Killed Laius," 216–17.

10. Curiously, Rank's *Das Inzestmotiv in Dichtung und Sage* supports Devereux's notion of what Freud leaves behind, notably the sexually aggressive parents, and especially fathers. In his chapter on father-daughter incest (300–37),

Rank demonstrates that in the overwhelming majority of myths and legends he reviews, the father is the sexual aggressor, and the daughter makes strenuous efforts to elude him, up to and including suicide. Daughters who attempt to leave with age-appropriate suitors are often punished severely by the father if caught. On the one hand, the stories and contemporary cases that Rank discusses involve older girls and young women, who in some cases have been forced to bear children by their rapacious fathers. This accords with the view that Freud "never denied the reality of incest." On the other hand, the contemporary cases reported in the newspapers which Rank cites all involve working men or at best "landowner"[s] when occupation is specified. This suggests the pattern of repression that allows that "such things" occur within the lower classes, and where the daughter is old enough to become pregnant. It leaves aside the question of Freud's female patients, wealthier and educated, where repression of the acts perpetrated in earliest childhood, as had his own, could lead to psychological disturbances. Such wealthy fathers had the presumption of law (*pace* Fournier) to protect them, along with Freud's need not to alienate those paying for his services.

11. Devereux, "Why Oedipus Killed Laius," 229.

12. Krüll, *Freud and His Father,* 61–63.

13. William A. Percy III, "Sexual Revolution 600 B.C.–400 A.D.: The Origins of Institutionalized Pederasty in Greece," reprinted in *Homosexuality in the Ancient World,* ed. Wayne R. Dynes and Stephen Donaldson, vol. 1 (New York: Garland Press, 1992), 378–79; also *Pederasty and Pedagogy in Archaic Greece* (Chicago: University of Illinois Press, 1996), 59–92.

14. David Cohen, "Law, Society and Homosexuality in Ancient Athens," *Past and Present* 117 (November 1987); *Law, Society and Sexuality: The Enforcement of Morals in Classical Athens* (Cambridge: Cambridge University Press, 1991), 186–87.

15. Constans, *La Legende d'Œdipe;* E. Bethe, "Die dorische Knabenliebe, ihre Ethic, ihre Idee," *Rheinische Museum* 62 (1907): 438–75; Licht, *Sexual Life in Ancient Greece;* Bernard Sergent, *Homosexuality in Greek Myth,* trans. Arthur Goldhammer (Boston: Beacon Press, 1984).

16. Licht, *Sexual Life in Ancient Greece,* 134.

17. Ibid., 139.

18. It is not inappropriate to speculate, given Freud's at times transparent autobiographical tendencies when developing theory, that Freud's diminution of Laius parallels the little stature Freud's father held in his own society, and the closeness between Freud and his mother, which excluded his father to a great extent. We should remember that Sigmund was a child of his father's third wife. Erich Fromm argues the point explicitly and cogently in *Sigmund Freud's Mission: An Analysis of His Personality and Influence* (New York: Harper and Brothers, 1959), 19–61.

19. Sergent, *Homosexuality in Greek Myth,* 67–68.

20. Ibid., 7–54; Percy, *Pederasty,* 59–69; "Sexual Revolution," 375–78; Cohen, *Law,* 195–201.

21. Percy, *Pederasty and Pedagogy,* 55–56.

22. Cohen, *Law;* K. J. Dover, *Greek Homosexuality* (Cambridge, Mass.: Harvard University Press, 1977).

23. Cohen rehearses the legal complexities very well in both *Past and Present* and *Law.*

24. Cohen, *Law,* 178–79.

25. Self-control was considered a supreme virtue by the Greeks. See Licht, *Sexual Life;* Cohen, *Law;* Bruce Thornton, *Eros: The Myth of Ancient Greek Sexuality* (Boulder: Westview Press, 1997); and Dover, *Greek Homosexuality,* on the expectation that erastes were always supposed to wait patiently for the sexual reward of the eremenoi (81–100).

26. Judith Herman and Linda Hirschman, "Father Daughter Incest," in *The Signs Reader: Women, Gender and Scholarship,* ed. Elizabeth Abel and Emily K. Abel (Chicago: University of Chicago Press, 1983), 262.

27. See, for example, Stewart, "Jocasta's Crimes," 424–30, and Graves, *The Greek Myths,* 2:10.

28. See Graves's commentary, ibid., 1:117; Sergent, *Homosexuality in Greek Myth,* 72.

29. Percy, *Pederasty,* 80–92; Dover, *Greek Homosexuality,* 73–100; Cohen, *Laws,* 194–195.

30. Sergent, *Homosexuality in Greek Myth,* 71.

31. Philip Slater, *The Glory of Hera* (Boston: Beacon Press, 1968), 11.

32. Slater, ibid., investigates this theme in his general discussion of the condition of women in ancient Greece.

33. See especially Sergent, *Homosexuality in Greek Myth,* 16–54.

34. Cohen explores the very complexities of these legal codes in Athens, and notes that in other city-states, there was a tendency for pederasty to be either completely accepted or rejected (*Law,* 180).

35. Sergent, *Homosexuality in Greek Myth,* 72, 82.

36. Rape equals penetration; penetration makes the victim a woman; women have no rights; sexual penetration equals the loss of substantial rights for any male citizen. Dover, *Greek Homosexuality,* 104–6, describes homosexual penetration as an expression of domination.

37. Percy, *Pederasty,* 64–72; Jan Bremmer, "An Enigmatic Indo-Europdean Rite: Paederasty," *Arethusa* 13, no. 2 (1980): 279–98.

38. Percy, *Pederasty,* 84–85.

39. Graves, *The Greek Myths,* 1:118.

40. Cohen, *Law,* 198.

41. Graves, *The Greek Myths,* 2:42.

42. Dover, *Greek Homosexuality,* 81–109; Cohen, *Law,* 196–200.

43. Graves, *The Greek Myths,* 2:41–42.

44. Licht, *Sexual Life,* 135.

45. Graves, citing the Scholiast on Euripides's *Phoenician Women,* Plutarch's *Parallel Stories,* Hyginus's *Fabulae,* and the Scholiast on Euripides's *Orestes,* 2:42.

46. Jean-Pierre Vernant, *Myth and Tragedy in Ancient Greece,* trans. Janet Lloyd (New York: Zone Books, 1988), 212.

47. Ibid., 71–72.

48. Seymour Chatman, *Story and Discourse,* (Ithaca, N.Y. : Cornell University Press, 1978).

49. Eugene O'Neill, Jr., "General Introduction," in *The Complete Greek Drama: All the Extant Tragedies of Aeschylus, Sophocles and Euripides, and the Comedies of Aristophanes and Menander, In a Variety of Translations,* ed. Whitney J. Oates and Eugene O'Neill, Jr., vol. 1 (New York: Random House, 1938), xxix, xxx, xxxii.

50. Constans, 35–42, in Masson, *Letters,* 304. Constans begins his discussion of Laius and the "beau fils de Pelops, Chrysippe," on page 11. Constans writes: "Eschyle semble en avoir traite toutes les parties. Welcker a constitue trois trilogies se rapportant a ce cycle avec les tragedies completes que nous avons de lui, et celles don't il ne nous reste que des fragments: 1° *Laius,* le *Sphinx, Oedipe;* 2° *Nemea,* les *Sept contre Thebes,* les *Phoeniciennes;* 3° les *Eleusiniens,* les *Argiens,* les *Epigones*" (17). A bit further, after rehearsing the standard Oedipus tale, Constans writes: "Cependant Laïus etait parti de Thèbes pour aller consulter le Pythie au sujet du fléau qui désolait la ville. Suivant le Pseudo-Pisandre (. . . .), le Sphinx aurait été envoyé aux Thébains par Junon du fond de l'Éthiopie, parce qu'ils n'avaient point puni Lauïs de son amour infame pour le beau Chrysippe, qu'il avait enlevé de Pise, abusant de l'hospitalité de Pélops, son père, et donnant le premier l'example d'un amour contre nature. L'enfant se tua de désespoir; son père Pelops maudit l'auteir de ce crime, Laïus, et l'effet de cette malédiction se porta sur le fils at les petit-fils de ce prince" (26).

51. Ruth Scodel, *Sophocles* (Boston: Twayne Publishers, 1984), 7–8; Licht, *Sexual Life,* 136–37; R. G. A. Buxton, *Sophocles* (Oxford: Oxford University Press, 1984), 4–5.

52. Lucy Byrne, "Fear in the Seven against Thebes," in *Rape in Antiquity,* ed. Susan Deacy and Karen F. Pierce (London: Duckworth, 1997), 143–62. Cohen citing Vlastos suggests the same thing; see *Law,* 198.

53. Constans, in Masson, *Letters,* 26.

Notes to Chapter Seven

1. See, for example, Percy, "Sexual Revolution," 380.

2. Florence Rush, *The Best Kept Secret: Sexual Abuse of Children* (Englewood Cliffs, N.J.: Prentice-Hall, 1980), 53.

3. As I mentioned in a note in chapter 5, when attempting to tally the instances the encyclopedic Graves records of such activities, I stopped at 50, well before the end of both his volumes of Greek mythology. Rush, ibid., discusses Talmudic and Christian arrangements for the sexual use of children by adults, including through child "marriage" (16–73). Gordon, *Heroes,* observed the "ordinariness" of incest in the Boston social work case histories she reviewed as well (227). Where incest was once considered an extremely rare occurrence, recently

we have come to see evidence of its being a much more widespread practice, in many cases condoned or accepted by nonoffending adult partners. See Louise Armstrong, *Rocking the Cradle of Sexual Politics: What Happened When Women Said Incest* (Reading, Mass.: Addison-Wesley, 1994); Herman, *Father-Daughter Incest;* Barbara G. Tabachnick and Kenneth Pope, "Therapist Responses to Recovered and Never-Forgotten Memories of Child Sex Abuse: A National Survey of Licensed Psychologists, *Violence Against Women,* 3, no. 4 (August 1997): 348–60. On treatment issues, see Christine Courtois, "Healing the Incest Wound: A Treatment Update with Attention to Recovered Memory Issues," *American Journal of Psychotherapy* 51, no. 4 (Fall 1997): 464–96; Tracy Robinson, "Making the Hurt Go Away: Psychological and Spiritual Healing for African American Women Survivors of Childhood Incest," *Journal of Multicultural Counseling and Development* 28 (July 2000), 160–76. For a historical perspective, see chapters 2 and 3.

4. Freud, "Freud on Oedipus," in *Oedipus: A Folklore Casebook,* ed. Lowell Edmunds and Alan Dundes (New York: Garland Press, 1983), 176–77.

5. See, for example, Russell, *The Secret Trauma,* esp. 231–68; also *Sexual Exploitation: Rape, Child Sexual Abuse, and Workplace Harrassment* (Beverly Hills: Sage Publications, 1987); Herman, *Father-Daughter Incest;* Rush, *The Best-Kept Secret;* David Finkelhor, *Child Sexual Abuse* (New York: The Free Press, 1984); Ward, *Father-Daughter Rape.*

6. See, for example, Russell, ibid., 194–98; Mic Hunter, *Abused Boys: The Neglected Victims of Sexual Abuse* (Lexington: D. C. Heath, 1990); Bass and Davis, *The Courage to Heal.*

7. Herman and Hirschman, "Father Daughter Incest," 262.

8. Freud, "Freud on Oedipus," 177.

9. Eva Keuls, *The Reign of the Phallus in Ancient Athens* (New York: Harper and Row, 1985); Sarah Pomeroy, *Goddesses, Wives, Slaves, and Whores: Women in Classical Antiquity* (New York: Schocken Books, 1975).

10. Girard discusses this dynamic in *The Scapegoat* (Baltimore: Johns Hopkins University Press, 1986). Ida B. Wells also made this the centerpiece of the evidence in her antilynching crusade in the United States of the 1890s. White Southern town newspapers often published both threats of lynchings and accounts of who carried them out because such men were the elected and unelected leaders of the community, and thus feared no reprisals.

11. Herman and Hirschman, "Father Daughter Incest," 36–63.

12. Dana Ferrin Sutton, *The Lost Sophocles* (Lanham, Md.: University Press of America, 1984), 143–44.

13. Girard, *The Scapegoat,* 1–23.

14. Rank, *Das Inzestmotiv,* 330–37; on Pelopia and the alleged mistaken identity, 323.

15. Graves, *The Greek Myths,* 2:45–48, emphasis added.

16. Rank, *Das Inzestmotiv,* 323.

17. Graves, *The Greek Myths,* 2:48.

18. Herman; Gordon, *Heroes;* van der Heijden, *Women as Victims.*

19. This is consistent with Gordon and van der Heijden, *Women as Victims.*

20. Graves, *The Greek Myths,* 1:69–71.

21. Rank, *Der Inzestmotiv,* 303.

22. Graves, *The Greek Myths,* 1:72.

23. Graves, *The Greek Myths,* 2:9–15.

24. Mary Foertsch (Marcel), *The Rhetoric of Feminist Object Relations Psychoanalysis: Chodorow, Greek Myth, and the U.S. Women's Movement* (Ph.D. dissertation, University of California at Berkeley, 1990).

25. Rudnytsky, *Freud and Oedipus,* 3–17.

26. "The Psychogenesis of a Case of Homosexuality in a Woman (1920)," in *The Standard Edition of the Complete Pyschological Works of Sigmund Freud,* vol. 18, trans. James Strachey et al. (London: Hogarth Press, 1962), 155.

Notes to Chapter Eight

1. Herman, *Trauma and Recovery,* 19.

2. Larry Wolff, *Postcards from the End of the World: Child Abuse in Freud's Vienna* (New York: Atheneum, 1988).

3. The closest might be Cupid, or Adonis, the child of father-daughter incest and the object of female desire as a child.

4. Cohen makes clear that forced sex with children in general seems to fall within the category of "hubris," or outrage, and thus would be prosecutable. See *Law,* 174–201; "Law," 6–9; and "Sexuality, Violence, and the Athenian Law of 'Hubris,' " *Greece and Rome,* 2nd ser. 38 (October 1991): 171–88.

5. Herman and Hirschman, "Father-Daughter Incest," 262.

Bibliography

Ahl, Frederick. *Sophocles' Oedipus: Evidence and Self-Conviction.* Ithaca, N.Y.: Cornell University Press, 1991.

Amada, Gerald. Review of *From Freud's Consulting Room: The Unconscious in a Scientific Age,* by Judith M. Hughes. *American Journal of Psychotherapy* 49, no. 3 (1995): 464–65.

Anderson, S. C. , C. M. Bach and S. Griffith. "Psychosocial Sequelae in Intrafamilial Victims of Sexual Assault and Abuse." Paper presented at the Third International Conference on Child Abuse and Neglect, Amsterdam, The Netherlands, 1981.

Anonymous. "Is Anatomy Really Destiny, Dr. Freud? — Freud and His Critics." *The Economist* 328, no. 7826 (1993): 83–84.

Anzieu, Didier. *Freud's Self-Analysis.* Translated by Peter Graham. London: Hogarth Press and the Institute of Psychoanalysis, 1986.

Apollodorus. *The Library of Greek Mythology.* Translated by Keith Aldrich. Lawrence, Kan.: Coronado Press, 1975.

Aristotle. *The "Art" of Rhetoric.* Translated by J. Freese. Cambridge, Mass.: Harvard University Press, 1926.

Armstrong, Louise. *Rocking the Cradle of Sexual Politics: What Happened When Women Said Incest.* Reading, Mass.: Addison-Wesley, 1994.

Ashby, LeRoy. *Dependency, Neglect and Abuse in American History.* New York: Twayne, 1997.

Balmary, Marie. *Psychoanalyzing Psychoanalysis: Freud and the Hidden Fault of the Father.* Translated by Ned Lukacher. Baltimore: Johns Hopkins University Press, 1982.

Bass, Ellen, and Laura Davis. *The Courage to Heal.* New York: Harper and Row, 1988.

Behlmer, Charles. *Child Abuse and Reform in England, 1870–1908.* Stanford, Calif.: Stanford University Press, 1982.

Bernard, Paul. *Des attentats à la pudeur sur les petites filles.* Paris: Octave Doin, 1886.

Bernfield, Siegfried, and Suzanne Cassirer Bernfield. "Freud's Early Childhood." *Bulletin of the Menninger Clinic* 8 (1964): 107–15.

Bernheimer, Charles, and Claire Kahane, eds. *In Dora's Case: Freud-Hysteria-Feminism.* New York: Columbia University Press, 1985.

Berrick, Jill Duerr, and Neil Gilbert. *With the Best of Intentions: The Child Sexual Abuse Prevention Movement.* New York: Guilford Press, 1991.

Bethe, E. "Die dorische Knabenliebe, ihre Ethic, ihre Idee." *Rheinische Museum* 62 (1907): 438–75.

Breger, Louis. *Freud: Darkness in the Midst of Vision.* New York: John Wiley and Sons, 2000.

Bremmer, Jan. "An Enigmatic Indo-European Rite: Paederasty." *Arethusa* 13:2 (1980): 279–298.

Briere, John. *Child Abuse Trauma: Theory and Treatment of the Lasting Effects.* Newbury Park, Calif.: Sage, 1992.

Brodsky, Annette M., and Rachel T. Hare-Mustin. *Women and Psychotherapy: An Assessment of Research and Practice.* New York: Guilford Press, 1979.

Brody, Benjamin. "Freud's Caseload." *Psychotherapy: Theory, Research and Practice* 7 (Spring 1970): 8–12.

Brookhiser, Richard. "The Final Analysis." *National Review* 50, no. 22 (1998): 41–44.

Brouardel, Paul. *Les Attentats aux Moeurs.* Paris: J. B. Ballière, 1909.

Brunner, Jose. *Freud and the Politics of Psychoanalysis.* New Brunswick, N.J.: Transaction, 2001.

Burke, Kenneth. *The Rhetoric of Religion.* Berkeley and Los Angeles: University of California Press, 1968.

Butler, Eliza. *The Tyranny of Greece over Germany: A Study of the Influence Exercised by Greek Art and Poetry over the Great German Writers of the Eighteenth, Nineteenth, and Twentieth Centuries.* Boston: Beacon Press, 1925.

Buxton, R. G. A. *Sophocles.* Oxford: Oxford University Press, 1984.

Byrne, Lucy. "Fear in the *Seven against Thebes.*" In *Rape in Antiquity,* ed. Susan Deacy and Karen F. Pierce, 143–62. London: Duckworth, in association with the Classical Press of Wales, 1997.

Chatman, Seymour. *Story and Discourse.* Ithaca, N.Y.: Cornell University Press, 1978.

Chu, James A. *Rebuilding Shattered Lives: The Responsible Treatment of Complex Post-Traumatic and Dissociative Disorders.* New York: John Wiley and Sons, 1998.

Cicchetti, Dante, and Vicki Carlson, eds. *Child Maltreatment: Theory and Practice on the Causes and Consequences of Child Abuse and Neglect.* Cambridge: Cambridge University Press, 1989.

Cohen, David J. *Law, Sexuality and Society: The Enforcement of Morals in Classical Athens.* Cambridge: Cambridge University Press, 1991.

———. "Law, Society and Homosexuality in Ancient Athens." *Past and Present* 117 (1987): 1–21.

———. "Sexuality, Violence, and the Athenian Law of 'Hubris,'" *Greece and Rome*, 2nd ser. 38 (October 1991): 171–88.

Constans, Leopold. *La Légende d'Œdipe: Étudiée dans l'antiquité au Moyen Âge et dans les Temps Modernes en Particulier dans Le Roman de Thèbes.* Geneva: Slatkine Reprints, 1974; originally published 1886.

Courtois, Christine. "Healing the Incest Wound: A Treatment Update with Attention to Recovered Memory Issues." *American Journal of Psychotherapy* 51 (Fall 1997): 464–96.

Crews, Frederick. *The Memory Wars: Freud's Legacy in Dispute.* New York: New York Review of Books, 1995.

Davies, G. "Research on Children's Testimony: Implications for Interviewing Practice." In *Clinical Approaches to Sex Offenders and Their Victims,* ed. Clive R. Hollin and Kevin Howells, 93–115. Chichester, N.Y.: John Wiley, 1991.

Dawes, Robyn. *House of Cards: Psychology and Psychotherapy Built on Myth.* New York: Free Press, 1994.

Deacy, Susan, and Karen F. Pierce, eds. *Rape in Antiquity.* London: Duckworth, in association with the Classical Press of Wales, 1997.

DeFrancis, V. *Protecting the Child Victim of Sex Crimes Committed by Adults.* Denver: American Humane Association, 1969.

deMause, Lloyd, ed. *The Evolution of Childhood.* New York: Psychohistory Press, 1974.

———. "The Universality of Incest." *The Journal of Psychohistory* 19, no. 2 (1991): 28 pages. Available at http://www.psychohistory.com.htm.06a1 incest.html; accessed June 24, 2002.

Devereux, George. "Why Oedipus Killed Laius: A Note on the Complementary Oedipus Complex in Greek Drama." In *Oedipus: A Folklore Casebook,* ed. Lowell Edmunds and Alan Dundes, 215–33. New York: Garland, 1983.

Dorne, Clifford. *Crimes against Children.* New York: Harrow and Heston, 1989.

Dover, K. J. *Greek Homosexuality.* Cambridge, Mass.: Harvard University Press, 1977.

Downing, Christine. *Mythos and Mysteries of Same-Sex Love.* New York: Continuum, 1989.

Dynes, Wayne, and Stephen Donaldson, eds. *Homosexuality in the Ancient World.* New York: Garland, 1992.

Eber, Alfred. *Die Blutschande: Eine kriminilogische Untersuchung unter besonderer Berucksichtigung der Tatsituation.* Liepzig: E. Wiegandt Verlagsbuchhandlung, 1937.

Edelson, Marshall. *Psychoanalysis: A Theory in Crisis.* Chicago: University of Chicago Press, 1988.

Edmunds, Lowell, and Alan Dundes, eds. *Oedipus: A Folklore Casebook.* New York: Garland, 1983.

Esterson, Allen. *Seductive Mirage: An Exploration of the Work of Sigmund Freud.* Chicago: Open Court, 1993.

Faller, K. Coullborn. *Understanding Child Sexual Maltreatment.* Newbury Park, Calif.: Sage, 1990.

Feldstein, Richard, and Judith Roof, eds. *Feminism and Psychoanalysis.* Ithaca, N.Y.: Cornell University Press, 1989.

Fel Tham, Colin. "Facing, Understanding and Learning from Critiques of Psychotherapy and Counselling." *British Journal of Guidance and Counselling* 27, no. 3 (1999): 310–11.

Finkelhor, David. *Child Sexual Abuse.* New York: The Free Press, 1984.

———. *Sexually Victimized Children.* New York: The Free Press, 1979.

Finkelhor, David, Richard Gelles, Gerald Hotaling and Murray Straus, eds. *The Dark Side of Families: Current Family Violence Research.* Beverly Hills, Calif.: Sage, 1983.

Foertsch (Marcel), Mary. *The Rhetoric of Feminist Object Relations Psychoanalysis: Chodorow, Greek Myth, and the U.S. Women's Movement.* Ph.D. Dissertation, University of California, Berkeley, 1990.

Fournier, Alfred. "Simulation d'attentats vénériens sur de jeunes enfants." *Annales d'hygiène publique et de médecine légale* 4, no. 6 (1880): 498–519.

Freeman, Elizabeth. "Honeymoon with a Stranger: Pedophiliac Picaresques from Poe to Nabokov." *American Literature* 70, no. 4 (1998): 863–97.

Freud, Sigmund. "The Aetiology of Hysteria." In *Standard Edition of the Works of Sigmund Freud,* vol. 3, translated by Alix Strachey, 189–221. London: The Hogarth Press and the Institute of Psycho-analysis, 1962.

———. "Charcot." In *Standard Edition of the Works of Sigmund Freud,* vol. 3, translated by Alix Strachey, 9–23. London: The Hogarth Press and the Institute of Psycho-analysis, 1962.

———. *Civilization and Its Discontents.* In *Standard Edition of the Complete Psychological Works of Sigmund Freud,* vol. 21, translated by James Strachey et al., 59–145. London: Hogarth Press and the Institute of Psycho-analysis, 1961.

———. *The Complete Letters of Sigmund Freud to Wilhelm Fliess 1887–1904.* Translated and edited by Jeffrey M. Masson. Cambridge, Mass.: Belknap Press of Harvard University Press, 1985.

———. *The Interpretation of Dreams* (1900) reprinted in *The Basic Writings of Sigmund Freud,* translated and edited by A. A. Brill. New York: Random House, 1938.

———. "On the Psychical Mechanism of Hysterical Phenomena." In *Standard Edition of the Complete Works of Sigmund Freud,* vol. 3, 27–39, translated by Alix Strachey. London: Hogarth Press and the Institute of Psycho-analysis, 1962.

———. "An Outline of Psychoanalysis." In *Standard Edition of the Complete Works of Sigmund Freud,* vol. 23, 141–207, translated by James Strachey et al. London: Hogarth Press and the Institute of Psycho-analysis, 1962.

———. "The Psychogenesis of a Case of Homosexuality in a Woman" (1920). In *The Standard Edition of the Complete Psychological Works of Sigmund Freud,* vol. 18, translated by James Strachey et al., 145–71. London: Hogarth Press and the Institute of Psycho-analysis, 1962.

———. "The Psychotherapy of Hysteria." In *Standard Edition of the Complete Works of Sigmund Freud,* vol. 2, translated by James Strachey et al., 255–305. London: Hogarth Press and the Institute of Psycho-analysis, 1955.

———. "Screen Memories." In *The Standard Edition of the Complete Psychological Works of Sigmund Freud,* vol. 3, translated by James Strachey et al., 301–22. London: Hogarth Press and the Institute of Psycho-analysis, 1962.

———. *Die Traumdeutung,* 8th rev. ed. Leipzig: Franz Deuticke, 1930.

Friedrich, W. N., A. J. Urquiza and R. Beilke. "Behavioral Problems in Sexually Abused Young Children." *Journal of Pediatric Psychology* 11 (1986): 47–57.

Fromm, Erich. *The Forgotten Language: An Introduction to the Language of Dreams, Fairy Tales and Myths.* New York: Grove Weidenfeld, 1951.

———. *Sigmund Freud's Mission: An Analysis of His Personality and Influence.* New York: Harper and Brothers, 1959.

Gallagher, Sister Vera. *Speaking Out, Fighting Back: Women Who Have Survived Child Sexual Abuse in the Home.* Seattle: Madrona Publishers, 1985.

Garcia, Emanuel, ed. *Understanding Freud: The Man and His Ideas.* New York: New York University Press, 1992.

Gardiner, Richard A. *Sex Abuse Hysteria: Salem Witch Trials Revisited.* Cresskill, N.J.: Creative Therapeutics, 1991.

Gay, Peter. *Freud: A Life for Our Time.* New York: W. W. Norton, 1988.

Gebhart, Hans-Ulrich. *Der Inzest im Schweiz. Strafrecht mit einem Verblick über seine strafrechtliche Behandlung in der Vergangenheit.* Zurich: Buchdruckerei Stampfenbach AG, 1947.

Gilman, Sander. *The Case of Sigmund Freud: Medicine and Identity at the Fin de Siècle.* Baltimore: Johns Hopkins University Press, 1993.

Girard, Rene. *Deceit, Desire and the Novel: Self and Other in Literary Structure.* Translated by Yvonne Freccero. Baltimore: Johns Hopkins University Press, 1965.

———. *The Scapegoat.* Translated by Yvonne Freccero. Baltimore: Johns Hopkins University Press, 1986.

———. *Violence and the Sacred.* Translated by Patrick Gregory. Baltimore: Johns Hopkins University Press, 1977.

Gordon, Linda. *Heroes of Their Own Lives: The Politics and History of Family Violence.* New York: Viking Penguin, 1988.

Graves, Robert. *The Greek Myths.* 2 vols. London: Penguin, 1955.

Green, Andre. *The Tragic Effect: The Oedipus Complex in Tragedy.*

Translated by Alan Sheridan. Cambridge: Cambridge University Press, 1979.

Greene, William Chase. *Moira: Fate, Good and Evil in Greek Thought.* New York: Harper Torchbooks, 1944.

Grünbaum, Adolf. *The Foundations of Psychoanalysis: A Philosophical Critique.* Berkeley and Los Angeles: University of California Press, 1984.

Halperin, David, John Winkler and Froma Zeitlin, eds. *Before Sexuality: The Construction of Erotic Experience in the Ancient Greek World.* Princeton, N.J.: Princeton University Press, 1990.

Hartman, Carol, and Ann Burgess. "Sexual Abuse of Children: Causes and Consequences." In *Child Maltreatment: Theory and Research on the Causes and Consequences of Child Abuse and Neglect,* edited by Dante Cicchetti and Vicki Carlson, 95–128. Cambridge: Cambridge University Press, 1989.

Harvey, Mary, and Judith Herman. "Amnesia, Partial Amnesia and Delayed Recall among Adult Survivors of Childhood Trauma." *Consciousness and Cognition* 3 (1994): 295–306.

von Hentig, Hans, and Theodor Viernstein. *Untersuchungen über den Inzest.* Heidelberg: Carl Winters Universitätsbuchhandlung, 1925.

Herman, Judith Lewis. "Crime and Memory." In *Trauma and Self,* edited by Charles B. Strozier and Michael Flynn, 3–17. Lanham, Md.: Rowman and Littlefield, 1996.

———. *Father-Daughter Incest.* Cambridge, Mass.: Harvard University Press, 1981.

———. *Trauma and Recovery: The Aftermath of Terror — From Domestic Abuse to Political Terror.* New York: Basic Books, 1992.

Herman, Judith, and Linda Hirschman. "Father-Daughter Incest." In *The Signs Reader: Women, Gender and Scholarship,* edited by Elizabeth Abel and Emily K. Abel, 257–78. Chicago: University of Chicago Press, 1983.

Herman, Judith, Diana Russell and Karen Trocki. "Long-Term Effects of Incestuous Abuse in Childhood." *American Journal of Psychiatry* 143 (October 1986): 1293–96.

Hooper, Carol-Ann. "Child Sexual Abuse and the Regulation of Women: Variations on a Theme." In *Regulating Motherhood: Historical Essays on Marriage, Motherhood and Sexuality,* edited by Carol Smart, 53–77. New York: Routledge, 1992.

Hughes, Judith. *From Freud's Consulting Room: The Unconscious in a Scientific Age*. Cambridge, Mass.: Harvard University Press, 1994.

Hunter, Mic. *Abused Boys: The Neglected Victims of Sexual Abuse*. Lexington, Mass.: Lexington Books, 1990.

Izenberg, Gerald N. "Seduced and Abandoned: The Rise and Fall of Freud's Seduction Theory." In *The Cambridge Companion to Freud*, edited by Jerome Neu, 25–43. Cambridge: Cambridge University Press, 1991.

Jackson, Louise. *Child Sexual Abuse in Victorian England*. London: Routledge, 2002.

Johnson, Miriam. *Strong Mothers, Weak Wives: The Search for Gender Equality*. Berkeley and Los Angeles: University of California Press, 1988.

Johnston, Moira. *Spectral Evidence — The Ramona Case: Incest, Memory and Truth on Trial in Napa Valley*. Boston: Houghton Mifflin, 1997.

Jones, Ernest. *Hamlet and Oedipus*. New York: Norton, 1949.

———. *The Life and Work of Sigmund Freud*, 3 vols. New York: Basic Books, 1953.

Justice, Blair, and Rita Justice. *The Broken Taboo: Sex in the Family*. New York: Human Sciences Press, 1979.

Kahr, Brett. "The Sexual Molestation of Children: Historical Perspectives." *The Journal of Psychohistory* 19 (Fall 1991): 191–214.

Kendall, P. C. "Social Cognition and Problem Solving: A Developmental and Child-Clinical Interface." In *Applications of Cognitive-Developmental Theory*, edited by B. Gholson and T. C. Rosenthal. New York: Academic Press, 1984.

Keuls, Eva. *The Reign of the Phallus: Sexual Politics in Ancient Athens*. New York: Harper and Row, 1985.

Kofman, Sarah. *The Enigma of Woman: Woman in Freud's Writings*. Translated by Catherine Porter. Ithaca, N.Y.: Cornell University Press, 1985.

Kretz, Irmgard, Ricki Reichel and Marguerite Zoechling. *Sexual Abuse of Children in Austria*. Vienna: Federal Ministry for Environment, Youth and Family, 1988.

Krüll, Marianne. *Freud and His Father*. Translated by Arnold J. Pomerans. New York: Norton, 1979.

Kurzweil, Edith. "One Hundred Years of Seductions." *Partisan Review* 65, no. 2 (1998): 185–94.

Lacassagne, Alexandre. "Attentats à la Pudeur sur les Petites Filles." In *Archives d'Anthropologie Criminelle et de Sciences Pénales* 1 (1886): 59–68.

Lakoff, Robin Tolmach, and Mandy Aftel. "In the Malcolm Archives." *The Nation*, December 16, 1996, 32–35.

Lear, Jonathan. "The Shrink Is In." *The New Republic*, December 25, 1995, 18–27.

Letters, F. J. H. *The Life and Work of Sophocles.* London: Sheed and Ward, 1953.

Licht, Hans. *Sexual Life in Ancient Greece.* Translated by J. H. Freese. London: Constable, 1994.

Marcel, Alejandro. Personal communication, June 2001.

Masson, Jeffrey Moussaieff. *Against Therapy: Emotional Tyranny and the Myth of Psychological Healing.* New York: Atheneum, 1988.

———. *The Assault on the Truth: Freud's Suppression of the Seduction Theory.* New York: Farrar, Straus and Giroux, 1984.

———. *A Dark Science: Women, Sexuality and Psychiatry in the Nineteenth Century.* New York: Farrar, Straus and Giroux, 1986.

McNaron, Toni, and Yarrow Morgan, eds. *Voices in the Night: Women Speaking about Incest.* Minneapolis: Cleis Press, 1982.

McOmber, James. "Silencing the Patient: Freud, Sexual Abuse, and the 'Etiology of Hysteria.'" *Quarterly Journal of Speech* 82 (1996): 343–63.

Miller, Alice. *For Your Own Good: Hidden Cruelty in Child-Rearing and the Roots of Violence.* Translated by Hildegarde and Hunter Hannum. New York: Noonday, 1990.

———. *Thou Shalt Not Be Aware: Society's Betrayal of the Child.* Translated by Hildegarde and Hunter Hannum. New York: Farrar, Straus and Giroux, 1984.

———. *The Untouched Key: Tracing Childhood Trauma in Creativity and Destructiveness.* Translated by Hildegarde and Hunter Hannum. New York: Doubleday, 1990.

Morris, Michelle. *If I Should Die Before I Wake.* New York: Dell, 1982.

Mrazek, Patricia Beezley, and C. Henry Kempe, eds. *Sexually Abused Children and Their Families.* Oxford: Pergamon, 1987.

Mullahy, Patrick. *Oedipus, Myth and Complex: A Review of Psychoanalytic Theory.* New York: Grove Press, 1955.

Neu, Jerome, ed. *The Cambridge Companion to Freud.* Cambridge: Cambridge University Press, 1991.

Newton, Peter. *Freud: From Youthful Dream to Mid-Life Crisis.* New York: Guilford Press, 1995.

Nussbaum, Martha C. "The Oedipus Rex and the Ancient Unconscious." In *Freud and Forbidden Knowledge,* ed. Peter Rudnytsky and Ellen Handler Spitz. New York: New York University, 1994.

O'Neill, Jr., Eugene. "General Introduction." In *The Complete Greek Drama: All the Extant Tragedies of Aeschylus, Sophocles and Euripides, and the Comedies of Aristophanes and Menander, in a Variety of Translations,* edited by Whitney J. Oates and Eugene O'Neill, Jr., xiii–xlix. New York: Random House, 1938.

Ostow, Mortimer, Marica Cavell, Allen Esterson and Colin McGinn. "'Freud under Analysis': An Exchange." *The New York Review of Books,* February 24, 2000, 46–48.

Pagelow, Mildred Daley, and Lloyd Pagelow. *Family Violence.* New York: Praeger, 1984.

Percy, William A. *Pederasty and Pedagogy in Archaic Greece.* Urbana: University of Illinois Press, 1996.

———. "Sexual Revolution 600 B.C.–400 A.D.: The Origins of Institutionalized Pederasty in Greece." Reprinted in *Homosexuality in the Ancient World,* edited by Wayne Dynes and Stephen Donaldson, 375–80. New York: Garland, 1992.

Pomeroy, Sarah. *Goddesses, Wives, Slaves, and Whores: Women in Classical Antiquity.* New York: Schocken Books, 1975.

Porter, Ray. "Madness and the Family before Freud: The View of the Mad-Doctors." *Journal of Family History* 23, no. 2 (1998): 159–72.

Poston, Carol, and Karen Lison. *Reclaiming Our Lives: Hope for Adult Survivors of Incest.* Boston: Little, Brown and Co., 1989.

Pucci, Pietro. *Oedipus and the Fabrication of the Father: Oedipus Tyrannus in Modern Criticism and Philosophy.* Baltimore: Johns Hopkins University Press, 1992.

Rank, Otto. *Das Inzestmotiv in Dichtung und Sage: Fundamentals of a Psychology of Literary Creation.* Translated by Gregory Richter. Baltimore: Johns Hopkins University Press, 1992. Originally published in 1912.

Reviere, Susan. *Memory of Childhood Trauma: A Clinician's Guide to the Literature.* New York: Guilford Press, 1996.

Robinson, Tracy. "Making the Hurt Go Away: Psychological and Spiritual Healing for African American Women Survivors of Childhood Incest." *Journal of Multicultural Counseling and Development* 28 (July 2000): 160–76.

Rudnytsky, Peter. *Freud and Oedipus.* New York: New York University Press, 1987.

Rudnytsky, Peter, and Ellen Handler Spitz, eds. *Freud and Forbidden Knowledge.* New York: New York University Press, 1994.

Rush, Florence. *The Best Kept Secret: Sexual Abuse of Children.* Englewood Cliffs, N.J.: Prentice-Hall, 1980.

Russell, Diane E. H. *The Secret Trauma: Incest in the Lives of Girls and Women.* New York: Basic Books, 1986.

———. *Sexual Exploitation: Rape, Child Sexual Abuse, and Workplace Harassment.* Beverly Hills, Calif.: Sage, 1984.

Rycroft, Charles. *Viewpoints.* London: The Hogarth Press, 1991.

Sachs, David. "In Fairness to Freud: A Critical Notice of *The Foundations of Psychoanalysis.*" In *The Cambridge Companion to Freud,* ed. Jerome Neu, 309–38. Cambridge: Cambridge University Press, 1991.

Sajner, Josef. "Drei dokumentarische Beiträge zur Sigmund Freud-Biographik aus Böhmen und Mähren." *Jahrbuch der Psychanalyse* 13 (1981): 143–52.

———. "Sigmund Freuds Beziehungen zu seinem Geburtsort Freiberg und zu Mähren." *Clio Medica* 3 (1968): 167–80.

Sangster, Joan. "Masking and Unmasking the Sexual Abuse of Children: Perceptions of Violence against Children in 'The Badlands' of Ontario, 1916–1930." *Journal of Family History* 25, no. 4 (2000): 504–26.

Schatzman, Morton. *Soul Murder: Persecution in the Family.* New York: Random House, 1973.

Schimek, J. et al. "The Unknown Freud: An Exchange." *The New York Review of Books,* February 3, 1994, 34–48.

Schneider, Hans Joachim. "Sexual Abuse of Children: Strengths and Weaknesses of Current Criminology." *International Journal of Offender Therapy and Comparative Criminology* 41, no. 4 (1997): 310–24.

Scodel, Ruth. *Sophocles.* Boston: Twayne, 1984.

Sergent, Bernard. *Homosexuality in Greek Myth.* Translated by Arthur Goldhammer. Boston: Beacon Press, 1984.

Shapiro, Barbara. *Probability and Certainty in Seventeenth Century England: A Study of the Relationships between Science, Religion, History, Law and Literature.* Princeton, N.J.: Princeton University Press, 1983.

Showalter, Elaine. *The Female Malady: Women, Madness, and English Culture, 1830–1980.* New York: Pantheon Books, 1985.

Simon, Bennett. *Mind and Madness in Ancient Greece: The Classical Roots of Modern Psychiatry.* Ithaca, N.Y.: Cornell University Press, 1978.

Simon, Bennett, and Rachel Blass. "The Development and Vicissitudes of Freud's Ideas on the Oedipus Complex." In *The Cambridge Companion to Freud,* edited by Jerome Neu, 161–74. Cambridge: Cambridge University Press, 1991.

Simpson, Anthony E. "Criminal Law: The 'Blackmail Myth' and the Prosecution of Rape and Its Attempt in Eighteenth-Century London: The Creation of a Legal Tradition." *Northwestern School of Law Journal of Criminal Law and Criminology* 77 (101), accessed via Lexis June 7, 2001, 40 pages.

———. "Vulnerability and the Age of Female Consent: Legal Innovation and Its Effect on Prosecutions for Rape in Eighteenth-Century London." In *Sexual Underworlds of the Enlightenment,* edited by G. S. Rousseau and Roy Porter, 181–205. Manchester: Manchester University Press, 1987.

Singer, Jerome, ed. *Repression and Dissociation: Implications for Theory, Psychopathology, and Health.* Chicago: University of Chicago Press, 1990.

Slater, Philip. *The Glory of Hera: Greek Mythology and the Greek Family.* Boston: Beacon Press, 1968.

Smith, Joseph H., and Morris, Humphrey, eds. *Telling Facts: History and Narration in Psychoanalysis.* Baltimore: Johns Hopkins University Press, 1992.

Sprengnether, Madelon. "Mourning Freud." In *Psychoanalyses/Feminisms,* edited by Peter Rudnytsky and Andrew M. Gordon, 11–37. Albany: SUNY Press, 2000.

———. *The Spectral Mother: Freud, Feminism, and Psychoanalysis.* Ithaca, N.Y.: Cornell University Press, 1990.

Stewart, Harold. "Jocasta's Crimes." *International Journal of Psychoanalysis* 42 (1961): 424–30.

Stone, Alan A. Review of *House of Cards: Psychology and Psychotherapy*

Built on Myth, by Robyn Dawes. *The American Journal of Psychiatry* 152, no. 7 (1995): 1090–91.

Strozier, Charles, and Michael Flynn, eds. *Trauma and Self.* Lanham, Md.: Rowman and Littlefield, 1996.

Sulloway, Frank J. *Freud: Biologist of the Mind: Beyond the Psychoanalytic Legend.* Cambridge, Mass.: Harvard University Press, 1979.

Suttie, Ian. *The Origins of Love and Hate.* Reprint of the 1935 edition with new prefaces by John Bowlby and Dorothy Heard. London: Free Association Books, 1988.

Sutton, Dana. *The Lost Sophocles.* Lanham, Md.: University Press of America, 1984.

Tabachnick, Barbara G., and Kenneth Pope. "Therapist Responses to Recovered and Never-Forgotten Memories of Child Sex Abuse: A National Survey of Licensed Psychologists." *Violence against Women* 3 (August 1997): 348–60.

Tardieu, Ambroise. "Étude Médico-Légale sur les Sévices et Mauvais Traitements Exercés sur des Enfants." In *Annales d'hygiène publique et de médicine légale,* 2nd ser., 13 (1860): 361–98.

Thoinot, L. *Medicolegal Aspects of Moral Offenses.* Translated by Arthur Weysse. Philadelphia: F. A. Davis, 1916.

Thornton, Bruce. *Eros: The Myth of Ancient Greek Sexuality.* Boulder: Westview Press, 1997.

Thucydides. *The History of the Peloponnesian War.* Translated by Rex Warner. London: Penguin Books, 1954.

Thurschwell, Pamela. "Ferenczi's Dangerous Proximities: Telepathy, Psychosis, and the Real Event." *Differences* 11, no. 1 (1999): 150–78.

Tierney, Kathleen J., and David Corwin. "Exploring Intrafamilial Child Sexual Abuse: A Systems Approach." In *The Dark Side of Families: Current Family Violence Research,* edited by David Finkelhor, Richard Gelles, Gerald Hotaling and Murray Straus, 102–16. Beverly Hills, Calif.: Sage, 1983.

Torrey, E. Fuller. "History of an Illusion." Review of *Why Freud Was Wrong: Sin, Science, and Psychoanalysis,* by Richard Webster. *National Review* 47, no. 25 (1995): 43–44.

van der Heijden, Manon. "Women as Victims of Sexual and Domestic Violence in Seventeenth-Century Holland: Criminal Cases of Rape, Incest and Maltreatment in Rotterdam and Delft." *Journal of Social History* 33, no. 3 (2000): 623–44.

Vernant, Jean-Pierre. *Myth and Tragedy in Ancient Greece*. Translated by Janet Lloyd. New York: Zone Books, 1988.

Wallerstein, J. S., and J. B. Kelly. *Surviving the Breakup: How Children and Parents Cope with Divorce*. New York: Basic Books, 1980.

Ward, Elizabeth. *Father-Daughter Rape*. New York: Grove Press, 1985.

Watters, Ethan, and Richard Ofshe. *Therapy's Delusions: The Myth of the Unconscious and the Exploitation of Today's Walking Worried*. New York: Scribner, 1998.

Webster, Richard. *Why Freud Was Wrong: Sin, Science, and Psychoanalysis*. New York: Basic Books, 1995.

Wilson, Elizabeth. "Not in This House: Incest, Denial and Doubt in the White Middle Class Family." *The Yale Journal of Criticism* 8 (1995): 35–58.

Winkler, John. *The Constraints of Desire: The Anthropology of Sex and Gender in Ancient Greece*. New York: Routledge, 1990.

Winnicott, D. W. *The Maturational Processes and the Facilitating Environment: Studies in the Theory of Emotional Development*. Madison: International Universities Press, 1965.

Wolff, Larry. *Postcards from the End of the World: Child Abuse in Freud's Vienna*. New York: Atheneum, 1988.

Zeal, Paul. Review of *Dr Freud — A Life, by Paul Ferris*. *International Journal of Psychotherapy* 4, no. 1 (1999): 94–97.

———. The Unknown Freud. Reviews. *The New York Review of Books* 40, no. 19 (1993): 55–65.

Index